Lockdown Shakespeare

SHAKESPEARE AND ADAPTATION

Shakespeare and Adaptation provides in-depth discussions of a dynamic field and showcases the ways in which, with each act of adaptation, a new Shakespeare is generated. The series addresses the phenomenon of Shakespeare and adaptation in all its guises and explores how Shakespeare continues as a reference-point in a generically diverse body of representations and forms, including fiction, film, drama, theatre, performance and mass media. Including sole authored books as well as edited collections, the series embraces a mix of methodologies and espouses a global perspective that brings into conversation adaptations from different nations, languages and cultures.

Series Editor:
Mark Thornton Burnett (Queen's University Belfast, UK)

Advisory Board:
Professor Sarah Hatchuel (Université Paul-Valéry Montpellier, 3, France)
Dr Peter Kirwan (University of Nottingham, UK)
Professor Douglas Lanier (University of New Hampshire, USA)
Professor Adele Lee (Emerson College, USA)
Dr Stephen O'Neill (Maynooth University, Ireland)
Professor Shormishtha Panja (University of Delhi, India)
Professor Lisa Starks (University of South Florida)
Professor Nathalie Vienne-Guerrin
(Université Paul-Valéry Montpellier 3, France)
Professor Sandra Young (University of Cape Town, South Africa)

Published Titles:
Adapting Macbeth, William C. Carroll

Forthcoming Titles:
Women and Indian Shakespeares
Edited by Thea Buckley, Mark Thornton Burnett,
Sangeeta Datta and Rosa García-Periago
'Romeo and Juliet', Adaptation and the Arts:
'Cut Him Out in Little Stars'
Edited by Julia Reinhard Lupton and Ariane Helou
Shakespeare, Ecology and Adaptation: A Practical Guide
Alys Daroy and Paul Prescott
Shakespeare and Ballet, David Fuller

Lockdown Shakespeare

New Evolutions in Performance and Adaptation

Edited by
Gemma Kate Allred,
Benjamin Broadribb and
Erin Sullivan

THE ARDEN SHAKESPEARE
LONDON • NEW YORK • OXFORD • NEW DELHI • SYDNEY

THE ARDEN SHAKESPEARE
Bloomsbury Publishing Plc
50 Bedford Square, London, WC1B 3DP, UK
1385 Broadway, New York, NY 10018, USA
29 Earlsfort Terrace, Dublin 2, Ireland

BLOOMSBURY, THE ARDEN SHAKESPEARE and the Arden Shakespeare logo
are trademarks of Bloomsbury Publishing Plc

First published in Great Britain 2022
This paperback edition published 2024

Copyright © Gemma Kate Allred, Benjamin Broadribb,
Erin Sullivan and contributors, 2022

Gemma Kate Allred, Benjamin Broadribb, Erin Sullivan and contributors have
asserted their right under the Copyright, Designs and Patents Act, 1988, to be
identified as the authors of this work.

For legal purposes the Acknowledgements on pp. xiii–xv constitute
an extension of this copyright page.

Cover design: Tjaša Krivec
Cover image © Big Telly Theatre Company; Katherine Bourne Taylor; Creation
Theatre Company; CtrlAltRepeat; Incognita Enterprises; The Shakespeare
Ensemble; *The Show Must Go Online* (robmyles.com/theshowmustgoonline)

All rights reserved. No part of this publication may be reproduced
or transmitted in any form or by any means, electronic or mechanical,
including photocopying, recording, or any information storage or
retrieval system, without prior permission in writing from the publishers.

Bloomsbury Publishing Plc does not have any control over, or responsibility for,
any third-party websites referred to or in this book. All internet addresses given
in this book were correct at the time of going to press. The author and publisher
regret any inconvenience caused if addresses have changed or sites have ceased
to exist, but can accept no responsibility for any such changes.

A catalogue record for this book is available from the British Library.

A catalogue record for this book is available from the Library of Congress.

ISBN: HB: 978-1-3502-4780-2
PB: 978-1-3502-4784-0
ePDF: 978-1-3502-4782-6
eBook: 978-1-3502-4781-9

Series: Shakespeare and Adaptation

Typeset by Integra Software Services Pvt. Ltd.

To find out more about our authors and books visit www.bloomsbury.com
and sign up for our newsletters.

CONTENTS

List of Illustrations   viii
Notes on Contributors   x
Acknowledgements   xiii
Note on the Text   xvi
Glossary   xvii

Introduction: Cultural Cartography of the Digital Lockdown Landscape   1
Gemma Kate Allred and Benjamin Broadribb

Part One: Analyses

1 The Screen Language of Lockdown: Connection and Choice in Split-Screen Performance   23
John Wyver

2 Lockdown Shakespeare and the Metamodern Sensibility   45
Benjamin Broadribb

3 Notions of Liveness in Lockdown Performance   65
Gemma Kate Allred

4 Creation Theatre and Big Telly's *The Tempest*: Digital Theatre and the Performing Audience   87
Pascale Aebischer and Rachael Nicholas

5   Immersion in a Time of Distraction: 'The Under Presents: *Tempest*'   107
    Erin Sullivan

6   *What You Will* in the Time of Covid-19: Exploring the Digital Arts, Race and Flexible Resistance   127
    David Sterling Brown and Ben Crystal

Part Two: Case Studies

7   'Shakespeare for everyone'   149
    The Show Must Go Online in conversation with Gemma Kate Allred and Benjamin Broadribb

8   *Ricardo II*: una producción bilingüe de Merced Shakespearefest   161
    William Wolfgang and Erin Sullivan

9   'Your play needs no excuse'   171
    CtrlAltRepeat in conversation with Gemma Kate Allred and Benjamin Broadribb

10 'Are we all met?': Responding to Shakespeare's Canon through Online Community Performance   185
    Jennifer Moss Waghorn, Katrin Bauer, Sarah Hodgson, Diane Lowman, Kathryn Twigg and Martin Wiggins

11 'Present fears are less than horrible imaginings'   195
    Big Telly Theatre Company in conversation with Gemma Kate Allred and Benjamin Broadribb

12 Teaching Shakespearean Performance in
     Lockdown 207
     *Andrew James Hartley, Sarah Hatchuel and Yu
     Umemiya in conversation with Erin Sullivan*

Part Three

Lockdown Digital Arts: An Extended Year in
Review 219
*Gemma Kate Allred, Benjamin Broadribb and
Erin Sullivan*
 Spring 220
 Summer 229
 Autumn 239
 Winter/Spring 250

Conclusion: Shakespeare after Lockdown 259
Erin Sullivan

Index 266

LIST OF ILLUSTRATIONS

1. Matt Smith and Claire Foy in the split screens of *In Camera: Lungs* directed by Matthew Warchus for The Old Vic. Screenshot 40
2. Puck (Anna Faye Lieberman) creating her picture-book night sky to the flute-playing of the fairy (Dana Liu) in Arden Theatre Company's *A Midsummer Night's Dream*. Screenshot reproduced courtesy of Arden Theatre Company 54
3. Andrew Pawarroo and Elizabeth Dennehy perform as Polixenes and Camillo in *TSMGO*'s Zoom-to-YouTube production of *The Winter's Tale*, as the digital groundlings conduct their textual 'singalong' of Queen's 'Bohemian Rhapsody' in the Live Chat. Screenshot reproduced courtesy of *The Show Must Go Online* 75
4. Ferdinand (Ryan Duncan) and Miranda (Annabelle Terry). *The Tempest*, dir. Zoë Seaton for Creation Theatre and Big Telly, 2020. Screenshot reproduced courtesy of Creation Theatre and Big Telly 95
5. An audience member shining a light on Prospero in the opening scene at the campfire in 'The Under Presents: *Tempest*'. Image reproduced courtesy of Tender Claws 117
6. Andrew (Hiroaki Kurata), Olivia (Renee Rose) and Maria (Amba Suhasini Katoch Jhala) in *What You Will*. Image collage created and reproduced courtesy of The Shakespeare Ensemble 137
7. Iras (Rebecca Brough), First Guardsman (Neelaksh Sadhoo), Charmian (Maya Cohen), Diomedes (Andrew Pawarroo), Cleopatra (Debra Ann Byrd), Third Guardsman (Alec Stephens III), Mark Antony (Mark Holden) and Second

Guardsman (Lois Abdemalek) in *TSMGO*'s Zoom-to-YouTube production of *Antony & Cleopatra*. Screenshot reproduced courtesy of *The Show Must Go Online* 154

8 Northumberland (Harker Hale), Henry Bolingbroke (Greg Ruelas), Ricardo II (Alejandro Gutiérrez) and Bagot (Katie Sylvester) in *Ricardo II*, 'Ep. 10: Rey de la nieve'. Screenshot reproduced courtesy of Merced Shakespearefest 166

9 Rob Starveling (James Dillon), Nic Bottom (Joanna Brown), Frances Flute (Olivia Caley) and Peter Quince (Tom Black) perform *Pyramus and Thisbe* in CtrlAltRepeat's Zoom-to-YouTube production *Midsummer Night Stream*. Screenshot reproduced courtesy of CtrlAltRepeat 175

10 A witch (Dharmesh Patel) prepares to deliver the theatrical prophecies during Big Telly's Virtual Theatre production of *Macbeth*. Image reproduced courtesy of Big Telly 201

11 Katherine (Robyn McHarry), The Princess of France (Alix Dunmore), Rosaline (Marianne Oldham) and Maria (Lanna Joffrey) hold ladle parasols and eat bananas in The Factory Theatre Company's *Love's Labour's Lost*. Screenshot reproduced courtesy of The Factory Theatre Company 233

12 Captain Cassiopeia Martinez (Joanne Pocsidio), Sergeant Emiliano (Kekai Mattos), Lieutenant Karen Johanson (Evangeline Lemieux) and Gunnery Sergeant Nathan Ohelo Moore (Stephen Richter) in Justina Taft Mattos's production of *Moore – A Pacific Island Othello*. Image reproduced courtesy of Stephen Richter 246

NOTES ON CONTRIBUTORS

Pascale Aebischer is Professor of Shakespeare and Early Modern Performance Studies at the University of Exeter. Her most recent book is *Shakespeare, Spectatorship and the Technologies of Performance* (2020), and she leads two projects that respond to the Covid-19 pandemic: *Digital Theatre Transformation* (2020) and *The Pandemic and Beyond* (2021–3).

Gemma Kate Allred is a doctoral researcher at the Université de Neuchâtel, Switzerland. Her research examines how Shakespeare in performance is sold and marketed particularly to new audiences. Her examination of celebrity and Shakespeare, '"Who's There?" Britain's Twenty-First-Century Obsession with Celebrity *Hamlet* (2008–2018)', was published in *Shakespeare Survey* (2020).

Katrin Bauer completed her PhD in English Literature on Shakespeare and early modern globalization at the Ludwig-Maximilians-Universität Munich in 2021, where she also worked as a research and teaching assistant at the Anglistik Department. She was a visiting researcher at The Shakespeare Institute, University of Birmingham, in winter 2019/2020.

Benjamin Broadribb completed his PhD at The Shakespeare Institute, University of Birmingham, in 2023. His research focuses on twenty-first-century screen adaptations and appropriations of Shakespeare, and how these create cultural artefacts. With Gemma Kate Allred, he is the co-founder of the *'Action is eloquence': (Re)thinking Shakespeare* blog (https://medium.com/action-is-eloquence-re-thinking-shakespeare).

David Sterling Brown – Shakespeare and premodern critical race studies scholar – is Assistant Professor of English at Trinity College, Connecticut, USA, and an ACLS/Mellon Scholars and Society

Fellow. His antiracist scholarship is published or forthcoming in Shakespeare Bulletin, *Shakespeare Studies*, *White People in Shakespeare*, *Hamlet: The State of Play* and other venues. His forthcoming book projects examine whiteness in Shakespearean drama.

Ben Crystal (www.bencrystal.com) is an actor, author, creative producer and explorer of original practices in Shakespeare rehearsal and production. He is the author of *Shakespeare on Toast* and *Springboard Shakespeare*, the co-author of *Shakespeare's Words* and *The Illustrated Dictionary of Shakespeare*, and the founder of theShakespeareEnsemble.com.

Andrew James Hartley is UNC Charlotte's Robinson Professor of Shakespeare studies and the author of books on dramaturgy, political theatre and the performance history of *Julius Caesar*. He edited collections on Shakespeare on the university stage, in millennial fiction and (with Peter Holland) on geek culture. He edited *Shakespeare Bulletin* for a decade.

Sarah Hatchuel is Professor of Film and Media Studies at the University Paul-Valéry Montpellier 3 (France) and former president of the Société Française Shakespeare. She has written extensively on adaptations of Shakespeare's plays and on TV series. She is general co-editor of CUP's *Shakespeare on Screen* collection and the online journal *TV/Series*.

Sarah Hodgson is a PhD student at The Shakespeare Institute, University of Birmingham. After completing her MA in Shakespeare Studies during the Covid-19 pandemic, her research interests include analysing digital adaptations of Shakespeare's plays and evaluating the possibilities of video conferencing software as a medium for dramatic performance.

Diane Lowman is a writer whose essays have appeared in many publications, including *O, The Oprah Magazine*, *Brevity Blog* and *When Women Waken*. She writes a weekly column called *Everything's an Essay* and her memoir, *Nothing But Blue*, was published in 2018. In 2019, she was named Westport, Connecticut's first Poet Laureate.

Rachael Nicholas is a researcher with expertise in theatre audiences, digital theatre and cultural value. She has researched audience experiences of online theatre before and during Covid-19, and is currently Postdoctoral Research Associate on the Pandemic and Beyond project at the University of Exeter.

Erin Sullivan is Reader in Shakespeare at The Shakespeare Institute, University of Birmingham. Her work on Shakespeare and twenty-first-century performance includes *Shakespeare on the Global Stage: Performance and Festivity in the Olympic Year* (2015, with Paul Prescott) and *Shakespeare and Digital Performance* (2022).

Kathryn Twigg is a doctoral researcher at The Shakespeare Institute, University of Birmingham. She is researching the trauma-informed teaching of Shakespeare, combining the fields of Shakespeare studies, education and developmental psychology. She aims to develop educational frameworks to support young trauma-survivors in their study of Shakespeare.

Yu Umemiya is an alumnus of The Shakespeare Institute, University of Birmingham, and former assistant professor at Waseda University, Japan. He received his PhD with a thesis on the textual study of *Hamlet* in February 2021. While conducting classes bilingually, he works as the artistic director of Waseda Institute Players.

Jennifer Moss Waghorn is a theatre music researcher, composer and musician finishing her PhD on the music of the King's Men at The Shakespeare Institute. She has composed for over thirty theatre productions and has developed online learning resources for the University of Warwick, Royal Shakespeare Company and Shakespeare Birthplace Trust.

Martin Wiggins is an Honorary Fellow of The Shakespeare Institute, Stratford-upon-Avon, and the author of *British Drama, 1533–1642: A Catalogue* (2012–).

William Wolfgang is a theatre practitioner and independent scholar. He has produced twenty-three Shakespeare plays with the OrangeMite Shakespeare Company as the founding executive director. Wolfgang has also directed and managed productions with Merced Shakespearefest and Shakespeare in Yosemite. His research interests include community-based arts and Shakespeare in bilingual performance.

John Wyver is a writer and producer with Illuminations, specializing in arts documentaries and screen adaptations of performance. He is the Royal Shakespeare Company's Director, Screen Productions, and Professor of the Arts on Screen, University of Westminster. His recent publications include *Screening the Royal Shakespeare Company: A Critical History* (2019).

ACKNOWLEDGEMENTS

This book started its life on Gemma and Benjamin's blog *'Action is eloquence': (Re)thinking Shakespeare* and through countless conversations as they navigated the 'new normal' of the pandemic.

We are grateful to all the colleagues and mentors who helped us develop the book by reading drafts, sharing unpublished work and giving invaluable advice. They include Pascale Aebischer, Hannah August, Katherine Steele Brokaw, Mark Thornton Burnett, Rebecca Bushnell, Emma Depledge, Barbara Fuchs, Emi Hamana, Russell Jackson, Elizabeth Jeffery, Peter Kirwan, Hyon-u Lee, Vladimir Makarov, Sonia Massai, Paul Prescott, Abigail Rokison-Woodall, Michiko Suematsu, Stephanie Shirilan and Caridad Svich. Mark Dudgeon, Lara Bateman and The Arden Shakespeare team supported us each step of the way and made the experience of bringing together a book in a little over a year as smooth as it could be.

So many creative practitioners helped us by granting interviews, graciously sharing images and performance recordings, and talking to us more informally about digital theatre-making. They include Lucy Askew, Cynthia Cantrell, Samantha Gorman, Adam Lenson, Jared Mezzocchi, Haylee Nichele, J Noland, Sinéad Owens, Stephen Richter, Natasha Rickman and Giles Stoakley. We are hugely grateful to Big Telly Theatre Company, CtrlAltRepeat, Merced Shakespearefest and *The Show Must Go Online*, including their wider members (and *TSMGO*'s digital groundlings) whose words are not in their respective case studies, but without whom those chapters would not exist. To the online digital theatre community – there are too many of you to name, but you know who you are. Thank you for providing friendship and support during these strange times. Finally, this book wouldn't have been possible without the family and friends who have supported us.

Gemma would like to thank Paul Taker, Nathaniel Taker and Obi who have joined and indulged her love of the digital arts, and for their unwavering support of her academic ventures. Her lobsters: Brian Allen, Lesley Bound, Claire Coast-Smith, James Cuffe, Lisa Deverson, Celia Gilbert, Phoebe Lambdon, Laura Pokorny and Justine Redfearn for their ongoing and unconditional support. Her parents Peter and Valerie Allred who were formative in her love of theatre and Shakespeare, and her brother James Allred. Finally, Benjamin, without whom the last long year would have felt so much longer.

Benjamin would like to thank his parents Graeme and Josephine Broadribb for their endless support and encouragement of his academic endeavours, his sister Charlotte and his grandma Iris. He would also like to thank his friend Sarah Dodd for cheering him on over the years in all his Shakespeare-related escapades. Lastly, Benjamin would like to thank Gemma for being the best collaborator and friend he could hope for.

Erin would like to thank Will and Ada, the best lockdown bubble she could have wished for, and all her family in the United States for the many years of video call training. Thank you to Gemma and Benjamin for welcoming her to the project and being such dedicated, kind collaborators.

Finally, Gemma and Benjamin would like to acknowledge that this book would not exist without Erin's belief, support and encouragement. They are incredibly grateful for her guidance, mentorship and level-headedness over the last year.

We are very grateful to the performers and image-holders who have generously allowed us to reproduce their images on our front cover: Maya Cohen as Adriana in *Shakespeare Republic: #AllTheWebsAStage (The Lockdown Chronicles)* (© Incognita Enterprises); Joanna Brown as Nic Bottom in CtrlAltRepeat's *Midsummer Night Stream* (© CtrlAltRepeat); Kristin Atherton as Hamlet in TSMGO's *Hamlet* (© The Show Must Go Online); Ashley Byam as Richard, Duke of Gloucester in TSMGO's *Henry VI Part III* (© The Show Must Go Online); Leo Atkin as Puck in *Shakespeare Republic: #AllTheWebsAStage (The Lockdown Chronicles)* (© Incognita Enterprises); Katrina Allen as Lady Macbeth in TSMGO's *Macbeth* (© The Show Must Go Online);

Anirudh Nair as 'Orsino: Vanitas' in *What You Will* care of The Shakespeare Ensemble (© The Shakespeare Ensemble); David Alwyn as Oberon in CtrlAltRepeat's *Midsummer Night Stream* (© CtrlAltRepeat); Annabelle Terry as Miranda in Creation Theatre and Big Telly's *The Tempest* (© Creation Theatre Company/Big Telly Theatre Company); Eugenia Low as R2-D2 in TSMGO's *William Shakespeare's Star Wars* (© *The Show Must Go Online*); Katherine Bourne Taylor as Snug in the Back Room Shakespeare Project's *A Midsummer Night's Dream* (© Katherine Bourne Taylor); and Dharmesh Patel as Mercutio in Creation Theatre's *Romeo and Juliet* (© Creation Theatre Company).

NOTE ON THE TEXT

All quotations from Shakespeare's plays refer to *The Arden Shakespeare Complete Works* (2021), R. Proudfoot, A. Thompson, D. S. Kastan and H.R. Woudhuysen (eds), London: Bloomsbury.

GLOSSARY

Lockdown Performance Types

Live-streamed	A production which is performed live and streamed to a digital platform such as YouTube or Vimeo.
Shakespeare in Pieces	Short-form adaptations, in which usually a single actor performs a passage from Shakespeare in isolation or hyper-condenses a scene or play.
Streamed	A production which has been pre-recorded, then streamed to a digital platform such as YouTube or Vimeo.
Virtual Theatre	A production which is performed live on Zoom with the audience joining the actors on the call, allowing the audience to interact with the performance.
Zoom-to-YouTube	A production which is performed via the video conferencing software Zoom and live-streamed (or, in rare instances, streamed) to YouTube for the audience to watch.

Zoom Functionality

The functionality of the video conferencing software Zoom is currently widely known and understood through its extensive use throughout the Covid-19 pandemic. However, we have included a glossary of Zoom's functionality commonly used in Zoom-based performance to aid readers unfamiliar with the software both now and in the future.

Breakout Room	A sub-meeting within a Zoom meeting where a smaller number of participants can meet and hold discussions before rejoining the main meeting.
Chat	A text-based function that allows participants to either message all participants or send a personal message to just one.
Gallery View	A viewing option where all Zoom participants' video feeds are shown on screen in rectangular windows.
Host	The person who created the Zoom meeting, and who is in charge of functionality such as Muting/Unmuting and Spotlighting.
Meeting	A standard Zoom video conference, also commonly referred to as a 'Zoom call'. Participants can join via a computer webcam, a smartphone or tablet device.
Mute/Unmute	The functionality to turn a participant's microphone off (Mute) and on (Unmute). This can be done by either the participant or the Host.
Speaker View	A viewing option where only the active speaker's video feed is showcased.
Spotlight	The functionality whereby an individual Zoom participant's video feed is showcased on screen by the Host. A participant who is showcased in this way is referred to as being 'Spotlighted'.
Webinar	In contrast to a standard Zoom meeting, a Zoom Webinar allows a performance to be broadcast to audience members who cannot see each other, only those performing. The Host can also choose to disable Chat. The performance can take place live on Zoom or can be live-streamed from an auditorium.

Introduction: Cultural Cartography of the Digital Lockdown Landscape

Gemma Kate Allred and Benjamin Broadribb

On Tuesday 16 March 2021, the Royal Shakespeare Company (RSC) released a short film on their YouTube channel, directed by artistic director Gregory Doran, entitled *Lament for a Year of Lost Theatre* (2021). The film marked one year since the company had closed its doors on Monday 16 March 2020 when, as the Covid-19 pandemic swept the nation, UK Prime Minister Boris Johnson told the British public to 'avoid pubs, clubs, theatres and other such social venues' (2020). Whilst the official order for theatres to close came five days later, for many venues 16 March marked the moment that they shut down.

The long-term closure of the historic theatre in Stratford-upon-Avon is of course a thing to lament; however, the title and tenor of Doran's film are characteristic of the solipsism that 'Big Theatre' – the major names and companies within the industry around the world, many of which are subsidized – showed both at the one-year mark of Covid-19 closure and when the industry began to open up once more a couple of months later. On 19 May 2021, Shakespeare's Globe Theatre tweeted a message from its artistic director, Michelle Terry, to mark the return of Sean Holmes's 2019 production of *A Midsummer Night's Dream* as the theatre's first in-person show of 2021:

> 'Is there no play to ease the anguish of a torturing hour?' For 429 days the answer has been no, but tonight the answer is yes. The anguish of this torturing year will ease as we once more watch, hear, feel a play. Tonight we will be allowed to hope & Dream again.
>
> (2021)

Whilst the 429 days equates to the amount of time that had passed since Shakespeare's Globe had shut its doors in 2020, the tweet frames the preceding fourteen months as a time when no theatre took place – a sentiment which is categorically untrue. This framing of the pandemic as a time without theatre went beyond Shakespeare. In a statement made on 18 June 2021 that the opening of his musical adaptation of *Cinderella* in June 2021 would not be part of the UK government's pilot scheme to reopen theatres at increased capacity, Andrew Lloyd Webber described *Cinderella* as 'the first world premiere of a new musical in this country [the UK] since the pandemic' – a statement which is, again, categorically untrue (2021). Only weeks earlier, a new musical, *Public Domain*, written and performed by Francesca Forristal and Jordan Paul Clarke, had made its West End debut at London's Vaudeville Theatre. Even more significantly, Forristal and Clarke had written *Public Domain* during lockdown.[1] The musical had premiered online in January 2021 as a live-streamed performance from Southwark Playhouse via the theatre's website, and was one of several live-streamed theatrical premieres from Southwark Playhouse since September 2020 – a number of which were also musicals.

The suggestion by Lloyd Webber, Terry and Doran that there had been no theatre since March 2020 both reflects and ingrains the wider misconception that this was the case. This misconception is furthered by the fact that many looking to get their theatre fix whilst physical spaces were closed turned to the streamed recordings of past productions which numerous Big Theatre companies worldwide made available online, often for free whilst asking for donations: Shakespeare's Globe and the National Theatre in the UK, Schaubühne Berlin and Thalia Theater in Germany, the Stratford Festival in Canada, the Folger Theater in the United States – the list goes on. Indeed, it literally does in our Extended Year in Review in Part Three of this book, which offers an analytical review of lockdown digital arts during the fourteen months in which the majority of theatres were closed in the UK (approximately March 2020 to May 2021). The prevalence of these streams, particularly in the early months of lockdown, created a subconscious association for the public of pandemic theatre being past rather than present. Whilst people were practising social distancing, those watching these streams also experienced cultural distancing through both the passage of time and the mediating presence of the screen. The sight of full houses and the traffic of the stage offered a nostalgic look back at audiences and actors less than two metres apart.

Let us be clear: this book, *Lockdown Shakespeare*, is not a lament for lost theatre. Nor is this book primarily focused on streamed theatre recordings, although they appear as a backdrop to the new work that was being created in digital spaces whilst analogue ones remained closed. The narrative of theatre shutting down during the pandemic is not only untrue, but also does a huge disservice to the numerous theatres, companies and practitioners who never stopped creating. It is those works, and the people behind them, that *Lockdown Shakespeare* most significantly recognizes, analyses and – perhaps most importantly – celebrates. As this volume testifies, the individuals and collectives who created digital productions during the pandemic did so out of a desire to carry on doing what they love against unimaginable restrictions, to keep theatre alive when physical theatre spaces were forced to close – but also out of a need to survive. They simply did not have the financial reserves or the funding to shut down indefinitely.

Before we go any further, let us also acknowledge that, whilst this book is primarily focused upon performance during the pandemic, it has of course been written during a period of unfathomable suffering, loss and grief around the world – a period which, whilst improving at the time of writing, is far from over. As of 1 November 2021, the official number of deaths across the globe due to Covid-19 has reached five million, with the World Health Organization suggesting the real global death toll could be two or three times higher than this ('Covid-19 deaths' 2021). Figures such as these are impossible to fully comprehend, as is the number of personal tragedies experienced by every single person who has lost someone they love. By exploring and celebrating the innovative approaches to performance in digital spaces during this period, we have never sought to minimize, trivialize or disrespect those who have died or the loved ones left behind to mourn them. *Lockdown Shakespeare* was written with Covid-19 and its dreadful impact worldwide as an inescapable presence – something of which we, and everyone who has contributed to the publication of this book, have been acutely conscious and continually respectful.

'What country, friends, is this?' (*Twelfth Night*, 1.2.1)

Whilst our primary focus is of course Shakespearean performance, you will find a considerable amount of non-Shakespearean productions throughout this collection. Indeed, John Wyver's chapter, which opens Part One, deliberately considers performance history far beyond Shakespearean borders. Shakespeare was an undeniable and continual presence throughout lockdown performance. But theatre never occurs in a vacuum. Other works created in lockdown echoed and were influenced (either consciously or unconsciously) by the Shakespearean performances going on around them; likewise, the non-Shakespearean influenced the Shakespearean. Our hope is to act as cultural cartographers: mapping the major landmarks and hidden beauty spots of the fourteen months of digital arts in lockdown this book encompasses; tracing the topographical features of their shared landscape; identifying connections within Lockdown Shakespeare – our umbrella term, as used in the title of this volume, for the extraordinary range and output of Shakespearean performance and adaptations created and shared in digital spaces during the pandemic – as well as between 'Shakespeare' and 'not Shakespeare'.

Although our map has become ever more detailed by the day, it remains tantalizingly unfinished. Lockdown digital arts have sprung up around the globe, and the technology that has allowed us to remain connected in a time of separation has also allowed us to learn about and experience performances on six of the seven continents (and, at the time of writing, we are aware of a hybrid project in development that will see in-person productions live-streamed from the seventh, Antarctica, to audiences both at home and in theatre spaces). That said, this collection was conceived and created as, to borrow a phrase from two of our contributors, a 'rapid-response Covid-19 project', with a fundamental aim of documenting and analysing digital performances as close to the moment of their production as possible, lest they be lost to the ever-expanding black hole that is the internet (Chapter 4: 87–8). In doing so, we are aware that, as mostly UK- and US-based, English-speaking scholars, our perspective will inescapably have been orientated towards productions emerging from the Anglophone world. We are also aware that, in moving quickly, areas of this collection have become weighted towards Anglo-American productions. That being said, what we have striven to achieve throughout the writing and editing of *Lockdown Shakespeare* is a map that, whilst inherently incomplete and presented from our own viewpoints and those of our contributors, is as egalitarian as possible: unconstrained by borders, preconceptions or privilege. Our map offers a detailed impression of digital performance in lockdown so far, onto which productions as-yet uncharted by us can be placed.

This analogy of uncharted territory is reflected in the language and perspectives of the creatives we have spoken to in the process of writing and editing this book. In three separate case studies within Part Two of this collection, contributors make comparisons between the digital theatre industry during the pandemic and the 'Wild West' – a new frontier to be explored, charted and cultivated (Chapter 7: 159; Chapter 9: 178; Chapter 11: 204). The sentiment is echoed further by actor Haylee Nichele, who describes Virtual Reality as the 'wild world' (Chapter 5: 120). The creatives who use this language do so with a sense of excitement, invention and, most importantly, optimism. Through the dark clouds of incredible loss, suffering and uncertainty the pandemic has brought, creatives who have embraced digital performance have seen a glimmer of hope and held onto it: that the decimation of their industry since March 2020 gives them an opportunity to rebuild it in a more accessible, equitable and open-minded way.

Creatives we have spoken to have talked about this moment as a levelling. Big Telly actor Dharmesh Patel speaks of the 'chance to flatten [the industry] and start again as an equal', noting that '[w]e're at a place of equality, and we need to drive that' (Chapter 11: 205). Lockdown digital arts have worked to showcase identity-conscious casting: Robert Myles, creator of *The Show Must Go Online* (*TSMGO*), one of the most prolific Lockdown Shakespeare projects, describes 'manually unpick[ing] the threads of exclusion that have been so tightly woven by cultural imperialists who have weaponized Shakespeare for generations' (Chapter 7: 155). For audiences too there are gains to be made – at its simplest, the ability to experience live performance from home can aid access for those with caring responsibilities or who are unable to travel to in-person theatre spaces. As Ben Crystal notes in Chapter 6, *TSMGO* heard from people 'in isolation, who are disabled, in palliative care, in hospital, who *never* have access to Shakespeare, or theatre in general, and were getting to see Shakespeare for the first time in their life, and in some cases, the last' (138).

Disability and neurodiversity have been embraced: digital technology allows for captioning across the board, not just for occasional access performances. Interpolation of British Sign Language interpretation has been included in *TSMGO's* productions of *Pericles,* Lyly's *Gallathea* and others, the nature of Zoom's Gallery View affording interpreter Janet Guest equal and equivalent space on screen. Members of CtrlAltRepeat speak of ensuring that their immersive work is accessible: James Dillon advises that while '[p]eople are comfortable at home ... you're still entering someone's personal space so it actually can be more intrusive than you think to have access to someone's Zoom screen'. This process, he notes, is 'work': formulating the experience so that the audience can participate on their own terms, giving them 'the space to have that freedom to not be Spotlighted on screen, so by the time they're going to say anything, they know they're in good hands. That takes a bit of work, but that's the rewarding part' (Chapter 9: 182). It is a sentiment echoed by Kathryn Twigg, who notes in her consideration of the educational benefits of play-readings on Zoom that the platform's Chat functionality 'could be used to facilitate understanding of Shakespeare's works with students who might need to ask for clarification throughout a reading ... [with an] added sense of community and peer-support engendered through the informal discussion' (Chapter 10: 190).

Whilst digital technology has in these respects and others placed creatives and audiences at 'a place of equality', it has in others starkly exposed the digital divide which exists both within individual nations and across different parts of the world. Mirca Madianou notes how '[t]he public health response to the Covid-19 pandemic led to the unprecedented situation of millions of people relying almost exclusively on communication technology to work, study, and socialize', but that 'any opportunities afforded by communication technologies are asymmetrically distributed' (2020). In the UK, higher income families were significantly more likely than lower income families to have the devices and internet access to allow adults to work remotely and children to complete schoolwork at home when schools were closed. Thus, 'digital technologies become part of a larger assemblage that perpetuates and increases social inequalities ... [and] become implicated with the stratified effects of the coronavirus' (ibid.). This inequality is inescapable when considering lockdown digital arts, for both audiences and creatives. Watching online, or performing online, presupposes *being* online. However, digital theatre in lockdown does not deserve to be solely held to account for highlighting the inequity that has been ingrained in the theatre industry more widely for decades, even centuries. To use the UK as an example once again, being able to experience a performance at the National Theatre presupposes the ability to afford a ticket, to travel to the theatre (or live in London), to access the auditorium – and to have the free time to do all of this in the first place. So, whilst we acknowledge the inherent imbalance of access to digital technology at the time of the pandemic, we strongly believe that the numerous issues of inequality in theatre that digital performance in lockdown has been able to tackle should not be overlooked due to those it has not.

Digital theatre throughout lockdown afforded creatives agility. Productions created in short time spans against the backdrop of a rapidly changing world could offer reactions in the moment to global events. Black Lives Matter (BLM) gained international attention in 2020 following the murder of George Floyd in Minneapolis, Minnesota, on 25 May, with protests in the United States and around the world in the months that followed. Creatives reacted quickly and powerfully, adding their voices to the global outrage, challenging the oppressive structures of racism that millions around the world were working, fighting and dying in order to dismantle. In the week following Floyd's murder, productions opened with messages of both anger and support. Amelia Parillon introduced *TSMGO*'s *A Midsummer Night's Dream* with an emotional account of her personal experience of racism; and both Fresh Life Theatre Company and Arden Theatre Company prefaced their own adaptations of *Dream* with clear statements of solidarity with BLM, including both information and donation links to support the movement. As the BLM protests continued, lockdown productions explicitly and critically engaged with systemic racism. In discussion with Crystal about the Shakespeare Ensemble's digital promenade production *What You Will*, David Sterling Brown highlights how 'the Ensemble was trying to be conscious about race(ism) and not simply reflect whiteness back to whiteness in the ways we are so used to seeing theatre companies do, in ways that some would actually consider a form of racial erasure or even racial violence' (Chapter 6: 141–2). Crystal recalls: 'While we were creating, we were listening very keenly to the state of the world. The pandemic, the racist state violence in America' (ibid.: 140). The Shakespeare Ensemble were not alone in doing this.

Part Three captures numerous productions which explicitly responded to issues of race in 2020. Saheem Ali's radio production of *Richard II* for the Public Theater places race at its core and exists as an artefact of the cultural moment immediately following Floyd's murder. During the recording of the production, '[BLM] protests were a constant presence in many of the actors' New York apartments in a manner that they would not be in sound-proofed recording studios' (Part Three: 237). *Moore – A Pacific Island Othello*, directed by Justina Taft Mattos, interrogated the intersections of race and gender, whiteness and ethnicity, in twenty-first-century America through a partially gender-flipped modern-day adaptation of Shakespeare's play (see Part Three: 245–6). The production was presented as being inherently linked to the 2020 moment: 'With the impending presidential election, rising social unrest, and our present reckoning about systemic racism in the United States, we felt it was high time to revisit Othello and examine what the play means here and now in America' ('About Moore'). Companies exploited the borderless nature of digital performance to throw the casting net wide. *TSMGO*'s Andrew Pawarroo and Lisa Hill-Corley speak to the 'global community' that the project built, and Myles notes how *TSMGO*'s production of *Othello* 'preserve[d] Othello's exceptional nature in the play without casting exclusively white people in all the other roles' and 'offer[ed] unique angles on the experiences of those with varied ethnicities navigating a white supremacist world' (Chapter 7: 158, 155). This was, as producer Sarah Peachey attests, work: *TSMGO* 'had to make and keep and continually reaffirm a commitment to inclusivity so people from under-represented backgrounds could see, week after week, that this is a place they could feel welcome' (ibid.: 155). This sense of work is echoed by Crystal who notes that, in addressing the racial inequalities brought to the fore by the BLM movement, he was led to (re)evaluate the diversity of the Shakespeare Ensemble. Crystal acknowledges that despite the 'multi-ethnic membership ... Global Majority members were only a third of the demographic'; he saw the 'imbalanced membership as an unconscious bias' leading the Ensemble to 'carefully consider who steps forward to play and how often a room is led by folx who look like me' (Chapter 6: 141).

However, whilst many Shakespearean and non-Shakespearean digital performances created between March 2020 and May 2021 actively engaged with and positively pushed against the issues of race, accessibility and social inequality both in the theatre industry and more widely, we fully acknowledge that the shift to digital spaces and platforms has not provided a panacea for these issues. In short, while offering *a* solution to some of these concerns, the digital arts can never be *the* solution. As Erin Sullivan notes in her conclusion, 'to suggest that going online democratised Shakespearean performance in a straightforward manner would be to gloss over how the internet reiterates and even magnifies existing inequalities' (261). What creatives have done, in the hardest of conditions, is to show time and time again that, with conscious work and awareness, the theatre industry can be changed for the better.

Features of the landscape: Zoom-to-YouTube, Virtual Theatre, Shakespeare in Pieces

Shakespeare has been an ever-present figure in lockdown digital arts and emerged as such almost immediately in both streams of pre-pandemic recorded theatre and newly created work. As Big

Theatre companies around the world put dozens of recordings of past Shakespearean productions online, creatives across the planet turned to Shakespeare to play with digital performance in lockdown. In the UK, three days before theatres had been instructed to close their doors, Myles tweeted about 'set[ting] up an online #Shakespeare play-reading group via Zoom or similar', with the message: 'We have to do what we can to stay connected and creative over this time' (2020). Myles's 'play-reading group' would go on to become *TSMGO*, an archetype of the Zoom-to-YouTube mode of performance which emerged in early 2020. Zoom-to-YouTube productions are, in almost all cases, performed live via the video conferencing software Zoom and streamed to YouTube for the audience to watch. A performance mode native to lockdown, Zoom-to-YouTube is a specific and particularly prevalent form of the wider category of live-streamed theatre which creatives have performed and directed live online (in contrast to *streamed* theatre, where pre-recorded performances are made available) during the pandemic. From one-person shows to full productions from Big Theatre's empty auditoria, the examples are too numerous to list here. Many examples can be found in Part Three and are acknowledged and explored again and again throughout this collection.

Myles was by no means the only creative to turn to Shakespeare in the early days of lockdown. On 31 March, less than two weeks after tweeting they were 'currently unable to generate any income from live performances', Oxford-based Creation Theatre Company began publicizing a production they had been working on with previous collaborators Big Telly Theatre Company from Portstewart, Northern Ireland, that would 'push the boundaries of this brave new world we find ourselves in, and embrace our new digital stage with gusto' (2020a, 2020b). That production was *The Tempest*, directed by Zoë Seaton, which would go on to international recognition. With *The Tempest*, Creation and Big Telly essentially invented the Virtual Theatre performance model which has emerged in lockdown: productions performed live on Zoom with the audience joining the actors on the call, allowing those watching to interact with the performance. Both Creation and Big Telly have gone on to become leading pioneers of digital performance in lockdown, with their numerous online productions created throughout the pandemic rightfully referenced and discussed in various chapters throughout *Lockdown Shakespeare*.

Much of the space between the new and pre-existing full Shakespearean productions was filled with Shakespeare in Pieces – our term for short-form adaptations, in which usually a single actor performs a passage from Shakespeare in isolation or hyper-condenses a scene or play. Arguably, the most celebrated example of Shakespeare in Pieces is Sally McLean's multi-award-winning *Shakespeare Republic: #AllTheWebsAStage (The Lockdown Chronicles)*, a web series edition of her existing Australian television series filmed and edited during the pandemic. Like Myles and Creation, McLean moved quickly: she invited actors from across the world to submit self-taped auditions in March 2020 and began rehearsals in April. 'Twenty four souls, six cities – one shared experience of being human', declares the tagline of *The Lockdown Chronicles*' cinema-style poster, capturing the essence of Shakespeare in Pieces, and indeed Lockdown Shakespeare, more widely ('About the project'). From McLean's web series, to the Shakespearean micro-content created by TikTok users, to Sir Patrick Stewart's 'sonnet a day' series on Twitter, individuals across the planet have turned to Shakespeare to find a way to remain connected in a time of enforced isolation.

Indicative of a genre in flux, there is some blurring at the edges of these definitions. Companies such as UK-based Cross-Stitch Theatre used the Zoom-to-YouTube model to offer a pre-recorded stream rather than performing live. Similarly, Fresh Life Theatre Company in the UK and the Back Room Shakespeare Project in the United States pre-recorded their respective free YouTube adaptations of *A Midsummer Night's Dream* to exploit, as Wyver notes in respect of Back Room's production, 'FaceTime recordings and filters, shots of web pages and animations [and] message feeds … [that] pushed the production … towards the hyper-visuality of music videos' (Chapter 1: 38). Shakespeare's Globe offered staged productions filmed in lockdown from the Sam Wanamaker Playhouse; and Southwark Playhouse, the Old Vic and others gave empty auditoria productions live-streamed in lockdown a second life as on-demand pre-recorded streams. This second life was equally afforded to many Zoom-to-YouTube live-streams such as *TSMGO* and CrtlAltRepeat's Shakespearean productions that continue to exist as YouTube videos. Play-readings, both amateur and professional, sprung up online: some through private groups such as The Shakespeare Institute 'marathon', featured in Chapter 10; others more widely accessible, such as those offered by the Red Bull Theater. While these did not offer fully staged productions, they adopted elements of the new conventions of Zoom as a performance space.

As lockdown digital arts have continued to emerge and evolve, they have garnered critical attention. This began with media coverage for individual projects: *TSMGO* was featured on the BBC's *Newsnight* current affairs programme on 20 March 2020; Creation and Big Telly's *Tempest* was reported in numerous UK newspapers and broke into the US news cycle via *The New York Times* and CNN. However, regular coverage of digital theatre throughout the pandemic has largely fallen not to professional journalists, but to amateur and academic bloggers. Amongst the most prolific amateur blogs have been Debbie Gilpin's *Mind the Blog* (https://pleasemindtheblog.wordpress.com) and John Chapman's *2nd from Bottom* (https://2ndfrombottom.wordpress.com), both of which have reviewed a wide variety of online productions in lockdown. Academic offerings have come from Peter Kirwan's long-running *Bardathon* (https://blogs.nottingham.ac.uk/bardathon), which has focused mainly on archive streams but has also ventured occasionally into newly created Lockdown Shakespeare; and our own *'Action is eloquence': (Re)thinking Shakespeare* (https://medium.com/action-is-eloquence-re-thinking-shakespeare), through which we have aimed to document and analyse the performance and adaptation of Lockdown Shakespeare from the first UK lockdown onwards, as well as formulating our thoughts about these rapidly evolving new performance mediums which sit somewhere between stage and screen, digital and analogue, together and apart. Twitter has emerged as an important space for discussion and debate, with creatives such as Jared Mezzocchi (@JaredMezzocchi), Adam Lenson (@AdamLenson), Caridad Svich (@Csvich) and Paula Varjack (@paulavarjack) working to define and document fast-moving developments. That it has fallen almost entirely to amateur enthusiasts and the extracurricular efforts of academics and creatives to chart the course of lockdown digital arts is yet another indicator of the wider erasure of the work of creatives throughout the pandemic. Whilst there has been sporadic coverage of lockdown performance in national media outlets, it has generally focused on the productions offered by Big Theatre (although *The New York*

Times offers a welcome exception to this). The overwhelming sense has been of theatre critics waiting for physical spaces to reopen, with limited interest in the exciting work that has been happening online. Critical engagement with lockdown digital arts has increasingly emerged in academic journals, however, with reviewers invited to write about not only the productions viewed but also their experiences of watching them during the pandemic, powerfully highlighting how the introspective quality of performance for those watching as well as those creating has been heightened by life in lockdown. As part of its November 2020 edition, *Cahiers Élisabéthains* included a special section, entitled 'Shakespeare under global lockdown', with an emphasis on the pre-pandemic recordings made available during the opening months of lockdown. *Shakespeare Bulletin* also compiled a special reviews section in 2020, released in 2021, similarly subtitled 'Shakespeare in Lockdown', which presented a more equal balance between pre-pandemic streams and new content.

Lockdown Shakespeare is by no means the only book-length examination of performance in the time of Covid-19, with other volumes on the horizon signposting a further shift towards in-depth academic and critical engagement with the period. We are honoured this publication will sit alongside other works, including Pascale Aebischer's *Viral Shakespeare: Performance in the Time of Pandemic*, Caridad Svich's *Toward a Future Theatre: Conversations during a Pandemic* and Barbara Fuchs's *Theater of Lockdown: Digital and Distanced Performance in a Time of Pandemic* in documenting, exploring and analysing this extraordinary time in the history of performance.

'I thank thee. Lead me on.'
(*Twelfth Night*, 1.2.61)

The opening three contributions within Part One of *Lockdown Shakespeare*, 'Analyses', take a panoramic view of the digital arts landscape to offer detailed explorations of the performance and adaptation of Shakespeare (and non-Shakespeare) in lockdown.

Together they explore the visual, cultural, aesthetic and receptive trends to be found across the wide spectrum of lockdown digital arts. In Chapter 1, John Wyver looks significantly beyond Shakespearean productions to explore not only how split-screen performance has become the screen language of lockdown, but also numerous forebears in film and television broadcast, delving into the origins of this visual aesthetic from the beginnings of moving image performance. In doing so, Wyver expands the temporal and transmedial parameters of our cultural cartography, providing a rich framework through which the many lockdown productions considered throughout this collection can be examined. Benjamin Broadribb narrows the focus to the twenty-first century in Chapter 2, assessing the ways in which Lockdown Shakespeare effuses the metamodern sensibility, the perceived cultural shift beyond late-twentieth-century postmodernism which permeates the opening decades of the 2000s. Considering the metamodern structures of feeling discernible in a range of productions, Broadribb draws lines between Lockdown Shakespeare and contemporary cinema and art, locating lockdown digital arts as essential artefacts in our wider cultural moment. In Chapter 3, Gemma Kate Allred considers how liveness exists in both Shakespearean performance and lockdown digital arts more widely. Considering pre-pandemic definitions of liveness and the event-connectedness of audiences, Allred explores how both creatives and audiences have created the sense of connection and ephemerality inherent to live performance whilst embracing the separation and mediation lockdown digital arts entail. In doing so, Allred's chapter convincingly makes a case for new forms of liveness to be recognized as digital performance continues within and beyond the pandemic.

The closing three contributions to Part One offer deep dives into three specific Lockdown Shakespeare productions. Pascale Aebischer and Rachael Nicholas analyse Creation and Big Telly's Virtual Theatre production of *The Tempest* in Chapter 4, considering how the production functioned as an archive of the companies' pre-pandemic in-person immersive *Tempest*, as well as an innovative new adaptation of the play in its own right. Aebischer and Nicholas also draw on their AHRC/UKRI-funded *Digital Theatre Transformation* project to explore how Creation and Big Telly generated both emotional connection and a sense of liveness for audiences early in lockdown when both seemed impossible. In

Chapter 5, Erin Sullivan investigates a very different but equally immersive adaptation of *The Tempest*, Tender Claws' Oculus Quest virtual reality experience 'The Under Presents: *Tempest*'. As well as reflecting on Tender Claws' transformation of Shakespeare's play for the VR environment and the participants entering it, Sullivan offers personal recollections of her experiences and frustrations engaging with performance in the pandemic, reflecting the wider emotional and psychological impact of life in lockdown. In Chapter 6, David Sterling Brown and Ben Crystal reflect on Crystal's experience working with the Shakespeare Ensemble on their *Twelfth Night*-inspired virtual theatrical promenade performance, *What You Will*. Vibrantly presented as a personal discussion between Crystal as a creative and Brown as a scholar of Shakespeare and critical race studies, together they consider vital issues of access, agency, race and whiteness, exploring the tensions between resistance and flexibility in relation to the creative response to the pandemic.

Part Two offers a series of case studies which together present a cross-section of lockdown digital arts. Three of these chapters are devoted to three UK-based creative collectives which, between them, have produced key examples of Lockdown Shakespeare. Our focus on these three collectives in no way implies that the work of other individuals, projects and companies, or emerging from other parts of the world, is of any less value or importance, with detailed discussion and analysis of numerous other examples throughout *Lockdown Shakespeare*. However, in focusing on these three collectives, our aim is to showcase the processes undertaken through different creative and philosophical ethea: *TSMGO* (Chapter 7), which offered Zoom-to-YouTube Shakespeare as weekly appointment viewing freely accessible to all; CtrlAltRepeat (Chapter 9), a company formed in lockdown which began with free Zoom-to-YouTube Shakespeare in order to explore the digital performance space in which they found themselves, leading to non-Shakespearean paid-for Virtual Theatre productions; and Big Telly (Chapter 11), an established theatre company which has been producing both Shakespearean and non-Shakespearean performances for years, whose existing ethos of experimentation and 'game theatre' led to paid-for Virtual Theatre productions of *The Tempest* (with Creation Theatre) and *Macbeth*, the latter of which is the focus of this case study. Each of these chapters is presented as an edited transcript of our discussions, with our own words included only to help frame and contextualize the conversations, allowing the words of the creatives involved in making Lockdown Shakespeare to stand as far as possible in unembellished form. They are intentionally closely based on conversations held as close to the moment of creation as possible, in order to represent and capture the emotional responses and reactions to creating digital performance during the pandemic.

These creative-focused case studies alternate with three community and education-focused chapters, which examine how lockdown digital performance practices were integrated into community-based theatres and classrooms around the world. In Chapter 8, William Wolfgang and Erin Sullivan reflect on Wolfgang's production for Merced Shakespearefest, *Ricardo II*, a bilingual adaptation of *Richard II* originally envisioned as an in-person performance which was pivoted to a serialized filmed adaptation released via YouTube. Featuring reflections from creatives involved in the production, the chapter charts the emotional impact of performing and creating an adaptation underscored by political and cultural division against the fractured backdrop of America in 2020. Chapter 10 offers a series of reflections from staff, students and alumni of The Shakespeare Institute, University of Birmingham, on moving their annual play-reading 'marathon' from its usual in-person model onto Zoom. What 'began as a digital substitute' ultimately 'heightened the communal experience of the plays, evoking greater shared pathos, surprise and (most often) mirth', offering a key example of the sense of connection online play-reading groups afforded their members around the world in lockdown (193–4). Chapter 12 brings together reflections from three educators from around the globe, considering how they have turned to digital spaces to continue teaching Shakespearean performance during the pandemic. All three contributors – Andrew James Hartley in the United States, Sarah Hatchuel in France and Yu Umemiya in Japan – offer valuable insights into the forms of digital performance adopted by their students, as well as the ways in which life in lockdown became ingrained in the pieces they created.

Part Three presents a detailed and expansive review of lockdown digital arts by the three editors of this volume: a chronological examination of adaptation and performance of Lockdown Shakespeare, alongside key non-Shakespearean examples, from approximately March 2020 to May 2021. Our hope in this section is to place the many different forms of digital performance and adaptation which have emerged during the pandemic in conversation with one another. It is here that our cultural cartography is inherently at its widest, viewing the digital lockdown landscape panoramically across cultures and continents to consider how and why trends in Shakespeare and beyond have emerged. Our aim here is not simply to list or catalogue productions but rather to analytically engage with these productions within their cultural moments.

For the creatives featured in this book, and many more around the world, lockdown has been a time of innovation and agility as they moved from physical to virtual spaces, pushing at the edges of the capabilities of digital technology and finding both its limitations and advantages. Much of the work created in lockdown was, by its nature, experimental, a work in progress reflecting the conditions of its creation. As Mezzocchi notes, 'the theatre industry [has been] thrust into a site-specific venue called the internet' during the pandemic, a venue which inspired creatives 'to define what makes theatre theatre and celebrate how our form can adapt to any space it inhabits' (2021). As the rules of lockdown flexed and changed, so too did the conventions of performance and adaptation. Lockdown performance is not a substitute for in-person performance – it is something different. In a time of isolation, Lockdown Shakespeare and digital arts more widely offered connection and showed time and time again what is possible when creatives embrace the possibilities of together-apart. In the words of Caridad Svich: 'Digital Theatre/performance: We were and are dreaming the present future' (2021). Theatre was never lost; it just moved to a different landscape.

Note

1 The *Oxford English Dictionary* offers a definition of 'lockdown' as 'a state of isolation, containment, or restricted access, usually instituted for security purposes or as a public health measure; [and] the imposition of this state' (2021). Since March 2020, the term 'lockdown' has been widely used with this meaning across the English-speaking world, in both the media and common parlance, to encompass the varying restrictive measures implemented by governments around the world, including stay-at-home measures, social distancing, quarantine requirements, travel bans and the

shutdown of individual businesses and whole industries. We have therefore used the term 'lockdown' throughout this collection in this more general sense. Our aim in doing so is not to homogenize the experience of the Covid-19 pandemic throughout the world – which has unquestionably been dictated by social, economic and geopolitical borders just as much as the virus itself – but rather to offer a continuity which would not be achieved by alternating between several different terms, some of which may be less widely understood by all readers.

References

'About Moore'. Available online: https://mooreworldpremiere.sites.ucsc.edu/production/ (accessed 28 November 2021).

'About the project'. Available online: http://allthewebsastage.com/about/ (accessed 28 November 2021).

'Covid-19 deaths pass five million worldwide' (2021), *BBC News*, 1 November. Available online: https://www.bbc.co.uk/news/world-59119731 (accessed 28 November 2021).

Creation Theatre Company (2020a), Twitter, 18 March. Available online: https://twitter.com/creationtheatre/status/1240306933975977985 (accessed 28 November 2021).

Creation Theatre Company (2020b), Twitter, 31 March. Available online: https://twitter.com/creationtheatre/status/1245017535982026754 (accessed 28 November 2021).

Johnson, B. (2020), 'Prime Minister's statement on coronavirus (COVID-19)', *gov.uk*, 16 March. Available online: https://www.gov.uk/government/speeches/pm-statement-on-coronavirus-16-march-2020 (accessed 28 November 2021).

'Lament for a Year of Lost Theatre' (2021), Royal Shakespeare Company. Available online: https://www.rsc.org.uk/news/lament-for-a-year-of-lost-theatre (accessed 28 November 2021).

Lloyd Webber, A. (2021), Twitter, 18 June. Available online: https://twitter.com/OfficialALW/status/1405900328311136261 (accessed 28 November 2021).

'lockdown, n.' (2021) *OED Online*, Oxford: OUP. Available online: https://www.oed.com/view/Entry/269145 (accessed 28 November 2021).

Madianou, M. (2020), 'A Second-Order Disaster? Digital Technologies during the COVID-19 Pandemic', *Social Media + Society*. Available online: https://doi.org/10.1177%2F2056305120948168 (accessed 28 November 2021).

Mezzocchi, J. (2021), 'The Technological Theatre Experimenters', *HowlRound*, 18 February. Available online: https://howlround.com/technological-theatre-experimenters (accessed 28 November 2021).

Myles, R. (2020), Twitter, 13 March. Available online: https://twitter.com/robmyles/status/1238543541741199361 (accessed 28 November 2021).

Shakespeare's Globe Theatre (2021), Twitter, 19 May. Available online: https://twitter.com/The_Globe/status/1395069240621867011 (accessed 28 November 2021).

Svich, C. (2021), Twitter. Available online: https://twitter.com/Csvich/status/1411348822916096000 (accessed 28 November 2021).

PART ONE

Analyses

1

The Screen Language of Lockdown: Connection and Choice in Split-Screen Performance

John Wyver

The first signs of a significant shift in the screen language of performance appeared soon after the start of the first Covid-19 lockdowns in Britain and elsewhere in mid-March 2020. Responding to the enforced closure of auditoria and the consequent loss of revenue, theatre and dance companies, orchestras and solo performers needed to find new ways of remaining in touch with their audiences. With broadcast television available to only a few organizations, social media and other online channels were quickly embraced.

One of the earliest examples of a new approach to online performance was the presentation of part of Beethoven's Ninth Symphony from Rotterdams Philharmonisch Orkest ('From us, for you' 2020). Introductions self-shot by players on their smartphones were followed by rapidly edited reflections about innovating to remain connected. 'Because if we do it together,' one of the musicians explained (in Dutch), before the frame fragmented into twelve headshots on a four-by-three grid as the whole group said, 'we'll succeed.' Single shots alternated with multiple shots in split-screen configurations. Increasingly complex visual patterns dominated the remainder of the four-minute arrangement until an unseen choir crashed in over a final eighteen-image irregular array. Released on 20 March 2020, the recording rapidly clocked up hundreds of thousands of views on YouTube and other platforms. A host of musical variants followed with musicians recording at home alone to a click track to keep time before being digitally edited together. Dancers soon followed with the Ballet de l'Opéra national de Paris collaborating with filmmaker Cédric Klapisch to express their thanks to frontline medical workers ('Dire merci' 2020). Fragments of rehearsal and performance were edited to the 'Dance of the Knights' section of Prokofiev's *Romeo and Juliet*. Shakespeare's drama of love, forced separation and loss, adapted as a ballet in Soviet Russia, was now reimagined as a visual tale of forced separation and hope. In the final moments, two dancers apparently in separate spaces and screens came together in a single frame where, presumably in their bubble, they embraced.

What these early lockdown performances and many others shared in filmic terms was a visual language of split screens: multiple moving images displayed simultaneously within the overall frame of the work. Similar split-screen visuals were at the same moment becoming familiar with the rapid take-up of video conferencing software for both professional and personal exchanges. Producers of screen drama quickly saw the potential of Zoom both as a production tool and as a conceptual framework for performance (see Turk 2020). The webisode 'Initial Lockdown Meeting' of BBC Television's comedy series *W1A* (dir. Morton 2020) was an early, recorded example of a Zoom call as a narrative device, and a similar idea was successfully developed in the comedy series *Staged* (dir. Evans 2020–1) with David Tennant and Michael Sheen. Theatre companies similarly began to explore the split-screen space of Zoom as a performance arena, including for live presentations, as in *The Tempest* co-produced by Creation Theatre and Big Telly (see Allred Chapter 3; Aebischer and Nicholas Chapter 4; Part Three).

The rapid take-up and subsequent ubiquity of the language of split screens for online performance has obscured just how radical a break this widespread usage is from the previously dominant screen language employed for almost all theatre, dance and classical music.

'Event cinema' broadcasts in the past decade, including Met Opera Live in HD, NTLive and others, have almost without exception used sequences of full-frame shots, as have countless examples, including the vast majority of Shakespeare productions drawn from stage presentations, across nearly a century of screen performance. Shots filling the frame are sequenced either live or in post-production editing to reveal interactions occurring within a real-world space. In contrast, with traditional production methods closed off in the spring of 2020, variants of a split-screen aesthetic were quickly established. Such was the prevalence of split-screen usage that this visual form emerged as the screen language of lockdown for digital performance.

Although this chapter may seem somewhat anomalous in a collection dedicated primarily to Shakespeare on screens during lockdown, it aims to explore the history and aesthetics of an alternative screen language to that of the tradition of screened Shakespeare performance. Developing from an initial discussion of the previously dominant sequential montage language of performance, it highlights precursors of split-screen language and considers the implications and possible meanings of this visual approach in the context of online theatre generally, especially in relation to ideas of connection and choice for the viewer. While it does not focus on extended experiments with split-screen language in Shakespeare performance in the past, it begins to apply its ideas to lockdown productions, and it is hoped that this offers some productive ideas for the more detailed discussions in subsequent chapters. Concluding remarks consider how the break that split screens represent for the dominant form of screen performance may impact on theatre and on the production of screen Shakespeare as cultural organizations emerge from the constraints of lockdown.

Breaking the frame

'Through most of the cinematic century,' Anne Friedberg has written, 'the dominant form for the moving image was, with striking consistency, a single image in a single frame.' Film extended the deep-seated understanding in Western systems of representation of the frame as a window into a world beyond. Friedberg has traced this metaphor back to the 1435 treatise on painting and perspective by Leon Battista Alberti, who 'famously instructed the painter to "regard" the rectangular frame of the painting as an open window' (2006: 1). Naturalized long before the cinema, and despite challenges by visual artists including Picasso and Braque in the early twentieth century, this conception of the frame was unquestioningly adopted by almost all film-makers. Nonetheless, Barry Salt has noted that alternatives in the form of split screens can be found in films as early as 1902 (1983: 72–3). Often associated with dreams or fantasy scenes, split screens were also used to visualize the mediated connection between two parties using the telephone, including in *Suspense* (1913), a drama directed by Phillips Smalley and Lois Weber. In Holger-Madsen's Danish drama *Balletens Datter* (1913) two characters speaking by phone are framed within oval vignettes on either side of a shot showing an elevated distant view of a modern metropolis. A better-known and more spectacular example of split screens from the silent period is the final reel of Abel Gance's epic *Napoléon* (1927) for which the director used the Polyvision process to film and project three images side by side.

Such split-screen sequences are examples of what the theorist Lev Manovich has defined as spatial montage, in which multiple images, often of different sizes and proportions, are juxtaposed on a screen at the same time. 'This juxtaposition by itself,' Manovich has noted, 'of course does not result in montage; it is up to the filmmaker to construct a logic that determines which images appear together, when they appear, and what kind of relationships they enter into with one another' (2001: 322). Spatial montage contrasts with the traditional temporal montage of cinema, whether in its deployment as the continuity editing of classical Hollywood cinema or in the more radical work of Soviet filmmakers, most notably Sergei Eisenstein. Employed in almost all film and television, including screen performance, temporal montage creates meaning from the sequencing of individual shots. Conjunctions and disjunctions across edits develop or disturb an unfolding narrative. By bringing together images often filmed non-continuously and in different real-world places, temporal montage creates recognizable space in time.

Employed most often as an attention-attracting special effect, spatial montage has had only a marginal presence in mainstream drama. A notable example from Hollywood in the 1950s is the 'Once Upon a Time' number from MGM's musical *It's Always*

Fair Weather (dirs. Kelly and Donen 1955), in which Gene Kelly, Dan Dailey and Michael Kidd, each in a different space, appear to dance side by side on screen. Michael Gordon's 1959 comedy *Pillow Talk* features a lightly eroticized mediatized conversation in a manner similar to *Suspense* nearly a half-century before. Here the characters played by Doris Day and Rock Hudson speak together on the phone while taking baths in their separate apartments. As they commune in telephonic space, their feet 'touch' across the boundary of the split-screen visualization. Such sequences have been understood by critics as a response to the apparent threat to the movies posed by television, an idea which is echoed in the more explicitly satirical presentation of the new medium in *It's Always Fair Weather*. In both cases, the spectacle of CinemaScope and Eastmancolor is complemented by special effects split-screening to demonstrate the visual and narrative pleasures the low-res, mostly monochrome domestic medium could not aspire to deliver. More than sixty years later, during lockdown in 2020, American musical theatre stars Katheryne Penny and Nathan Lucrezio demonstrated the easy availability via mobile phones and tablets of production techniques that were complex and expensive in 1950s Hollywood by posting to Facebook a home-produced video employing exactly the 'Once Upon a Time' technique (Falls Patio Players 2020).

A decade after *It's Always Fair Weather,* a group of mainstream films also made extensive use of split screens, including John Frankenheimer's motor racing drama *Grand Prix* (1966), the heist film *The Thomas Crown Affair* (dir. Jewison 1968), the serial-killer narrative *The Boston Strangler* (dir. Fleischer 1969), the festival documentary *Woodstock* (dir. Wadleigh 1970) and George Lucas's *American Graffiti* (1973). Jim Bizzocchi proposed that the split screens of this moment were a response to the vibrancy of youth culture, and most notably the centrality of pop and rock music. Split-screen sequences in the majority of these films were prominently associated with music, which supports Bizzocchi's proposal of the split screen as 'a cinematic attraction that was capable of "blowing the minds" and capturing the attention of a youth culture comfortable with expanded consciousness and oriented towards the visceral pleasures of the sensorium' (2009: 7). And while *Grand Prix* does not have an explicit address to a younger audience, its multiplied images, serial repetitions and near-abstract patterning across inset windows, coupled with the intense soundtrack, illustrate how split screens can suggest the heightened perceptions of immersive involvement in a sports context. Here too there is a direct engagement with 'the visceral pleasures of the sensorium'.

More than fifty years later, split screens, music and youth culture are once again brought together, this time with a strong participatory component, in the Duets function on TikTok. This facilitates a user recording their own video alongside an original, with the new recording being posted most often in the left-hand panel of a split screen. Initially introduced in 2017 as a way of users singing along with friends or responding as fans to well-known musicians, the function's potential for developing connections has, according to Alexis Bondy, 'created a unique capacity for community building, meaningful interactions, and support' (2020). TikTok saw what the trade magazine *Variety* described as 'meteoric' growth in 2020 with more than 100 million users across the world during lockdown and with rapidly increasing multi-generational use (Littleton 2020) (see Part Three).

Liberating the eye

Split screens faded from prominence in mainstream movies of the later 1970s, not least because of the complexity and expense of the optical printing techniques required to create them. But the availability of digital post-production methods at the turn of this century facilitated a number of independent films employing the device prominently, including work by Peter Greenaway and several features directed by Mike Figgis. Greenaway's most extended exploration to date is his digital film *The Pillow Book* (1996), although prior to this the director had used split screens, composite and overlapping images, and the collision of multiple visual and aural sources in his work for broadcast television, most notably in *A TV Dante* (co-created with Tom Phillips, 1990, Channel 4). The visualization of the first eight cantos of the *Divine Comedy* was supplemented by commentators who appeared in inset split-screen frames in a form of footnotes. In *The Pillow Book,* Greenaway conjured up an even more complex text, as Benedict Morrison has proposed:

[T]he film's form plays with both structure and meaning through a sustained use of layered frames: multiple frames coincide and compete, some eclipsing others. These complex mosaics – which make use of digital technologies to create intermedial collisions between images, texts, and sounds – transform the familiar sequential and sutured structures of narrative film editing into collages that are defined, instead, by complex simultaneity.

(2020: 1)

Figgis's sustained engagement with split screens began in *Miss Julie* (1999), elements of which he shot with two cameras running simultaneously. In post-production, a recently introduced digital editing system showed the two shots side by side, and Figgis displayed them in this way in an extended sequence of the final film. As he said: 'The eye was suddenly liberated, you weren't just a prisoner of the edit' ('Evolution of Split-Screen' 2021). In *Timecode* (2000), Figgis developed the possibilities of the visual language of split screens by running four stories simultaneously in real time in screen quadrants, a technique made possible not only by digital editing but also by the use of exceptionally lengthy, uninterrupted takes. These too were now achievable thanks to the recording capacities of new digital cameras. Figgis planned and choreographed his shoot so as to coordinate significant narrative events achieving prominence at particular moments in one or other of the frames. The eye may be liberated to roam across the four channels, but attention is directed by specific visual cues and also by the audio privileging significant elements. Figgis spoke of *Timecode* and of this narrative technique as a kind of fugue (ibid.). He also stressed the influence on these films of his work with live performance, not least in their use of uninterrupted takes, and also of theatre productions by the Wooster Group, which have often matched staged action with film or television recordings run on monitors set within the playing area. Figgis continued his split-screen experiments in *Hotel* (2002), a comedy drama about a British film crew shooting a screen version of John Webster's *The Duchess of Malfi* in Venice. One split-screen sequence features a night journey by gondola through Venice, the film's director getting medical attention after being shot, and a performance of Schubert's lied 'Der Doppelgänger.'

In the two decades since Figgis's experiments, split screens have also been employed by filmmakers closer to the mainstream. Ang

Lee's *Hulk* (2003) developed a complex screen language of panels that overlap spatially and temporally to parallel the graphical format of comics. Frank Miller and Robert Rodriguez's *Sin City* (2005) and Edgar Wright's *Scott Pilgrim vs the World* (2010) used split screens in a similar manner, while Steven Soderbergh's heist movie *Ocean's Thirteen* (2007) fragmented and recombined images of diegetic spaces in strikingly fluid ways. On occasions in the film, the split screen of the digital image is employed, as Malte Hagener has argued, 'to flesh out a different, non-classical and ambiguous space … It thus also reflects on the flexibility, modularity and potential transformations of the image in the computer – its overall unstable nature' (2008).

Small-screen split screens

From its beginnings in the late 1920s, television was understood, as John Caughie has detailed, as 'a technology for relay and adaptation … the service aesthetic seemed to define the horizons of aesthetic ambition' (2000: 41). Television brought that which was distant into proximity, seemingly with minimal mediation. As a consequence, as Friedberg has written, 'the televisual image largely followed the cinema's conventions of a single-screen format and sequential flow' (2006: 192). This was in part a consequence of television being broadcast live, at least until the gradual introduction of recording through the 1950s, and even when this was technically possible, the protocols of live production remained dominant for many years afterwards.

The process of multi-camera production, whether in the studio or as an outside broadcast, has in essence remained the same from the earliest days. Continuous feeds from the cameras are displayed simultaneously on a complex of screens; from these the screen director 'mixes' the selection to create the broadcast. The trace of a split-screen presentation, realized on physical monitors in the control rooms of the past and now more often on a single large digital screen, thus sits behind and makes possible a broadcast's sequence of single-screen frames. Conventional television broadcasts, of performance as well as of news and sports, involve creating a temporal montage from this hidden spatial montage, itself created from different simultaneous full-frame views of an event.

Split-screen television in a more familiar form, with two or more images (rather than monitors) embedded on the screen at the same time, was only possible technically from the late 1960s. The American producer Roone Arledge is credited with introducing the technique into sports broadcasting, including for skiing at the 1968 Grenoble Winter Olympics and then for baseball and American football. Understood as enhancing spectacle and excitement, split-screen techniques have been a staple of televised sports ever since. Split-screening is also familiar in news broadcasts, with a studio presenter calling up a correspondent 'on the spot' who appears in a separate frame. News channels have refined this form so as to feature multiple contributors to a discussion in a split-screen frame. In sports broadcasts, the idea persists that we are seeing two images from the same real-world space – the darts champion throwing and the close-up of the treble twenty on the board. News programming, by contrast, works unproblematically with the convention that the contributors are meeting in an electronic media space of connection. This is part of the reason why news and current affairs programmes adjusted comparatively easily to lockdown by displaying Zoom or its equivalents on screen – and also possibly why, in reverse and because we are familiar with a version of it on television, there was a rapid acceptance of the metaphor of the Zoom interface for meetings and online socializing. In sports and news, it might also be noted, there is the expectation that – for most of the time at least – we are seeing what is on the split screens *now*. Spectacle and self-reflexivity are key elements of television news and sport, but liveness is at least as fundamental to both types of broadcasting.

Single frames and self-reflexivity

Thinking specifically about dramatic performance, fixed, full-frame scenes presented in sequence was the screen language of performance from the first films. As Judith Buchanan has documented, this was the visual form of the earliest known Shakespeare production on film. In 1899, the British Mutoscope and Biograph Company shot at least three scenes of Herbert Beerbohm Tree's staging of *King John* (2009: 57–73). Each key moment was recorded on celluloid in a static wide shot that echoed the visuals of earlier media such as *tableaux vivants*, engravings and lantern slides. Numerous short performance films worked with this model, although a Shakespearean counter-example, the Clarendon company's *The Tempest* (dir. Stow 1908), used a layered shot combining two separately exposed images to illustrate Prospero and Miranda watching a storm-tossed ship through their cave's entrance. But the use of a split screen here, supposedly diegetically motivated but also comparable to other moments of dreaming or fantasy in early film, was rare in stage adaptations for the cinema, and has remained so to the present. Writing of productions of Shakespeare from what film historians characterize as the 'transitional' era (c.1907–13), Buchanan identified an increasing use of editing and camera movement, in common with almost all other genres of film in these years. But at the same time as the near-universal adoption of 'classical' narrative conventions, there was also the continuation of 'strict adherence to theatrical forms of representation ... [and] a sustained allegiance to the material's medium of derivation' (2009: 76). The presentation of performance on screen had to remain as direct and as unmediated as possible so as to simulate closely the spectator's presumed engagement with an artist playing upon a stage. This conception was carried across to television from the 1930s onwards. The presentation, for example, of a stage play, ballet or opera from a theatre was understood by television practitioners as comparable to an outside broadcast of a football match. This did not mean attempting to mimic a fixed viewpoint of a particular audience member but rather showcasing the stage performance through a visual language that was effectively 'invisible', as if the broadcast were unmediated. And while the screen language of sports and news programming responded to new technological possibilities, especially after the arrival of digital post-production, performance on television continued to be presented by a stream of consecutive single frames, whether the broadcast was the Proms, *Strictly Come Dancing* or Shakespeare. Image definition and audio quality have seen radical improvements, as has the mobility of cameras, but, in almost all essentials, concerns to achieve 'immediacy' and invisible mediation have continued to shape a conservative screen language that carried through to the event cinema broadcasts of the 2010s. The prevailing ethos was that performance is best and most respectfully served by a visual language of conventional continuity editing.

One performance form developed for television, however, broke radically with this ethos. Music video as a form is now ubiquitous across the whole range of screens, but its modern form developed with the cable channel MTV (Music Television), officially launched in 1981. Andrew Darley has argued that music video as a form is 'constructed upon an intensification and augmentation of modes of image combination or montage' (2000: 103), and split-screening – facilitated again by the arrival of digital technologies – is just one of its hypervisual modes. There are countless examples, among which are 'Emotion' by Destiny's Child (2001), in which director Francis Lawrence employs vertical split-screening; and Joseph Kahn's video for Blink-182's 'Always' (2004), which splits the screen horizontally. In direct contrast to the conservative screen language of most television performance, music video is a pre-eminently self-reflexive form. Among many critics who have developed variants of this argument, Darley has written that 'music videos make little or no pretence at hiding their eclectic media saturated dependence on other forms. They are definitively and conspicuously *about image*: about creating an image for a sound, a performer or performers, and (as often as not) for a performance' (2000: 116).

In conventional screen performance, however, the self-reflexivity of split screening is thought to impede in some way the viewer's direct experience of the drama or the dance. In this framework, the performance broadcast is focused on relaying a musician's interpretation or an actor's Iago, and is most certainly not about drawing attention to the image. One personal experience can perhaps illuminate this further. In 2008, I watched in the Clapham Picturehouse cinema a Met Opera Live in HD broadcast of Wagner's *Tristan und Isolde* (2008). Viewing this great music drama on the big screen I was surprised by the use of split-screen close-ups inserted into wide shots for the long, largely static duets, and thought this was an effective interpretative technique. As the credits rolled, however, and the name of the screen director, Barbara Willis Sweete, came up on screen, several people in the row behind me started to boo. When I asked the booers to explain, they said they wanted 'Wagner pure and simple' and did not appreciate the performance being 'messed about with' with the inserts. They loved, as it were, seeing the New York stage now, but they had no interest in anything suggesting self-reflexivity.

Only connecting

Before lockdown, split-screen techniques comparable to those employed in *Tristan and Isolde* were used exceptionally rarely in screen adaptations of theatre productions. But over the past decade and more, a developing body of stage performance has integrated screens within live production in increasingly sophisticated ways, as in the work of director Katie Mitchell. In a number of her productions the audience watches live action, camera operators filming that action and, on one or more screens above or to the side, the camera's digital feed. The live action and the screened feed split the stage space, and Sarah Atkinson has proposed parallels between Mitchell's work in *Forbidden Zone*, first staged for the Salzburg Festival in Austria in 2014, and the split-screen aesthetic of Figgis and others:

> [T]he overall formal quality of Mitchell's stage production creates a visual multi-screen picture-in-picture effect, invoking a digital aesthetic (a trope in various multi-screened films that proliferated in the early 2000s with the advent of digital editing, and an aesthetic of digital postproduction edit interfaces). The viewer is positioned as voyeur and is witness to the various screened vignettes, reminiscent of Alfred Hitchcock's *Rear Window* (1954).
>
> (2018: 198)

Paralleling Mitchell's work, although often conceived on a grander scale, have been productions by Ivo van Hove for his company Toneelgroep Amsterdam. Their large-scale multi-play stagings 'after William Shakespeare' of *Roman Tragedies* (first performed in 2007) and *Kings of War* (2015) integrate into their immersive settings a dense display of screens presenting archival news footage and graphical representations of data feeds as well as live elements from the drama. Sarah Hatchuel has identified the 'hyper-mediatization' of these productions, noting that French critics of *Roman Tragedies* compared the production to the Fox series *24* (2001–10), a television thriller that made extensive use of split-screens (2011: 54). In January and February 2021, Internationaal Theater Amsterdam (ITA) live-streamed multi-camera versions of both of these large-scale stagings. The visual density of the interplay between staged action and video feeds within the playing space was extended to the screen of the stream, which featured a dense flow of diegetic pictures-in-picture as well as selections from the video elements being displayed on the screen. Split-screen visuals were created both by cameras displaying multilayered action including a range of screens and by digitally edited compositions.

In *Julius Caesar*, for example, the conversations on the night before the assassination between Brutus (Roeland Fernhout) and Portia (Ilke Paddenburg), played out on one sofa in the setting, and between Caesar (Hugo Koolschijn) and Calpurnia (Janni Goslinga) on another, were run in parallel on the stage, but displayed on screen in a digital composition of four frames. This composition was played full frame in the stream for some moments but also presented on one or more of the on-stage monitors and as a projection, which could at times be glimpsed in a wider framing for the stream. As Holger Syme has commented on this moment in the stage production, '[b]locking and videography provide something like an analytical commentary on the parallels between the scenes and the characters, even as the two pairs of actors perform their dialogue as if they were in fact alone, and as if they were in greater physical proximity than they actually are' (2017). Throughout the stream, rather than there being, as is almost always the case with a screen version of a theatre work, the sense of a pre-existing staging being adapted and mediatized in a distinct process for the screen, the stream, with split images from both stage and video mix, felt as if it was a central, entirely integrated element of a singular intermedial project.

Developing the comparison with the television thriller series, Hatchuel argued that, 'Just as in *24*, Ivo van Hove's screen must not necessarily be seen as "split", but rather, as Monica Michlin argues, as "a web of images, *connected* rather than *separated* by the lines that criss-cross the TV screen"' (2011: 54). Michlin in her own detailed engagement with the narrative strategies and visual style of *24* has developed this key point about the language of split screen (which is also implicit in Manovich's term 'spatial montage'): that it is invariably used to make connections, between the three returning veterans in *It's Always Fair Weather*, between the developing narrative lines of *Timecode*, and indeed between the physically distanced players of Rotterdams Philharmonisch Orkest and the dancers of Ballet de l'Opéra national de Paris (2009). With the overwhelming majority of cultural connections in lockdown moving from physical spaces to media spaces, split screens realized and visualized those connections in effective and affecting ways.

Complementary to the idea of split-screen visuals connecting the disparate elements within the frame is the argument that split-screen language offers a distinctive and perhaps more democratic viewing experience. Figgis's comment about *Miss Julie*, that 'you weren't just a prisoner of the edit,' was echoed by Deborah Jermyn writing about *24*: 'it invites the viewers to embrace the act of editing for themselves' (2007: 51). Discussing screened performance, Bernadette Cochrane and Frances Bonner have argued that 'the primary virtue of the live experience [is] the ability, indeed the right, of each audience member to select and compile his or her own edit of the proceedings.' For Cochrane and Bonner, this ability is significantly constrained when watching a conventional presentation of a dramatic performance on screen, such as is offered in an NTLive presentation:

> For the relay, the NT Live Director for the Screen (albeit in consultation) decides what we see and when we see it. No longer do we the audience choose where, when, or towards whom we turn our gaze. Now, the screen close-up focuses on the speaker; now, a reaction shot; now some pertinent element of the set. A relevant prop may occupy the screen, reflecting or anticipating a mention in the current speech. But all of this is decided for us; we have ceded our rights of reception to the Director.
>
> (2014: 127)

Might then the use of split-screen techniques in performance restore to the spectator aspects of this ability to compile their own edit, and to wrestle back from the screen director elements of the right of reception? In a final section I consider further examples of split-screen use in recent lockdown presentations, drawing together elements associated with the form including the use of long takes, the idea of connection, hyper-visuality, self-reflexivity and the question of the spectator's rights of reception.

Views and hyper-visuals

CtrlAltRepeat's *Midsummer Night Stream*, directed by Sid Phoenix in April 2020, was one early production that used Zoom as both a production tool and as connected playing space with combinations of between one and five screens appearing and disappearing within the overall frame. Whenever a character was 'on stage', a continuous long take kept them within one of the inset streams, offering the viewer the freedom to focus attention as they wished across the visible characters. As in many such split-screen Zooms, in comparison to the single frame sequencing of conventional stage performance, the eye was liberated, albeit to only a modest degree, since the viewer's attention was focused by the audio of the character who was speaking. This echoes Figgis's techniques in *Timecode* in which he used the intensity of action and especially audio levels to impose a kind of edit for the spectator across the four simultaneous narratives. The split-screen interface was also exploited by what Gemma Allred identified as 'metatheatrical nods to the conventions of Zoom calls [which] added a reality to the production', and the playful use of names on screens and Snug's flipping between Virtual Backgrounds enhanced the inevitable self-reflexivity of Zoom (2020: 425).

Zoom designates the mode when multiple feeds are on the viewer's screen simultaneously as Gallery View, and while this may have been applied because the images are arrayed like paintings on a wall in an art space, it also suggests the area of a television production studio known as the gallery where the director monitors and selects from multiple camera feeds. Gallery View effectively positions the viewer as the screen director, monitoring all of the feeds and selecting from and sequencing them in a mental operation rather than a technical one. In contrast, in Speaker View the software makes an automated choice of a single feed by following a session's audio, but there is invariably a lag in this being applied and the operation is inconsistent (which is likely why very few online performances have opted to work with this). Creation Theatre has attempted to overcome these problems by using the streaming software package vMix to emulate the work of the screen director in a conventional multi-camera broadcast. This was apparent from the controlled and innovative use of split screens in the company's

The Duchess of Malfi in May 2021, which established a graphical screen space quite distinct from the Zoom interface and exploited the positioning of frames, colour washes and overlays to conjure an online world appropriate to Webster's nightmare. In the spatial montages in Gallery View, or when human control is directing the visuals, or indeed when the glitches of Speaker View expose the imperfect workings of the software, aspects of the artifice of production are revealed and embraced. In this self-reflexivity, as well as in the use of long takes and the connections between the frames which bring the cast into a virtual and electronic playing space (much like the telephone calls of *Suspense*, *Ballatens Datter* and *Pillow Talk* discussed earlier), *Midsummer Night Stream* employed many of the key aspects of spatial montage. As did the production of *A Midsummer Night's Dream* from The Back Room Shakespeare Project, although here the added use of FaceTime recordings and filters, shots of web pages and animations, message feeds and more also pushed the production, which used a partially modernized text, towards the hyper-visuality of music videos (2020).

Only a minority of online performances that employed the language of split-screens, however, aspired to the hyper-visuality demonstrated by the *Dream* from The Back Room Shakespeare Project. Another was the exceptionally achieved production of Caryl Churchill's *Mad Forest* directed by Ashley Tata (2020). For this, Tata's collaborators customized Zoom's code to create a modified version to allow for real-time camera editing, effectively transforming it into a video production suite. With more than one hundred Virtual Backgrounds, the production created a visually dazzling screen world for Churchill's drama of the 1989 Romanian Revolution, referencing a wide range of contemporary images and constantly moving between an integrated screen and multiple frames duplicating and echoing each other in constantly shifting patterns. Contrasted with most lockdown performance, the intricacy and inventiveness of this live production of *Mad Forest* demonstrated that while the use of split-screen language elsewhere might have been extensive, it was for the most part only moderately imaginative. Limited budgets, together with minimal experience within the performance sector of the technology or the ability to 'hack' it, have acted as constraints on its use, and arguably there has been no lockdown performance employing split screens in a manner as extended or as radical as the work discussed above by Greenaway or Figgis.

Nonetheless, the awareness and exploration of split screens, and their broad use and acceptance across lockdown performance, has offered a challenge to the previously dominant conventions of sequentially edited full-frame presentation. That split screens will be a mainstream rather than a marginal option beyond lockdown was suggested by two small-scale *In Camera* productions in the summer of 2020 from the Old Vic. The two-hander *Lungs* by Duncan Macmillan, with Claire Foy and Matt Smith, and Stephen Beresford's monologue *Three Kings*, written for and played by Andrew Scott, were both presented live online from the theatre's stage. Two camera feeds for the former and three for the latter were choreographed by Matthew Warchus, directing for both stage and screen, in mixes that made extensive use of split screens, despite there being no separation-imposed necessity to do so. In *Three Kings*, two and later three feeds of Scott in split-screen configurations were used to complement his playing of multiple characters, and as the reviews indicated the technique was accepted as appropriate and indeed naturalized. Jesse Green wrote that Warchus 'sometimes splits the screen as if [Scott's character] Patrick were coming apart, [as] Scott fearlessly leaps from one stage of his fragmenting personality to another' (2020).

In *Lungs*, the paired camera shots were present within the overall frame throughout, which meant both characters could be seen and scrutinized throughout the exceptionally rapid dialogue exchanges. Given the rich detail of the performances, this was an especially welcome 'liberation of the eye'. In the opening frame, with a keyed graphic thanking viewers for supporting the Old Vic, the two actors walked on opposite diagonals across the stage. On the cut, as they turned to face the two cameras, the graphic disappeared and each was digitally inserted into an identical inset frame now separated by only a thin border. Unlike any other screened performance they were positioned within, or rather at the borders between, both a stage space and a distinct screen space, and this was underlined when they on occasions again crossed the stage to be positioned within the frame taken by the other moments before. They returned only to the stage space for bows at the close, uneasily presented to pre-recorded applause, but again with the keyed graphic, as if the production wished to avoid embracing fully the auditorium.

The live-stream productively exploited the liminality of stage and screen as it unfolded, with the cameras following the characters, constantly adjusting shot sizes, sometimes matching and

FIGURE 1 *Matt Smith and Claire Foy in the split screens of* In Camera: Lungs *directed by Matthew Warchus for The Old Vic. Screenshot.*

sometimes contrasting them, and both anticipating and responding to the actors' movements. In one sequence, they sat back to back, brought into an electronic intimacy comparable to that of Hudson and Day in their *Pillow Talk* baths. At another moment, charged with eroticism, the inset frames melded the actors' bodies 'across' a split screen. Throughout, the use of the split screens was expressive rather than decorative (since the visual language might otherwise only have been employed to liven up the sparse staging of a modest two-hander), and the selection and spatial montaging of the shots constantly enhanced the text's complex engagement with ideas of connection and separation. In the closing moments, after we had lived right through their life together, and against intimations of ecological catastrophe, the death of one of the couple and the consequent alone-ness of the other, was made all the more poignant by the fade to black in one frame and the pitiless continuation of life in the other.

One other indication of a fundamental shift in the screen language of performance was Young Vic director Kwame Kwei-Armah's announcement that, rights permitting, all of the company's productions would in future be live-streamed. Moreover, the streams would permit viewers to choose between the camera feeds across a show. 'What do I love about the live experience?', he said.

Even though the director pushes me in the direction of where he or she wants me to look, I have the final say. I can choose to look at the person who is stage left. I can choose to look at the person who is stage right. I can choose to look at my fellow audience members. That's really where the idea was born – of giving the audience the choice to change seats.

(Brown 2021)

Kwei-Armah is not – yet – proposing split-screen feeds, but he is indicating his sense of a need to liberate the eye. As the theatre ecology emerges from lockdown, the innovations of Warchus and Kwei-Armah are likely to contest the space of screen performance with the more conventional and familiar forms. Indeed, the Young Vic employed their innovative multi-feed technology for their live-streams of *Hamlet*, with Cush Jumbo as the Prince, in late October 2021. As this plays out, the historical examples of split-screen languages and the imperatives that lay behind them, together with the explorations developed during lockdown, should be valuable touch points for theatre and broadcast creatives to consider, both in the screen presentations of Shakespeare and across the full spectrum of performance.

References

Allred, G. K. (2020), 'Review of Shakespeare's *A Midsummer Night's Dream* (titled *Midsummer Night Stream*)', *Shakespeare*, 16 (4): 424–6.

Atkinson, S. (2018), 'Synchronic Simulacinematics: The Live Performance of Film Production', in L. Feiersinger, K. Friedrich and M. Queisne (eds), *Image-Action-Space: Situating the Screen in Visual Practice*, 191–201, Berlin: De Gruyter.

Bizzocchi, J. (2009), 'The Fragmented Frame: the Poetics of the Split-Screen', draft paper, School of Interactive Arts and Technology, Simon Fraser University. Available online: http://web.mit.edu/comm-forum/legacy/mit6/papers/Bizzocchi.pdf (accessed 28 November 2021).

Bondy, A. (2020), 'Why Is TikTok So Obsessed With Duets?', *Medium*, 18 October. Available online: https://medium.com/swlh/why-is-tiktok-so-obsessed-with-duets-b0d1cc44149c (accessed 28 November 2021).

Brown, M. (2021), 'Young Vic to livestream all future productions, says artistic director', *Guardian Online*, 6 May. Available online: https://

www.theguardian.com/stage/2021/may/06/young-vic-to-livestream-all-future-productions-says-artistic-director (accessed 28 November 2021).

Buchanan, J. (2009), *Shakespeare on Silent Film: An Excellent Dumb Discourse*, Cambridge: Cambridge University Press.

Caughie, J. (2000), *Television Drama: Realism, Modernism and British Culture*, Oxford: Oxford University Press.

Cochrane, B. and F. Bonner (2014), 'Screening from the Met, the NT, or the House: what changes with the live relay', *Adaptation*, 7 (2): 121–33.

Darley, A. (2000), *Visual Digital Culture: Surface Play and Spectacle in New Media Genres*, London: Routledge.

'"Dire merci": Message de soutien du Ballet de l'Opéra national de Paris' (2020), YouTube, 16 April. Available online: https://youtu.be/OIiG14Ggmu0 (accessed 28 November 2021).

'The Evolution of Split-Screen Cinema' (2021), YouTube, 15 February. Available online: https://youtu.be/WkCEkqSkyKI (accessed 28 November 2021).

'Falls Patio Players: Nathan Lucrezio is with Katheryne Penny' (2020), Facebook, 28 May. Available online: https://www.facebook.com/fallspatio/posts/check-this-out-friends-/10158414467788279/ (accessed 28 November 2021).

Friedberg, A. (2006), *The Virtual Window: From Alberti to Microsoft*, Cambridge, MA: MIT Press.

'From us, for you: Beethoven Symphony No. 9' (2020), YouTube, 20 March. Available online: https://youtu.be/3eXT60rbBVk (accessed 28 November 2021).

Green, J. (2020), 'Review: In *Three Kings*, Hot Priest Sheds His Cassock', *New York Times*, 6 September. Available online: https://www.nytimes.com/2020/09/06/theater/review-three-kings-andrew-scott.html (accessed 28 November 2021).

Hagener, M. (2008), 'The Aesthetics of Displays: How the Split Screen Remediates Other Media', *Refractory* 14 (24), December. Available online: https://webarchive.nla.gov.au/awa/20091001064435/http://blogs.arts.unimelb.edu.au/refractory/2008/12/24/the-aesthetics-of-displays-how-the-split-screen-remediates-other-media-%e2%80%93-malte-hagener/ (accessed 28 November 2021).

Hatchuel, S. (2011), *Shakespeare and the Cleopatra/Caesar Intertext: Sequel, Conflation, Remake*, Vancouver, BC: Fairleigh Dickinson University Press.

In Camera: Lungs (2020), [Online performance], presented by The Old Vic, 26 June–4 July.

In Camera: Three Kings (2020), [Online performance], presented by The Old Vic, 3–5 September.

Jermyn, D. (2007), 'Reasons to Split Up: Interactivity, Realism, and the Multiple-Image Screen in *24*', in S. Peacock (ed.), *Reading 24: TV Against the Clock*, 49–57, London: I.B. Tauris.

Littleton, C. (2021), 'Why TikTok's popularity exploded during the pandemic', *Variety*, 27 January. Available online: https://variety.com/2021/digital/news/tiktok-popularity-covid-1234893740/ (accessed 28 November 2021).

Mad Forest (2020), [Online performance], presented by Theater for a New Audience and Fisher Center at Bard, 22 May.

Manovich, L. (2001), *The Language of New Media*, Cambridge, MA: MIT Press.

Michlin, M. (2009), 'Narrative and Ideological Entrapment in *24*: Plotting, Framing, and the Ambivalent Viewer', *GRAAT 9*, December.

Midsummer Night Stream (2020), [Zoom-to-YouTube], presented by CtrlAltRepeat, YouTube, 11 April. Available online: https://youtu.be/iEls9I4tSLs (accessed 28 November 2021).

A Midsummer Night's Dream (2020), [Film], presented by The Back Room Shakespeare Project, 21 April. Available online: https://youtu.be/j2gOa7jjzEw (accessed 28 November 2021).

Morrison, B. (2020), 'Dismembered Frames: Dialectic Intermedia in Peter Greenaway's *The Pillow Book*', *Open Screens*, 3 (1): 1–31.

Salt, B. (1983), *Film Style and Technology: History and Analysis*, London: Starword.

Syme, H. (2017), 'British Theatre under the Influence', *dispositio*, 25 March. Available online: http://www.dispositio.net/archives/2418 (accessed 28 November 2021).

Turk, V. (2020), 'Zoom took over the world. This is what will happen next', *Wired*, 6 August. Available online: https://www.wired.co.uk/article/future-of-zoom (accessed 28 November 2021).

2

Lockdown Shakespeare and the Metamodern Sensibility

Benjamin Broadribb

Together/Apart

The nature of our existence during the Covid-19 pandemic is paradoxical. Stopping the spread of the virus requires us to be physically apart; but in order to get through times of global crisis, it is essential for humanity to feel more connected than ever. Our social spaces – restaurants, places of worship, theatres – have both become meaningless through dormancy, closure and the human void within them; *and* taken on greater resonance as monuments to the human connection they facilitated pre-Covid, their emotional significance robbed of depth yet deeper than ever in the same instant.

Rather than inaugurating this concurrent togetherness and separation, the pandemic has amplified and catalysed this sensibility which already defined the opening decades of the twenty-first century. The creation and reception of Shia LaBeouf, Nastja Säde Rönkkö and Luke Turner's 'live-streamed durational artwork' HEWILLNOTDIVIDE.US throughout its four-year timespan offers a touchstone of this wider sense of together-apartness, at least within the Western world (Turner n.d.). HEWILLNOTDIVIDE.US ran for the entirety of US President Donald Trump's time in office 'as a show of resistance and insistence, opposition and optimism, guided by the spirit of each individual participant and the community' (ibid.). The artwork began as a 'participatory performance' in which members of the public delivered the phrase 'He will not divide us' into a wall-mounted camera, later changed to a live-stream of a continuously flying flag emblazoned with the same phrase (ibid.). Writing four days after its initial installation at the Museum of the Moving Image in New York, William Earl described the artwork as 'a melting pot of ages, races, genders, sexualities, and beliefs ... [an] impromptu community, in which people you'd never know or notice became fellow warriors, dance partners, chant buddies, and family' (2017). However, LaBeouf, Rönkkö & Turner's installation instigated discord as well as harmony: Earl reported instances of Trump supporters aggressively attempting to disrupt the performance and goad those taking part (ibid.). Two months later, the exhibit closed in New York after it became 'a flashpoint for violence and was disrupted from its original intent', resulting in the first of several changes of venue over its duration ('Statement from Museum of the Moving Image' 2017). The case of HEWILLNOTDIVIDE.US offers a microcosmic reflection of how Trump's presidency epitomized twenty-first-century together-apartness: uniting humanity through commonalities, whilst simultaneously dividing them further through a lack of empathy.

LaBeouf, Rönkkö & Turner identify themselves as proponents of 'metamodernism', a term proposed by cultural theorists Timotheus Vermeulen and Robin van den Akker for the predominant cultural sensibility that has emerged since the turn of the millennium (2010: 2). Vermeulen and van den Akker describe metamodernism as 'a structure of feeling that emerges from, and reacts to, the postmodern', characterized by the return of historicity, affect and depth following the inauthenticity, detachment and depthlessness identified by Fredric Jameson as defining features of the postmodern Western world (2017: 5). They adhere to Raymond Williams's definition of a structure of feeling, which they explain as 'a sensibility that everyone shares, that everyone is aware of, but which cannot easily, if at all, be pinned down. Its tenor, however, can be traced in art, which has the capability to express a common experience of a time and place' (ibid.: 7). According to Vermeulen and van den Akker, postmodern artists '"recycled" popular culture, canonised works and dead Masters by means of parody or pastiche'; in contrast, 'metamodern artists ... increasingly pick out from the scrapheap of history those elements that allow them to resignify the present and reimagine a future' through the '"upcycling" of past styles, conventions and techniques' (ibid.: 10). In doing so, metamodernism is 'characterised by an oscillating in-betweenness' which offers 'not a balance but a pendulum swinging between various extremes' (ibid: 11). These include, but are not limited to, 'a modern enthusiasm and a postmodern irony, between hope and melancholy, between naïveté and knowingness, empathy and apathy, unity and plurality, totality and fragmentation, purity and ambiguity' (Vermeulen and van den Akker 2010: 5–6). Turner states that '[t]he metamodern generation understands that we can be both ironic and sincere in the same moment; that one does not necessarily diminish the other' (2015). He also identifies numerous cultural works he recognizes as metamodern, including (but not limited to) the films of Spike Jonze and Miranda July, the music of Donald Glover and Janelle Monáe, the TV series *Parks and Recreation* and *BoJack Horseman*, and the novels of David Foster Wallace and Zadie Smith (ibid.).

It is my contention that the heightened separateness and connection of humanity that have gone hand in hand throughout lockdown offer a marker of our metamodern era; and that the way in which Shakespeare has been performed and adapted online in lockdown evinces a metamodern sensibility to create cultural artefacts of twenty-first-century society both during and beyond the pandemic. The remainder of this chapter offers a journey through adaptations and performances of Lockdown Shakespeare which, I argue, provide examples of the metamodern structure of feeling our Covid-19 cultural moment has magnified. In identifying these works as metamodern, I am conscious of James MacDowell's observation that the label 'risk[s] impoverishing the phenomena [it] describe[s] if defined carelessly or applied indiscriminately' (2017: 27). In short, I will not be suggesting that each work creates a metamodern aesthetic in the same way, or even creates the same sensibility. Just as the postmodern structure of feeling of the late twentieth century manifested itself in multifarious ways – the *King Lear* adaptations of Peter Brook (1971) and Jean-Luc Godard (1988) are both recognized as examples of postmodern cinema, as are *Monty Python and the Holy Grail* (dirs. Gilliam and Jones 1975), *Blade Runner* (dir. Scott 1982) and *Pulp Fiction* (dir. Tarantino 1994), but all five are clearly very different films – so the manner in which the metamodern sensibility can be identified and interpreted is also varied. However, in exploring the metamodern qualities of a selection of examples of Lockdown Shakespeare, I aim to newly consider (and hopefully in some way answer) a question Douglas Lanier posed about Shakespeare in popular culture nearly two decades ago: 'What is Shakespeare doing here?' – simultaneously asking what function Shakespeare plays in pop culture, and what business he has being there at all (2002: 2). Or, to put it another way, I hope to elucidate both how and why Shakespeare has been employed in lockdown to reflect and fit into the sense of together-apartness which permeates the wider cultural moment of the Covid-19 pandemic.

To be/Not to be

Sofa Shakespeare's first production, *Romeo and Juliet*, opens with Julia Giolzetti, the project's creator, at home in Poway, California, appropriately on her sofa. She sits cross-legged in jogging bottoms and a T-shirt with a quote from the play – 'Then I defy you, stars!' (5.1.24) – printed on it. Giolzetti's dog sits beside her. Behind her is the everyday detritus of family life – a throw blanket, discarded clothing – presumably moved to the back of the sofa to give her space to sit. Giolzetti begins to perform the Prologue, but is interrupted after four lines by her young daughter from behind the camera, prompting a calm but firm extratextual 'Rosie, quiet!' She continues, pulling two soft toys from behind a cushion to demonstrate the 'star-crossed lovers tak[ing] their life' (Prologue.6). A couple of lines later, her dog gives her a few licks to the chin. When Rosie interrupts again, Giolzetti invites her daughter to join her on the sofa for the final lines of the Prologue. Fade out. Fade into Darcy Porter, in her bedroom at home in Orange County, California, performing the opening exchange of Act 1 Scene 1, holding tarot cards up to either side of the screen to demonstrate each change in character. Like Giolzetti, Porter makes no effort to hide her everyday life, as clothes spill onto the floor from a wardrobe behind her. A minute later, Kalina Jones picks up the role of Sampson from her home in Parkersburg, West Virginia, whilst an uncredited family member awkwardly reads the lines of Gregory for her – their 'naked weapon[s]' (1.1.32) a long cardboard tube and walking stick respectively. Another minute passes, and we move to Ashley Engleman at home in San Diego, California, voicing a bottle of whiskey 'playing' Sampson (labelled 'Booze-son'), whilst, over Skype, Larissa Ryan voices another whiskey bottle seen on a laptop screen 'playing' Abraham ('Boozraham'). A minute later, and we are in Jenna Brucoli and Isaiah Tanenbaum's home in Brooklyn, New York, where the scene continues as a crude sock puppet show, the pair using both their hands and feet to represent different characters.

And so *Sofa Shakespeare*'s adaptation continues as a crowdsourced full text production of *Romeo and Juliet*. Each approximate minute of the play was allocated to a performer who had signed up to contribute, recorded in isolation, then sent to Giolzetti to edit together with the other contributions. The adaptation was made available for free on YouTube to watch as individual scenes, as well as a complete film lasting just under three hours. Giolzetti created fourteen productions in this way from March 2020 to March 2021. *Sofa Shakespeare*'s approach to Shakespearean adaptation is fundamentally postmodern: by dividing the plays up into one-minute sections, performed by different people without continuity of actor, performance style or aesthetic, it detaches the adaptation as a whole from any deeper meaning a production with a continuous cast and approach might have. The individual minutes exist as discrete adaptations, but often lack meaning if watched in isolation. Sections such as Engleman's whiskey bottles and Brucoli and Tanenbaum's sock puppets in particular approach Shakespeare with irreverence, presenting a Shakespearean pastiche in the manner of Jameson's idea of postmodern pastiche as 'blank parody', offering 'the imitation of a peculiar or unique, idiosyncratic style ... [but] a neutral practice of such mimicry, without any of parody's ulterior motives, amputated of the satiric impulse' (1991: 17). Edited together, Giolzetti's *Romeo and Juliet* offers a postmodern patchwork adaptation, the constant shifting between modes and settings highlighting the artifice of the production and presenting Shakespeare incongruously at times to the point of incoherence. Characters are passed from one performer to another, their identity likely to become lost as one clip switches to the next. The format forces the audience to constantly recalibrate their conception of character and form throughout – even audience members who know the play well will likely need to take a moment to work out which new performer is playing which character.

Whilst being inherently postmodern in its deconstruction of Shakespeare and explicit artifice, *Sofa Shakespeare* is undoubtedly imbued with authenticity of a different kind. Giolzetti states her intention was 'to create an opportunity for anyone who was game to perform Shakespeare for a global audience from the confinements of their living rooms. The joy in watching the storytellers change every minute is in seeing all of us at home; with our pets, kids, messy bedrooms, wet hair, finger puppets, and T-Rex costumes' ('What is Sofa Shakespeare?'). The aim of each *Sofa Shakespeare* production is not to create a Shakespeare adaptation of continuity or even coherence. Shakespeare functions as a unifying textual conduit to enable those taking part, and those watching, to achieve connection in a time of separation. Contributors were given some simple technical guidelines by Giolzetti on how to record their performance (those using smartphones were instructed to film in landscape, for example) as well as a window of between eighteen and forty-eight hours to film and submit their minute of the play, but other than that were told: 'You do you. As long as the video has the words and it's a minute, you're golden' ('Actor FAQs'). As a result, whilst one contributor will have made different aesthetic choices to the next, each clip is affectively linked by the sincerity of the performers in committing to their low-tech aesthetic and real-world surroundings. Nobody hides behind a façade of domestic perfection, but earnestly creates their minute of the play in their homes – with real life creeping in however and whenever it chooses to do so.

Examining the adaptation of Act 3 Scene 1 of *Hamlet*, *Sofa Shakespeare*'s final production, reveals the metamodern oscillation which can be experienced throughout Giolzetti's project. The scene begins with the Newman family – specifically their four children – performing the opening dialogue. Their sequence is notably postmodern through its inclusion of intertextuality (Rosencrantz wears a *Rosencrantz and Guildenstern are Dead* T-shirt), Shakespearean in-jokes (fruit on the table is labelled 'Rotten' and 'Not rotten') and pop culture references (Polonius is 'played' by a cardboard stand-up of US politician Bernie Sanders, specifically that of him seated in a large coat and mittens at the inauguration of President Joe Biden which became an internet meme in early 2021). Ashleigh Ehren continues the scene through a crude puppet show using plastic Muppet toys. The pop culture status and inherent humour of the Muppets gives her performance a sense of postmodern pastiche; but the well-worn appearance of the toys, perhaps childhood keepsakes (Kermit, playing Claudius, is missing an eye), and the low-tech charm of the puppetry lend Ehren's segment sincerity. Next, the audience is thrust into a Zoom-style aesthetic by Patrick McGuire, Justin Charles, Kathia Torres and Kelly Neuls. Recorded separately, their four performances are edited together to resemble a video conference call, complete with the characters 'turning off' their cameras when they exit to parallel the convention of Zoom performance in lockdown.

The scene then shifts suddenly from the explicit artifice of the Zoom aesthetic to unfiltered reality, as Giolzetti herself delivers the opening lines of Hamlet's 'To be, or not to be' speech (3.1.55). The actress lies on her bed, her heavily pregnant belly exposed, her performance one of sincere vulnerability. Hamlet's speech is famous to the point that its meaning can easily become obscured by its ubiquity; but hearing it delivered by Giolzetti in this way breathes life into Hamlet's words. Phrases such as 'the thousand natural shocks that flesh is heir to' (3.1.61–62) take on new meaning as Giolzetti caresses her belly with one hand throughout her performance. Dathan B. Williams continues the speech, his mouth filmed in extreme close-up in high-definition black and white. The filming choice brings the audience uncomfortably close to Hamlet's words, which again resonate anew: spoken by an American actor of colour, Williams's opening line – 'The pangs of despised love, the law's delay' (3.1.71) – inexorably echoes the injustices that drove the Black Lives Matter protests in the United States and beyond during the height of the pandemic. The scene continues, actors at home shifting from one performance style and set-up to another, creating a metamodern patchwork *Hamlet* which oscillates between postmodern deconstruction and pastiche, and modern sincerity and affect.

Make/Believe

Perhaps the defining signifier of our together-apart existence during the pandemic is the stratospheric rise of Zoom. Developed as a business video conferencing tool, Zoom was rapidly repurposed in lockdown as a virtual social, familial and – most importantly for this volume – theatrical space. Zoom has emerged as a metamodern technosocial marker of the pandemic: simultaneously facilitating affective connection, heightened further by our wider historical and cultural moment; *and* reducing our friends, our families, ourselves, into depthless low-definition digital duplicates. Whilst creating a sense of togetherness for people worldwide, Zoom's now-familiar Gallery View interface also serves as a persistent reminder of our enforced physical distance.

As a result, Zoom offers an inherently metamodern performance space, a sensibility which Zoom-based Lockdown Shakespeare productions have embraced in different ways. CtrlAltRepeat overtly acknowledged the platform in their two Shakespearean adaptations, setting the plays on Zoom to create a sense of real-world authenticity. As Artistic Director Sid Phoenix notes, '[i]t's very hard to think of something that's more of today than Zoom. ... The more that we can ground [the production] in everyone else's experience, the more resonance we're going to find in [Shakespeare's] words' (Chapter 9: 174). In contrast, *The Show Must Go Online* (*TSMGO*) treated Zoom more like a bare early modern stage, directing the audience's attention towards the performance rather than the digital space in which it was taking place. *TSMGO*'s metamodern sensibility came through what Master of Props Emily Ingram describes as a 'homespun aesthetic' – unapologetically low-tech props and costumes created by the cast and crew which offered 'physical, tangible things at a time when so much of our lives are very digital and intangible' (Chapter 7: 156). Artistic Director Rob Myles emphasizes the power of 'collective belief' in *TSMGO*'s productions – as Ingram observes: 'if you believe it's not cardboard and tinfoil, then the audience will believe as well' (ibid.: 151, 156).

Matt Pfeiffer's Zoom-to-YouTube production of *A Midsummer Night's Dream* for Philadelphia-based Arden Theatre Company (ATC) on 5 June 2020 offered a distinct example of the metamodernism of Zoom performance. The production began with Puck (Anna Faye Lieberman) tapping the lens of her webcam, then glancing around at her performance space. Puck's apparent awareness in these opening moments of her existence as a character being performed by an actor into a webcam postmodernistically acknowledged Pfeiffer's *Dream* as both a theatrical performance and its mediation through Zoom, drawing attention to its inherent artifice. This irony then swung towards sincerity as Puck sounded a chord on an unseen piano, then waited expectantly. Nothing. A second chord, a hopeful look around. A third chord, and a second Zoom window appeared as Lysander (Bryan Freedman) entered with a guitar. He strummed in reply, a look of joy spreading over Puck's face at having another person in her world. As Lysander took over musical duties, the rest of the cast appeared on screen, turning their cameras on one by one to create a grid of tessellated Zoom windows. Once all eleven cast members were present, Lysander's guitar-playing paused; Puck conducted the cast in taking one silent, synchronized breath in and out – shared air, in a time when such a thing felt impossible. Lysander strummed a final chord, and all but Theseus (Justin Mitchell) and Hippolyta (Brittany Onukwugha) turned their cameras off to begin the opening scene. The sequence simultaneously acknowledged the cast's apartness, their performances inherently separated by their Zoom windows, whilst facilitating an overwhelming sense of togetherness through musical and respiratory synchrony.

Following her omniscient introduction, Puck emerged as the main agent of the production's metamodern sensibility, most acutely demonstrated through the transition from the court of Athens at the end of Act 1 to the forest realm at the start of Act 2. As in the opening moments, music facilitated synchronous togetherness through the flute-playing of Dana Liu's fairy. As Liu began her tune, Puck reappeared, again staring straight down her camera lens to acknowledge her audience and the Zoom performance space. Paralleling the desire for tangibility and authenticity of both CtrlAltRepeat and *TSMGO*, Pfeiffer chose not to use Virtual Backgrounds, instead opting for a low-tech minimalist aesthetic with the cast performing against simple backdrops: plain surfaces or sheets hung to obscure – but importantly not mask entirely – the actors' domestic settings. Seemingly unsatisfied with the dark blue wall behind her, Puck first hung a string of colourful fairy lights. She then reached off camera and held up a paper plate simply decorated with felt pen to look like the moon, which she stuck to the wall above the fairy lights – crafting her own rudimentary night sky backdrop. As Puck fastidiously checked her fairy lights were hung to her satisfaction, Liu switched off her camera feed, although her audio continued. The sounds of her flute transformed from a tune to sound effects, with Lieberman's mime-like performance giving the

FIGURE 2 *Puck (Anna Faye Lieberman) creating her picture-book night sky to the flute-playing of the fairy (Dana Liu) in Arden Theatre Company's* A Midsummer Night's Dream. *Screenshot reproduced courtesy of Arden Theatre Company.*

impression the fairy had entered her own frame – music magically transcending the separation of the two characters. Puck traced her finger in the air to 'follow' the fairy as Liu played a descending scale, before flicking the fairy off her shoulder to a high-pitched squeal. After briefly exiting the frame, Puck returned to deliver 'How now, spirit, whither wander you?' (2.1.1) with comedic annoyance as Liu's flute-playing resumed to confirm she had not been dispatched after all.

Puck's construction of her scenery in front of the audience drew attention to the artifice of the performance as a whole. And yet, in the same moment, the brightly coloured balls of light and crudely drawn moon, the playful flute score and cartoonish sound effects, channelled both the low-tech aesthetic and collective belief of performer and audience inherent to Zoom performance. Pfeiffer's aesthetic choices for this sequence in particular also brought to mind what MacDowell has identified as the 'quirky sensibility', a key example of metamodernism in cinema (2012: 8). MacDowell suggests that 'as well as conveying knowingness, the [quirky] style also hints towards a kind of *naïveté*' through a 'boldness and simplicity [that is] often seemingly intentionally purified, bespeaking an effort to remake the world in a less chaotic form' (ibid.: 9). He notes how '[b]right, block colours can be key to this sense' as well as music with 'a sound and feel reminiscent of the tinkling purity of a child's music box' (ibid.). Lieberman's performance throughout was characterized by childlike sincerity and enthusiasm: a finger in the air when she had an idea; carefully placing the fairy lights just so; gleefully presenting her crudely drawn moon; cracking her knuckles with satisfaction when her work was complete; dusting off her hands after flicking the fairy off her shoulder. Puck acknowledged the camera in front of her, but this never undermined the authenticity of her performance or the play's world. Puck sincerely believed in the abstract, fanciful setting she had created, like a child playing make-believe constructing an imaginary world. Indeed, Puck's costume – a floral waistcoat over a plaid shirt, bright yellow round-rimmed spectacles and an orange beanie hat – made her feel just as much a part of that world. MacDowell argues that '[p]erhaps more than anyone, [Wes] Anderson exemplifies one extreme of the [quirky] sensibility's visual style' (ibid.). Anderson's unnaturalistic yet sincere picture-book aesthetic in films such as *The Royal Tenenbaums* (2001) and *The Grand Budapest Hotel* (2014) has become a hallmark of the director's work; the childlike nature of Lieberman's Puck and her overtly simplistic and crafted world felt like a lockdown cousin of Anderson's films and quirky cinema more widely, imbuing Pfeiffer's *Dream* with a distinctly metamodern sensibility.

Black/White

As the fifth episode of Sally McLean's web series *Shakespeare Republic: #AllTheWebsAStage (The Lockdown Chronicles)* begins, on-screen captions tell us we are in Lancashire, England, in May 2020. A news-bulletin-style voiceover, read by McLean, sets the scene further: with UK pubs remaining closed, many in Britain are 'resistant to change'. Leo Atkin enters the frame wearing a Manchester United football shirt under a zip-up hoodie, clutching a half-drunk pint of beer. Settling into a chair in his suburban Lancashire back garden, he assures us: 'I'll put a girdle round the earth in forty minutes!' (2.1.175–6), before taking a swig. Coming from Atkin's distinctly un-fairylike Puck – a world away from Lieberman's version – the claim has perhaps never been less convincing. Atkin proceeds to deliver Puck's earlier speech – 'I am that merry wanderer of the night' (2.1.43) – not as a supernatural sprite, but as a pub bore forced out of his natural habitat, similarly displacing Shakespeare's words from their original time and place and into the world of 2020 – a choice characterized by a postmodern sense of deconstruction and irony. Alongside this, however, there are choices throughout by both Atkin and McLean which offer palpable sincerity, affect and depth. Foremost amongst these is McLean's decision to present the episode – and indeed the entire series – in black and white. For a project facilitated by the abundance of handheld digital camera technology available to isolated actors on three different continents, the aesthetic is both prominent and distinct – especially true when considering that the first two series of *Shakespeare Republic*, filmed pre-Covid for Australian television, were broadcast in colour.

Filmmakers who have made black-and-white films in the twenty-first century have given numerous reasons for doing so. Geoff Andrew has noted black-and-white cinema's link to nostalgia, describing Alexander Payne's *Nebraska* (2013) as a film that 'isn't actually set in the past, but it's very much about the past … It's a very nostalgic film' (Fox 2013). Payne himself highlights black and white's severe aesthetic, saying it lent *Nebraska* 'a visual style as austere as the lives of the people in the film' (ibid.). On a practical level, black and white has logistical advantages: speaking about his 2013 film *A Field in England*, Ben Wheatley notes that black and white allows 'a lot more latitude for shooting outdoors and matching shots together than you have in colour' (ibid.). Whilst Wheatley's film is set in the past during the English Civil War, its black-and-white aesthetic adds to *A Field in England*'s surreal nature, the lack of colour taking it one step further from reality. Jay Hunter, cinematographer on Joss Whedon's film adaptation of *Much Ado About Nothing* (2012), describes the impact choosing to shoot Shakespeare in black and white had in similar terms. Whilst he and Whedon 'wanted it to be very natural', they also 'thought it would be a cool way to tell the story in a modern setting and also throw it into this alien universe of monochrome. Taking a text that's hundreds of years old, bringing it into the modern world, then sending it back another 40 years' (Patches 2013). Black and white can therefore act as a conduit for metamodern cinema: inducing affective connections to the places, people and periods depicted or evoked, whilst also undermining their depth through transforming them into colourless echoes. It simultaneously augments and undermines the authenticity of the world the director creates – somehow too real and not real in the same moment.

It is likely that McLean chose black and white for her 2020 series at least partially to overcome some of the practicalities of shooting remotely during lockdown: it lends the finished episodes both a cinematic gloss and visual harmony colour footage would not achieve. However, the aesthetic inescapably creates a sense of melancholic nostalgia for our pre-pandemic past, whilst also creating distance by drawing attention to the cinematic artifice of what we are watching. Performing as Puck, Atkin is clearly sitting in his actual back garden – evidently inhabiting our world, but drained of the vibrancy that makes it real. This is heightened further by McLean's choice to include brief establishing shots which situate Puck as being surrounded by nature (including, appropriately, a robin). McLean shoots these with documentary realism, presenting a recognizable and authentic version of contemporary England, highlighting the natural over the man-made world to suggest a focus on purity as well as a nostalgic link to the country's pre-industrial past. The black-and-white aesthetic simultaneously augments this sense, whilst also undermining it through working as an overt reminder of the episode's status as a crafted piece of cinema.

Whilst Atkin's casting as Puck and his choice not to play the role as a magical being make the artifice of *The Lockdown Chronicles* overt, the final moments of his performance create the episode's most palpably metamodern section. As in the play, Puck joyfully concludes his speech with the assertion: 'A merrier hour was never wasted there' (2.1.57); Atkin then laughs heartily as he reminisces and takes another sip of beer. His laughter gradually subsides, however, giving way to a wistful expression of longing, the moment of theatrical comedy transforming into one of realistic sadness. Atkin's affective sincerity in mourning the loss of a way of life very much in living memory reflects the wider emotional challenges many in the audience are likely to have experienced themselves. We arguably stop viewing Atkin as Puck, seeing in him an authentic reflection of ourselves and the affective toll of the pandemic. The final shot/reverse shot first cuts to Atkin's dog Eddie staring at him – complete with a cone collar – offering a brief moment of visual humour. However, Eddie's expression is clearly one of concern for his master, simultaneously offering both comic relief and a conduit for the audience's own concern for Atkin in this moment. McLean then cuts back to Atkin, now in close-up, appearing to avoid Eddie's (and the audience's) eye, instead dejectedly looking to the ground. It is a melancholic ending which contrasts Atkin's previous jollity, reframing it as a surface-level performance of happiness in contrast to the wordless emotional depth of the episode's final moments.

This oscillation between authenticity and artifice pervades McLean's web series more widely. Episode 6, set in Melbourne, Australia, features Israeli actress Maya Cohen as Adriana from *The Comedy of Errors*, performing the character's 'Ay, ay, Antipholus, look strange and frown' speech (2.2.118-154). Whilst Kent Cartwright describes Adriana's speech as 'earnest and moving … for its evocation of lapsed love', he notes nonetheless that it 'variously shifts towards comedy' (Shakespeare [1595] 2017: 186). This sense of earnestness is amplified, and the humorous elements diminished, through McLean removing Adriana's speech from its original comedic context; like Atkin's Puck, Cohen's Adriana gains a deeper sense of sincerity. In the play, Adriana's speech is rendered comical through misunderstanding and mistaken identity – not only is her husband not being unfaithful to her, but she is also not speaking to her husband at all. In McLean's film, however, Adriana is restlessly waiting at home for Antipholus. A series of jump cuts shows her anxiously checking her phone, adjusting a homemade 'Happy Anniversary' banner hanging behind her, checking her phone again, seated with her feet up on the empty chair next to her – a visual reminder of her absent husband. She sips a glass of wine, then sets it on a table next to a bread and cheese board – a celebratory date genuinely missed by Antipholus, rather than the comedy mix-ups of the play. The unassuming yet sincere handicraft of the 'Happy Anniversary' banner suggests Cohen's Adriana and her Antipholus's relationship was formerly one of playfulness and innocence (creating a parallel with the childlike aesthetic of ATC's *Dream*). However, McLean's black-and-white aesthetic robs the presumably brightly painted letters of this sense, the banner simultaneously existing as a signifier of former joy and current heartache. Much of Cohen's performance is filmed in mid shot so that a second item hanging on the wall – a heart-shaped chalkboard with 'I love you … ' handwritten upon it – appears in shot over her shoulder. Like the anniversary banner, the chalkboard appears as a reminder of her former love, the ellipsis perhaps signifying the oscillation between her conflicting past and present feelings for her husband.

In addition to delivering her speech with sincerity throughout the film, at two points Cohen speaks lines from Adriana's speech translated into her native Hebrew, a decision which directly feeds into the metamodern nature of the episode. The two translated lines – 'As take from me thyself, and not me, too' (2.2.137) and 'For if we two be one, and thou play false' (2.2.150) – both relate to the coalescent identity of husband and wife, a shared being which Adriana believes has been tainted by Antipholus's infidelity. The Hebrew lines importantly do not offer self-contained sentences: both they and the English lines surrounding them need each other to become complete, a linguistic representation of Adriana's language of the married couple as 'undividable, incorporate' (2.2.130). Switching between languages also lends the performance a sense of earnestness, as if Cohen's Adriana is at times moving into her mother tongue in order to give more heartfelt voice to her feelings – and also attempting to re-establish part of her own separate identity. However, whilst this grants Adriana a sense of depth, the choice simultaneously highlights the inherent artifice of Cohen's performance. Much as we see Atkin the actor sitting in his English garden, the lines force the audience to see the Israeli actress more than they see the character she is playing in these moments. This artifice then oscillates back to a different form of authenticity: that of the real isolated actress, performing Shakespeare alone in lockdown from her living room. Furthermore, as with all episodes in the web series, these forms of authenticity are simultaneously enhanced and destabilized by being filtered through McLean's black-and-white aesthetic. As a result, Cohen swings between multiple poles of depth and depthlessness, authenticity and artifice – a metamodern Adriana for our lockdown cultural moment.

Lockdown/Shakespeare

Having explored the metamodern sensibilities of my chosen Lockdown Shakespeare examples, I return to the question posed in this chapter's opening section: what is Shakespeare *doing* in lockdown? Terence Hawkes argues that '[w]e use [Shakespeare's plays] in order to generate meaning. ... Shakespeare doesn't mean: *we* mean *by* Shakespeare' (1992: 3). Turning to Shakespeare during the pandemic, as so many on both sides of the fourth wall have done, is the latest example of human beings looking to Shakespeare's plays in an attempt to make sense of living through a period in which many of the ways we give our lives meaning have suddenly, and indefinitely, been removed. The meaning that is being generated in *Sofa Shakespeare*'s productions, ATC's *Dream* and *Shakespeare Republic: #AllTheWebsAStage (The Lockdown Chronicles)* is specifically tied to our lockdown structure of feeling, which I consider to be distinctly metamodern. Acting as a familiar constant in a time defined by unfamiliar and unpredictable variables, Shakespeare has become the conduit through which creatives are, to cite Vermeulen and van den Akker once again, 'express[ing] a common experience of a time and place' – in this case, the experience of living during the Covid-19 pandemic.

Whether through *Sofa Shakespeare*'s patchwork adaptations, ATC's playful acknowledgement and transcendence of its Zoom windows, or *The Lockdown Chronicles*'s heightened artifice and realism, our together-apart existence permeates all three projects to reflect our metamodern state of being. In doing so, rather than depthlessly recycling Shakespeare with cynicism, creatives have upcycled his works 'to resignify the present and reimagine a future' beyond the pandemic. The metamodern sensibility is not restricted to the examples of Lockdown Shakespeare discussed here, however – other productions have created their own metamodern sensibilities. I recognize Zoom performance in particular as inherently metamodern, so any Lockdown Shakespeare created through Zoom will likely offer its own flavour of metamodernism. For example, Big Telly's *Macbeth* (dir. Zoë Seaton), which I have argued 'captured the simultaneous realness and unrealness of virtual theater', takes in elements of all three modes of metamodernism presented here, as well as undeniably offering its own (Broadribb 2022: 283; see Chapter 11). In this way, Lockdown Shakespeare contributes to the wider metamodern structure of feeling which permeates twenty-first-century culture, and which the experience of pandemic life has heightened.

Shakespeare is not essential to our metamodern sensibility. But the abundance of Lockdown Shakespeare suggests that, since March 2020, creatives and audiences have looked to him to generate meaning for themselves. Whilst both the work of other writers and newly written pieces have been performed in lockdown, as Pascale Aebischer notes, 'Shakespeare emerges from this period as a common reference point and source of comfort, as well as a focal point for community building and manic cultural activity' (2021: 11). Our lives since early 2020 have been metamodern: oscillating between different planes of existence; simultaneously discovering new depths and losing something of ourselves; cynically questioning the events of the present whilst sincerely hoping for a brighter future; embracing new creative and connective outlets whilst yearning for the old ones to return. With routines disrupted, human contact limited and time itself seemingly more elastic as countries around the world tighten and loosen lockdown restrictions, what Shakespeare is doing in lockdown is providing an anchor – something that, from the perspective of those creating and consuming Lockdown Shakespeare in our Covid-19 world, has always been there.

References

'Actor FAQs'. Available online: https://sofashakespeare.com/actor-faqs (accessed 28 November 2021).

Aebischer, P. (2021), *Viral Shakespeare: Performance in the Time of Pandemic*, Cambridge: Cambridge University Press.

Broadribb, B. (2022), 'Review of *Macbeth*', *Shakespeare Bulletin*, 39 (2): 279–83.

Earl, W. (2017), 'Shia LaBeouf's "HE WILL NOT DIVIDE US": Here's What It's Like To Peacefully Exorcise Trump's Bad Vibes', *IndieWire*, 24 January. Available online: https://www.indiewire.com/2017/01/shia-labeouf-he-will-not-divide-us-livestream-chant-review-1201772138/2/ (accessed 28 November 2021).

Fox, K. (2013), 'How black-and-white movies made a comeback', *The Observer*, 30 June. Available online: https://www.theguardian.com/film/2013/jun/30/black-and-white-movies-comeback (accessed 28 November 2021).

Hamlet (2021), [YouTube] *Sofa Shakespeare*, 17 March. Available online: https://youtu.be/9uhlCCmM_Ac (accessed 28 November 2021).

Hawkes, T. (1992), *Meaning by Shakespeare*, London: Taylor & Francis Group.

Jameson, F. (1991), *Postmodernism, or, the Cultural Logic of Late Capitalism*, Durham: Duke University Press.

Lanier, D. (2002), *Shakespeare and Modern Popular Culture*, Oxford: Oxford University Press.

'LONDON: Puck (A Midsummer Night's Dream) – Leo Atkin (UK)', *Shakespeare Republic: #AllTheWebsAStage (The Lockdown Chronicles)* (2020), [Web series] dir. Sally McLean. 15 August. Available online: https://www.facebook.com/1405128449782920/videos/309428430137957 (accessed 28 November 2021).

MacDowell, J. (2012), 'Wes Anderson, tone and the quirky sensibility', *New Review of Film and Television Studies*, 10 (1): 6–27.

MacDowell, J. (2017), 'The Metamodern, the Quirky and Film Criticism', in R. van den Akker, A. Gibbons and T. Vermeulen (eds), *Metamodernism: Historicity, Affect, and Depth After Postmodernism*, 25–40, London: Rowman & Littlefield.

'MELBOURNE: Adriana (The Comedy Of Errors) – Maya Cohen (Australia)', *Shakespeare Republic: #AllTheWebsAStage (The Lockdown Chronicles)* (2020), [Web series] dir. Sally McLean. 19 August. Available online: https://www.facebook.com/1405128449782920/videos/1429788333871363 (accessed 28 November 2021).

A Midsummer Night's Dream (2020), [Zoom-to-YouTube] Arden Theatre Company, 5 June. Available online: https://youtu.be/7ApwMSbvEGo (accessed 28 November 2021).

Patches, M. (2013), '"Much Ado About Nothing" and Why the Future of Monochrome Photography isn't Black & White', *MTV News*, 5 June. Available online: http://www.mtv.com/news/2770744/much-ado-about-nothing-black-and-white (accessed 28 November 2021).

Romeo and Juliet (2020), [YouTube] *Sofa Shakespeare*, 25 March. Available online: https://youtu.be/qNLurIlYAsw (accessed 28 November 2021).

Shakespeare, W. ([1595] 2017), *The Comedy of Errors*, ed. K. Cartwright, London: Bloomsbury Arden Shakespeare.

'Statement from Museum of the Moving Image on closure of HEWILLNOTDIVIDE.US' (2017). Available online: http://www.movingimage.us/exhibitions/2017/01/20/detail/hewillnotdivide-us/ (accessed 28 November 2021).

Turner, L. (n.d.), 'HEWILLNOTDIVIDE.US'. Available online: https://luketurner.com/works/hewillnotdivideus (accessed 28 November 2021).

Turner, L. (2015), 'Metamodernism: A Brief Introduction', *Notes on Metamodernism*, 12 January. Available online: http://www.metamodernism.com/2015/01/12/metamodernism-a-brief-introduction/ (accessed 28 November 2021).

van den Akker, R. and T. Vermeulen (2017), 'Periodising the 2000s, or, The Emergence of Metamodernism', in R. van den Akker, A. Gibbons and T. Vermeulen (eds), *Metamodernism: Historicity, Affect, and Depth After Postmodernism*, 1–19, London: Rowman & Littlefield.

Vermeulen, T. and R. van den Akker (2010), 'Notes on metamodernism', *Journal of Aesthetics & Culture*, 2 (1). Available online: https://www.tandfonline.com/doi/full/10.3402/jac.v2i0.5677 (accessed 28 November 2021).

'What is Sofa Shakespeare?'. Available online: https://sofashakespeare.com/about (accessed 28 November 2021).

3

Notions of Liveness in Lockdown Performance

Gemma Kate Allred

The debate over what constitutes liveness and its application to digital arts is not new. Peggy Phelan argues for liveness to exist only in the here and now, that a '[p]erformance's only life is in the present' ([1993] 2005: 147). Furthermore, Phelan argues that streamed productions, even live-streamed productions, 'can give us something that closely resembles the live event but they nonetheless remain something other than live performance' (2003: 295). Key to Phelan's argument is what Erika Fischer-Lichte has termed 'the bodily co-presence of actors and spectators' ([2004] 2008: 28). In contrast, Erin Sullivan draws on Philip Auslander's contention that:

> [I]t may be that we are now at a point in history at which liveness can no longer be defined in terms of either the presence of living human beings before each other or physical and temporal relationships.
>
> (2012: 6)

Sullivan argues for moving away from definitions of liveness based on bodily co-presence and towards definitions formulated by reference to event-connectedness – through online interaction or congregation of audiences in cinemas, in each case physically distanced from the actors. Doing so allows definitions of liveness to focus on the 'phenomenological experience that foregrounds interactivity and a feeling of togetherness' rather than 'technical requirements about time and place' (2018a: 61). Interactions on social media such as live tweeting could fulfil the need for event-connectedness. Joanna Bucknall and Kirsty Sedgman argue that online interaction leads audience members to feel as if they are 'part of the event', enabling 'the experience of liveness to travel outside the confines of physical co-presence' (2017: 124).

Discussions to date have, generally, presupposed a physical proximity between the actors: that the performance itself meets Phelan's requirements for the here and now, and that attendance in person to a shared air experience is theoretically possible. The debate has focused on whether productions streamed 'as live' such as Globe on Screen or NTLive Encore performances allow for a sense of liveness notwithstanding the temporal distance of performance and reception. Where lockdown productions differ is in the absence of touch. Actors are, predominantly, socially distanced and performing in isolation to temporally proximate yet physically distanced audiences. Where productions have been performed in and streamed from a shared space, such as the RSC's *Swingin' The Dream* in January 2021 or the Old Vic's 2020 *In Camera* season, blocking has ensured the actors remain socially distanced. The space between actors gains dramaturgical significance – shared distance rather than shared proximity. Traditional streamed theatre – the established 'live' theatre broadcast – retains an echo of the performance, of the sense of bodies moving in shared space: an audience visibly, physically present, or the suggestion that they could be. Lockdown performance draws attention to its lack of in-person audience: productions live-streamed from empty theatres use establishing shots of empty auditoria. When live-streaming *Romantics Anonymous* from Bristol Old Vic, Emma Rice introduced the production by walking through the auditorium, the equipment needed to live-stream replacing an in-person audience. The Old Vic *In Camera* season placed the actors facing the rear of the stage, the empty seats acting as the backdrop. Performing at home, the rectangular Zoom boxes frame the actors' private domestic spaces.

Mike Alfreds contends that theatre is the 'double process of transforming the here-and-now into the there-and-then, and bringing the there-and-then into the here-and-now' (2009: 13). In common with Phelan, he presupposes co-presence. However, his notions of liveness are founded in terms of audience participation – a contract wherein 'actors initiate a transaction, the audience completes it ... [through] a shared act of imagination' (ibid.). While Alfreds pushes against indiscriminate use of technology, he concedes that it can be consciously used to amplify the 'language of theatre: metaphor, transformation, imagination' (ibid.: 16). Lockdown performance exploits these amplifying possibilities to underscore its liveness. Embedded markers of ephemeral performance reveal production processes – actors merge into their green screen Virtual Backgrounds; ring lights and tripods are placed in view; actors physically build sets around them on screen.

Analysing a range of lockdown productions this chapter responds to Laura Collins-Hughes's assertion in the *New York Times* that:

> Digital theater isn't theater: it's a way to mourn its absence. The industry's show-must-go-on smile masks a harder truth: that there is no substitute for the live interaction between performer and audience.
>
> (2020)

An assertion I refute through examining immersive Virtual Theatre, where the audience is present via a Zoom call; Zoom-to-YouTube performance, where the audience reacts via Live Chat; and the aesthetic choices of live-streamed performance. Exploring what happens to notions of liveness when theatre embraces the possibilities of together-apart, I argue that the temporal proximity of actor and audience, and the embedded markers of ephemeral performance, afford digital theatre the equivalent quality of liveness as in-person theatre notwithstanding the absence of physical proximity.

Immersive Virtual Theatre

April 2020. Nathaniel, my four-year-old son, is jumping on the sofa, squawking. He's holding a puppet of a bird we have made from coloured paper and straws. He stops. 'Mummy, I'm on television!'. We've been Spotlighted. Selected from the gallery of virtual audience members to be featured on screen in a moment of audience participation by the 'Zoom Wizard' behind Creation Theatre's interactive The Tempest (dir. Zoë Seaton). The image changes, Madeleine MacMahon's Sebastian stumbles into shot, her hair in disarray, bird poop over her face. Nathaniel giggles in glee. Cause and effect.

When theatres closed in March 2020, Zoom quickly emerged as the medium of choice for digital theatre. Actors and audiences gathered, framed in a mosaic of rectangular Zoom boxes. The quirks of Zoom required audience members to actively unmute themselves in order to grant the host control of their microphones, the unexpected side effect being the gentle hum of pre-show conversation as audience members took their places on sofas and arranged last-minute drinks. Creation's *Tempest* co-opted the audience as Ariel's (Itxaso Moreno) spirits, helping create her magic (see Aebischer and Nicholas Chapter 4). Clicking fingers suggested rainfall, stamping feet created thunder. A tangible action creating intangible magic. While not explicitly set on Zoom, Seaton's Island exploited the surveillance possibilities of multiple cameras and screens: Prospero (Simon Spencer-Hyde) appeared in front of a wall of surveillance screens as he monitored his island, a device taken from the 2019 in-person production that felt prescient in 2020 when the world moved online. The surveillance cameras were then turned onto the audience as Alonso (Al Barclay) hacked the feed and joyously addressed the audience directly as a stream of 'furry friends' were offered up to the screen. It would be easy to dismiss the audience participation as pantomime-like silliness within a light-hearted production. However, I suggest that its impact goes to the core of liveness creating the event-connectedness Sullivan claims is needed in physically distanced performance.

As I have previously noted in respect of this production:

> [A]udience participation created a sense of community, a rare opportunity in a socially distanced world to come together with strangers and act as one. As the spotlight focused on members of the audience, it offered a glimpse into other people's locked-down homes. I saw individuals, couples, and families like mine staring back, joining in, all participating and working together to create this imaginary world.
>
> (Allred 2021: 537)

Congregation and co-creation, an ephemeral moment of shared time between actor and audience.

October 2020. I'm (virtually) sitting at the Macbeths' table, the edge of my sofa at home in Champéry, Switzerland, occasionally glitching into view. Banquo (Dharmesh Patel) appears on screen over my shoulder. A witch (Lucia McAnespie) fills the goblet on the table in front of me with wine. Further along the table sits my Dad. I can see light reflecting off his glasses, and I know he's sitting in his chair by the window at home in Shrewsbury, UK, his laptop on his knee.

Big Telly's *Macbeth* (dir. Seaton) played with the expectations of Zoom-based theatre. The production opened with what had, by October 2020, become the norm in Virtual Theatre: the audience gathered on Zoom and were asked to join in an audience participation task. As part of a political press conference, the Chief Science Advisor (McAnespie, a witch in disguise, unbeknownst to the audience) instructed audience members to hold a piece of paper up to the camera stating their location. Those Spotlighted were tested for 'witchcraft' – a fantastical threat equivalent to Covid-19, offering a light-hearted introduction playing on the serious real-world pandemic. The audience was instructed to light a candle, close the curtains, and not open the door – a nod to the three-step slogans of UK government Covid-19 advice. The impact was to influence the audience's viewing conditions, offering a suggestion of a commonality of space – dispersed households all watching in similar dimmed lighting, together-apart. As audience members were Spotlighted, the flickering candlelight in their homes played on the screen. Crissy O'Donovan, a producer at Big Telly, notes, 'when you're asked to turn off your lights and light a candle, for seventy-five minutes your room becomes somewhere different, so you're actually transporting your environment'. It is a recreation of the theatre environment within your own domestic space.

Framed as a *Truman Show*-style narrative in which the Macbeths were trapped in a world created and manipulated by the witches, the edges of the world flexed and contracted as it was never clear what was real and what was an illusion. Seaton exploited vMix Open

Broadcaster Software (OBS) to allow isolated actors to appear together on screen, creating the illusion of physically shared space. As Seaton notes, she avoided naturalism, opting instead for mismatched Virtual Backgrounds that were often out of scale – giant stairs loomed in the Macbeths' hallway as the composite OBS images glitched slightly at the edges (Chapter 11: 202). As the Macbeths were pulled further into the manipulated world of the witches, so too were the audience. Seaton placed audience members at the Macbeths' table and then later in the box of the empty Theatre Royal Brighton, where the witches delivered their prophecy to Macbeth (Dennis Herdman). This was more than the brief flutter of excitement of a momentary starring role. The audience were placed within the world alongside Macbeth, adding a sense of equivalency. Whilst Spotlighting offered an image of the audience in their own home as spectator, embedding their images within the scene reframed the audience as actor and co-creator.

'TAKE THE SHOT, ARCHER'. *It's April 2021, over a year into the pandemic. I'm dressed in my 1980s finest, crimped hair, drinking a Piña Colada with a tiny little umbrella. It's the final performance of digital theatre company CtrlAltRepeat's non-Shakespearean immersive '80s action movie-inspired* Viper Squad: Remastered. *Our sniper on the scene has encountered Neville, an out-of-place coffee repairman caught in the midst of a bank heist. My suspicions are raised. I give the order to shoot. He's hit. Falls. I'm called back to Control to be chastised. Too hasty, trigger happy. We now have an injured civilian whose trust we need to regain. This wasn't the way the production played out last week when I wasn't the person calling the (literal) shots.*

Viper Squad tasked audiences with neutralizing a Wall Street hostage situation. The production drew on the company's extensive experience as immersive theatre practitioners – and, as with in-person immersive theatre, no two performances were the same, with different story arcs influenced in the moment by the audience's actions. Through a 1980s action movie aesthetic, the production reframed Zoom in a time-out-of-joint fashion as *Viper Squad*'s proprietary 'Zero Oversight Optimal Messaging' system. The decisions made in Breakout Rooms impacted the wider audience experience. Simple choices – such as placing marksman Archer (David Alwyn) at a distance or up close – immediately changed the available information. The dialogue was different every night as audience members negotiated directly with bank robbers and the actors improvised responses. That's not to say there wasn't a guided narrative; however, once a choice was taken, all other options fell away, and the narrative arc changed. As with *The Tempest* and *Macbeth,* the audience participation had a real-time influence, with the temporal proximity of actor and audience working together in Alfreds's contract of shared imagination (2009: 13).

I would suggest, however, that for lockdown performance, which is by its nature physically distanced, the absence of temporal proximity between actors and audience prevents any sense of liveness, even where the audience is tasked with making decisions and influencing narrative arcs. In November 2020, Fresh Life Theatre's *Mortal Fools* was adapted from *A Midsummer Night's Dream* by director Charlie Day. Marketed as a 'Decision making game', it offered a series of pre-recorded videos on YouTube, each ending with a choice. As Sullivan notes, aesthetic 'works are fundamentally participatory in their design: they are brought to life not simply by the artist who creates them, but also by the auditor or spectator who receives them' (2018b: 120–1). 'Brought to life' – but not live. *Mortal Fools's* launch video casts the audience as a participant 'asked to make decisions and to help [Oberon Entertainment] understand what humans would do when put in extraordinary scenarios'. Day placed the participant in a position of power – ostensibly offering control of their experience. Fresh Life's Twitter feed encouraged the audience to '[m]ake decisions for the characters and shape your story. Order or chaos? It's your choice' (2020). It's an attractive sales pitch: the opportunity to step into the play and make changes. However, as the game progresses, it is increasingly clear that it is an illusion of agency: a seductive offer of autonomy that crumbles under closer inspection. The game is structured such that all paths ultimately lead to a common crossroads with essentially compulsory videos.

While there are fifty routes and ten endings, all are pre-recorded: they only ever existed on YouTube, waiting for me to click and watch, to make the choice. The route I take may be self-determined, but the alternative endings and routes nevertheless still exist within a multiverse. My choices, while impacting my experience, cannot influence anybody else's. Nor do my choices offer finality: I can replay the game either as a single narrative or as a 'do-over', going back and changing my choices – the same videos rearranged. However, the echoes of the multiverse exist and persist. I know in the moment this is not live, that it is not trying to be live. *Mortal Fools* does not capture the echoes of a performance but is rather a series of scenes, waiting to be assembled into a coherent narrative. Lacking temporal proximity, the experience will never be live, nor can it offer the sense of a live performance recorded to be experienced afresh. As with *Viper Squad*, decisions I make change my experience in the moment, but these changes importantly lack the ephemeral nature of performance. The edited and pre-recorded videos exist not as a moment captured but as one created.

Digital groundlings

March 2020. I'm waiting for The Show Must Go Online's *first Zoom-to-YouTube production – The Two Gentlemen of Verona – watching the number of viewers slowly increase. In the chat my fellow, unseen, audience members announce their locations:* 'Arizona', 'London' 'St. Petersburg', 'Bucharest'. *As Rob Myles introduces himself and the actors, excitement builds in the chat:* 'Wow!!!', 'YAY, very happy'. *Producer Sarah Peachey introduces herself on screen and simultaneously writes in the chat:* 'WELCOME EVERYONE! Wonderful to have you here from all corners of the world'.

Rob Myles's *The Show Must Go Online (TSMGO)* was one of the first purveyors of Lockdown Shakespeare: an ambitious project to perform all of Shakespeare's First Folio productions (see Chapter 7). Each production was marketed as a live event; while not visible on the performance screen, the audience was far from invisible. YouTube's 'Watching now' ticker at the bottom left of the screen offered a sense of congregation, each digit an audience member watching with you, live in the moment. However, it was in the Live Chat that those digits gained significance as audience members commented on and reacted to the production. *The Two Gentlemen of Verona* mirrored the experiences Sullivan notes in respect of live theatre broadcasts. Viewers gathered ahead of the show offering words of greeting, announcing their location and sharing anticipation for the show: 'This is one of the 5 Shakespeare plays I haven't seen. So excited', 'can't wait to see how this is done!'. The effect was to create, as Sullivan notes, 'a mental map of the geographically dispersed but experientially united broadcast audience' (2018a: 65). The difference here though was the lack of in-person congregation. For live theatre broadcasts there is a sense of physical proximity, an audience physically present and visible on screen. In contrast, the *TSMGO* audience is disparate in its entirety. In the absence of a physical theatre space, the Live Chat acts as an ersatz auditorium in which the audience gathers.

The *TSMGO* audience are affectionately referred to as the 'digital groundlings'. The Live Chat became a space of immediate reaction offering the unruly sense of the yard at Shakespeare's Globe Theatre, as Dominic Brewer (*TSMGO* actor and digital groundling) notes:

> From week one, anytime someone was wearing a hat people in the chat would shout (in capitals, type) 'HAT'. Anytime there was a dog, everyone would shout 'DOG'. From *Henry VI Part 1* onwards, 'SAUCY PRIEST' became a regular. How many saucy priests are there in Shakespeare? Lots, as it turns out!

The presence, albeit digitally, of a temporally proximate audience allowed for immediate feedback to the performers. Peachey joined the YouTube chat during *Two Gents*, posing questions and taking feedback on screen names: 'would be nice to list character name next to actor's name on lower left screen' suggested one groundling; Peachey offered to 'have them updated at the interval'. Moments later, Luke Barton entered as Proteus, his screen name already changed. After the interval, all actors had formatted their screen name as their character in capitals followed by their own name in brackets, in what would become standard *TSMGO* house style.

10 June 2020. Rob Myles made his much-anticipated TSMGO *debut playing Bottom in* A Midsummer Night's Dream *last week, joined by regular digital groundlings Scarlett Archer (Peaseblossom), Annabelle Higgins (Moth) and Mark McMinn (Snout). This week it's*

King John. *I navigate to YouTube to see the chat in full flow:* 'Hello friends', 'hi all hope everyone is fine'. As Scarlett, Annabelle and Mark join the chat, they're greeted with a chorus of congratulations: 'Great job last week!', 'You star'. In turn, they retake their usual weekly position: 'Nice to be a groundling again'.

The *TSMGO* community grew organically. Valerie Clayman Pye suggests that the groundlings have 'branched out into fandom' (2021: 6). Key to this fandom is familiarity. In respect of traditional live theatre broadcasts, Sullivan notes that online communication can turn 'individual experiences of aliveness ... into something more collective' (2018a: 72); for the most part those are fleeting online connections. In contrast, the *TSMGO* digital groundlings offered a community nurtured over time. As discussed in Chapter 7, *TSMGO* offered appointment viewing, a regular event at a fixed time; certainty in a time of uncertainty. The Live Chat became a place of familiarity and friendship. As Pye notes, the digital groundlings used:

> [T]he chat feature to create amongst them a shared experience that could not exist in a quiet theatre, where codes of behavior would prohibit the simultaneous engagement of both the play and the communal theatre-going experience.
>
> (2021: 4)

Key to Pye's observation is the duality of focus, what I describe as controlled inattention – the sense that being in the Live Chat is as much of an event as the production itself. As theatre moved online in 2020 and the 'watch party' concept became ubiquitous, audience attention was rarely fully on the play. An active Live Chat controls inattention, providing an acceptable outlet for distraction. Audience members may not be giving the production their undivided attention, but they are engaged with it. Joining the *King John* chat, one groundling announced, 'Yay just in time' to be met with 'as always, waiting for you', to which she retorted 'it's a running gag now'. And a running gag it is. Last week for *Dream* the same groundling joked: 'Hi everyone! Got my drink ready and everything'. The response from one of her fellow groundlings: 'You mean to say you're on time?!'. Light-hearted, familiar banter between friends within a community in which the regulars take a role: some offer dramaturgical support or textual nuance, others

NOTIONS OF LIVENESS IN LOCKDOWN PERFORMANCE 75

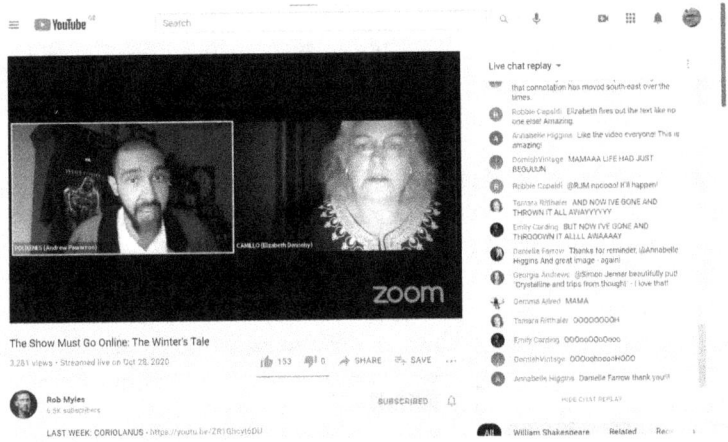

FIGURE 3 *Andrew Pawarroo and Elizabeth Dennehy perform as Polixenes and Camillo in* TSMGO's *Zoom-to-YouTube production of* The Winter's Tale, *as the digital groundlings conduct their textual 'singalong' of Queen's 'Bohemian Rhapsody' in the Live Chat. Screenshot reproduced courtesy of* The Show Must Go Online.

comedic commentary. Martin Barker suggests that this sense of physically distanced co-presence leads audiences to 'communally produce new ways of "doing liveness"' and 'the rise of new manners of participation' (2013: 71). This observation is echoed by Brewer:

> Some people were there just to chat, because they needed something to do or they wanted to communicate with people. It grew as its own community.

In contrast to the online communities formed during traditional 'live' theatre broadcasts, the Live Chat was not solely focused on the production and was, at times, easily derailed. During *The Winter's Tale*, talk turned to Bohemians: the question 'when did "Bohemian" stop meaning "people from Bohemia" and start meaning "scruffy but kind of artistic"?' was met with the response: 'the instant Freddie Mercury first sang "Mama, just killed a man ..."'. This started a textual 'singalong' of Queen's 'Bohemian Rhapsody' as one groundling after another typed song lyrics. On the production screen, Camillo (Elizabeth Dehenny) discussed Leontes's (Colin Hurley) erratic behaviour with Polixenes (Andrew Pawarroo);

in the chat, Mercury's lyrics sat alongside discussions of *Moulin Rouge* and Dehenny's 'crystalline' diction. The liveness of the moment created surreal juxtapositions, as one groundling noted: 'The Groundlings are howling Bohemian Rhapsody in the back of this scene ... superb'.

It is clear that the Live Chat was more than just a fan space; it offered connection between the audience and performers. *TSMGO* Associate Producer Matthew Rhodes monitored the conversation during each performance, feeding back filtered positive comments to the actors via Zoom's own Chat function. For him, the YouTube Live Chat offered the 'feeling of the audience': he recalls that 'the chat went silent a couple of times. It was very rare, but the chat would go silent, and we would think "Oh, we got them!"'. The Live Chat also became a performance space. As Rhodes recalls:

> We did use the chat for some dramatic purposes. We had the lovers from *A Midsummer Night's Dream* in the chat, responding to Pyramus and Thisbe. We also put Rosencrantz and Guildenstern in the chat [during *Hamlet*]. We used it like walking into the house [of a theatre auditorium].

This dual usage reinforced notions of the Live Chat as an auditorium space with the performance screen as stage. Breaking the fourth wall and engaging with the groundlings directly, rather than through the mediated screen space, strengthens the sense of liveness. As Ben Crystal notes, 'Those moments were like dropping down into the yard in the Globe and doing something amidst the crowd'.

June 2021. I'm writing this chapter, revisiting moments of TSMGO productions that, watched live months earlier, now echo in my memory. I have several tabs open on my internet browser as I scroll through chats, searching for half-remembered conversations. I pause, rewind, re-watch scenes. My past self is already in the chat, suggesting that the alpacas appearing in The Winter's Tale *sheep-shearing menagerie are 'Drama Llamas'. It's a joke I don't recall making, but it makes me smile as I fondly remember the unruly Queen singalong.*

It was Myles's intent to create a lasting resource of Shakespeare in performance, his mantra 'Shakespeare for everyone, for free, forever' inextricably linked to both the live performance and the enduring YouTube recording ('Our Story'). Unlike traditional live theatre broadcasts, and indeed the streaming of pre-recorded productions during lockdown, *TSMGO*'s productions are not ephemeral or time-limited. Sullivan suggests that, in respect of traditional theatre broadcasts, 'temporal synchronicity is helpful but not essential in the generation of liveness', concluding that a pre-recorded performance can hold the same sense of liveness as a live-stream even where an audience is physically distanced (2018a: 62). However, this analysis relies on a sense of event-connectedness, a group of disparate people coming together and interacting. Sedgman suggests that theatre requires '"concentration" meaning both assemblage and attentiveness. By *concentrating* people into a confined space and time, theatre demands that we *concentrate* together' (2018: 65). Echoing Alfreds's notion of a contract of imagination, Sedgman argues for a 'communal agreement to work *for* the performance rather than *against* it' (ibid.: 35). I would argue that Sedgman's notions of 'confined space' support physically distanced audiences, as the digital groundlings were *concentrated* into the Live Chat during the performance each week. However, *TSMGO* replays lack the temporal proximity of an audience to support a sense of liveness.

Each YouTube recording of a *TSMGO* production exists as an echo of two live performances: the recorded production, and the live audience reaction to it. Much as traditional live theatre broadcasts record and overtly include audience reaction to the in-person event, these digital performances are likewise tethered to a digital response. Importantly, those responses exist as snapshots of moments in time throughout the year. In the chat, groundlings reference their everyday lives, weather conditions and changes to lockdown. Recommendations for other performances sit alongside immediate reaction to the current live *TSMGO* production and anticipation for forthcoming productions. Wider cultural and societal events are referenced. *TSMGO*'s second performance, *The Taming of the Shrew* on 26 March 2020 worked the first 'Clap for our Carers' (a weekly UK-wide social movement to applaud National Health Service workers) into the production: the whole cast appeared on screen to applaud, and audience members posted clapping emojis in the chat. The week after the murder of George

Floyd, actress Amelia Parillon introduced *A Midsummer Night's Dream* with a powerful and personal account of racism and a call to action. Pye describes a 'bifurcated performance experience' in which 'a record of the dialogical response to the live event through the chat feature … replays in perpetuity alongside the performance' (2021: 8). The absence of temporal proximity, however, inhibits any sense of liveness, offering instead merely an echo of a moment passed. In this I depart from Pascale Aebischer's assertion that, with respect to traditional live theatre broadcasts, there is 'a conviction that the broadcasts offer a "same", first-hand experience of the performance in which "liveness" performs a central role' (2020: 152). Here I suggest that, whereas traditional live theatre broadcasts focus on the invisibility of the mechanics of broadcast by 'pushing the traces of remediation offstage', the replays of *TSMGO* offer clear markers of the time of performance, rendering the moment passed visible (ibid.: 151).

Markers of ephemeral performance

April 2020. I should be on a large social Zoom call. After a week of home-schooling, it's the last thing I want to do. Instead, I join a Zoom-to-YouTube live performance, CtrlAltRepeat's Midsummer Night Stream. *The production starts: Peter Quince (Tom Black) launches a video call and the mechanicals appear – out of focus, upside down, fingers tapping the screen as they mute, unmute and adjust their images.*

Lockdown performance developed its own specific aesthetics, conventions, and adaptive approaches shaped both by a world in pandemic and by the remote technology which directors and performers have used out of necessity. It would be easy to pre-record a performance, to offer an 'as live' stream – as costume coordinator Suzanne Knight recalls when CtrlAltRepeat's *Stream* was in development:

> There was a debate about whether to just film it and pretend it's live. Why was [director] Sid [Phoenix] so driven to make this an actual live performance when, if we filmed a Zoom production, no one would really know? But I feel like you *do* know, it makes a difference.

Notably, Shakespeare's Globe's *Macbeth: A Conjuring* (dir. Hastie and Terry 2020) and the RSC's *Winter's Tale* (dir. Whyman 2021) offered 'as staged' productions made in lockdown expressly for audiences at home; these were pre-recorded and edited productions rather than a single-take, shared-time experience. The productions never held a sense of liveness, nor did they claim to be anything other than a filmed production of actors working in a shared space – albeit subject to the contemporaneous rules of social distancing.

For many live-streamed performances, Zoom became both a performance space and narrative setting drawing from the Zeitgeist, reflecting the new normal of a socially distanced world. As Phoenix notes, setting *Stream* during the pandemic and

> Having Zoom as our medium made everything more immediate. By doing it live, warts and all, you could counteract the fact that anything on screen does sacrifice a little bit of immediacy.

This recognition of the world of the play as being a plausible version of the present allows the audience to process and accept the artificiality of actors trapped in individual rectangular Zoom frames without any physical proximity. The sense of a world interrupted permeated CtrlAltRepeat's Zoom-to-YouTube productions. Similarly, in their live productions both Northern Comedy Theatre's *Doing Shakespeare* in June and Cross-Stitch Theatre's *Henry V Take 2* in November offered metatheatrical takes on putting on Shakespeare in lockdown. Much as *Stream's* mechanicals met on Zoom to prepare for their performance, Cross-Stitch's Miscaster Theatre Group and Northern Comedy's Felching Players (affectionate parodies of amateur theatre companies) prepared to pivot to 'Zoom theatre'. Overtly set now (*Henry V Take 2* opened with a montage of real-world newspaper reports detailing the closure of theatres), both productions offered a behind-the-scenes viewpoint, playing with both the established conventions of traditional theatre and the new conventions of 'Zoom theatre'.

Doing Shakespeare included a running gag about whether a convoluted ritual is needed each time the play *Macbeth* is named in this Virtual Theatre space: Ebon (Kieran Maleedy) may be 'in virtual theatre virtually but [he's] actually in [his] actual spare bedroom'. The audience was simultaneously watching an actor both at home in their private domestic space and at work in the constructed world of the play, reflecting lockdown in the real world where both work life and social life moved online, blurring the lines between public and private. The effect was to strengthen the sense of shared experience and temporal proximity. While not on Zoom with the performers, the viewer experienced the Zoom call live, complete with its fallibility. As *Henry V Take 2* returned from the interval, the viewer interface had switched to Speaker View and the screen bounced dizzyingly between actors. The view quickly changed back to the more stable Gallery View, the actors side by side. Director Beth Atkinson apologized in the chat: 'Zoom and YouTube don't always like calibrating with each other'. In *Stream*, actor Edward Cartwright's internet connection faltered; so too did his character Demetrius's as he froze and unfroze, the judders adding dramaturgical strength to readings of his inconstant love for Helena. Experientially the flaws acted as a marker of ephemeral liveness, the lasting recording a moment of fallibility caught in time.

May 2021. The early hours of the morning. I've stayed up to watch the live-stream of Fake Friends' non-Shakespearean production This American Wife, *a satirical take on the popular* Real Housewives *reality TV franchise. Michael Breslin, Patrick Foley and Jakeem Dante Powell are arguing over an anecdote – both Michael and Patrick have told Jakeem the same personal anecdote. They've moved into the garage of the 'McMansion' where they're performing, the green screens visible behind them as producers set up virtual backgrounds. With the backgrounds up, someone closes the electric garage door – a pull cord handle moves slowly across the screen, undermining the illusion.*

There is a common made-at-home aesthetic to lockdown performance – actors working with props and sets constructed using items readily available at home (see also Broadribb Chapter 2). The world of Big Telly's *Macbeth* was created by making the tangible craft of the actors visible on screen. The witches spread out green cloth, painted swatches of green paint and poured green liquid to create the surfaces onto which the imaginary world of the Macbeths appeared through Virtual Backgrounds. The fortifications of Macbeth's castle were unmistakably cardboard boxes painted grey. In *TSMGO*'s *Love's Labour's Lost*, the Princess and her entourage constructed a makeshift camp using bed sheets and broom handles. There is a tangibility to the action of actors building their own sets, constructing the world of the play in the moment. For Seaton:

> Showing the working is really important because that makes it feel like it's theatre. If we were doing a show involving puppets, we wouldn't hide the people operating them. It's the same thing.

Fake Friends offer what they describe as 'livestream multi-camera internet theater' ('This American Wife'). Breslin and Foley's 2020 production *Circle Jerk*, a finalist for the 2021 Pulitzer Prize in Drama, was filmed within a New York theatre space. The live-stream saw Breslin, Foley and Catherine Rodríguez play nine roles between them with on-screen costume changes made on the fly as they ran between sets. It would have been simpler to have momentarily empty sets to allow these changes to occur 'off stage'; however, the frenetic energy of fast changes amongst visible broadcasting equipment marked the production as live, a continuous take in a single unit of time shared with the audience. It was a device further exploited in *This American Wife*. Performed on location in a Long Island, New York 'McMansion', the action moved through the house, drawing on tropes from reality TV by filming in closets, bathrooms and pantries. At the end of a scene in which Breslin and Powell were shot in close crop in the bathroom, a wide shot revealed tripod-mounted smartphones in ring lights placed in front of the bathtub. The action moved in one shot to the hallway as Foley passed an open door, revealing the monitors and mixing desks. Much like the garage door that closed on screen, these touches were choices rather than accidents, as Nicole Serratore notes:

> [T]he garage door pull slowly chugs along the top of the frame taking its own sweet time to exit. While I am sure this was intentionally included in the frame (or as my film teacher always said, once you put it on screen it becomes intentional), I laughed hardest at this moment of situational reality intruding on someone's staged reality.
>
> (2021)

The 'situational reality' here is an ephemeral moment of performance: a choice to undermine and dismantle the world of the production. Here the world-breaking door pull played a similar dramaturgical role as Seaton's world-creating witches. A key trait of live lockdown performance is 'showing the working' – pulling back the curtain, so to speak. Whether on Zoom or live-streamed from a physical theatre space, digital theatre is necessarily mediated through screens – a physical barrier acting to separate audience from performer, drawing attention to the lack of physical proximity between performance and reception. These markers of situational reality act to signify the liveness of the moment, with the roughness affording tangibility to an intangible digital world.

February 2021. I'm watching Nick Evans's made-in-lockdown film Romeo & Juliet. *Rather than focusing on the script or the actors, I'm trying to work out the size of a computer-generated sofa. It seems to be changing: it's as deep as a double bed when Juliet (Emily Redpath) lies down, yet when the Nurse (Lucy Tregear) joins her its dimensions seem to shift. I'm distracted by the uncanny nature of the computer-generated virtual world.*

Evans's *Romeo & Juliet* sought to exploit technology to create an illusion of shared space rather than acknowledging the conditions of production. Technological innovation was placed above everything else. With the exception of a brief scene between Sam Tutty's Romeo and Redpath's Juliet, actors were filmed individually against green screens then edited into a computer-generated theatre setting to create the appearance of sharing the same space. Producers Ryan Metcalfe and Simon Gordon describe 'using cutting-edge technology to truly redefine what was possible with virtual theatre productions' (2021: 2). There are moments where the effect is pleasing – the Capulet ball employs sweeping cinematic camerawork to lend vibrancy to capturing the together-apart performers 'on' the virtual stage. However, there are many more where the illusion does not hold up well enough, with the CGI backgrounds regularly draining the life from the actors' performances; as Peter Kirwan notes, 'there is no dynamic space between the actors, no sense of energy' (2021).

Lockdown performance is the first performance medium born out of a situation where the performers inherently cannot be in the same physical space. Whereas the majority of lockdown productions have embraced that dynamic, Evans's film feels as though it is pushing against this fundamental element. *Romeo & Juliet* ends up frustratingly offering a production which constantly reminds its audience of what they are not watching – neither a traditional theatre production, nor a fully realized cinematic adaptation – rather than embracing a lockdown set-up and aesthetic to both effectively and affectively tell the story. The sanitized, edited world lacks authenticity: actors' eyelines are regularly not quite right and, despite seemingly standing in close proximity, the absence of touch is palpable. A lack of emotional intent reveals its somewhat artificial conditions of creation. There is a contrast here with Seaton's artificially manipulated world of *Macbeth*, with its overtly out-of-scale backgrounds and digitally created proximity. I return to Sedgman's 'communal agreement' and 'shared focus, directed towards the work of art' (2018: 35). *Romeo & Juliet* never existed as a performance – the film lacks the temporal proximity needed to create any sense of liveness.

Throughout the pandemic, creatives turned to digital theatre, embracing notions of together-apart. Working to overcome the restrictions of social distancing, they found ways to engage and embrace an at-home audience not as a substitute for in-person theatre but as a live event on its own terms. Audiences interacted with performers on Zoom calls and through Live Chat functionality influencing the performance in real time. Live-streamed productions made visible the mechanics of performance, the embedded markers of ephemeral performance that foreground liveness. As Fake Friends' Breslin and Foley state:

> We don't see this as a poor substitute for "the real thing" or something we're only doing until it's safe to gather again. We're building on the traditions that have come before as we create a new genre, and we're so thrilled you're coming along on the ride with us.
>
> (2021)

Returning again to Collins-Hughes's opinion piece, the writer claims:

> What theater people do is put on a show; what audience members do is gather. It's ritual; it's reflex. It is also, in any conventional sense, largely inoperable right now. So we take the closest substitute we've got.
>
> (2020)

However, this underplays the power of virtual congregation, event-connectedness based on temporal rather than physical proximity. Alfreds's contention that theatre is the 'double process of transforming the here-and-now into the there-and-then, and bringing the there-and-then into the here-and-now' holds true for digital performance (2009: 13). Both actor and audience meet in a digital space, transformed by a contract of liveness identified by Big Telly's Crissy O'Donovan as being 'between the audience and the actor … agreeing to be together in that time'. Notwithstanding the absence of physical proximity, it is the temporal proximity of actor and audience, and the embedded markers of ephemeral performance, that afford digital theatre a new quality of liveness equivalent to in-person theatre.

Notes

1. YouTube chat comments have been anonymized.
2. Quotations from Crissy O'Donovan and Zoë Seaton are from a conversation with cast and crew of Big Telly's *Macbeth*, 29 October 2020.
3. Quotations from Dominic Brewer, Ben Crystal and Matthew Rhodes are from a conversation with cast and crew of *TSMGO*, 1 February 2021.
4. Quotations from Sid Phoenix and Suzanne Knight are from a conversation with CtrlAltRepeat, 26 January 2021.

References

Aebischer, P. (2020), *Shakespeare, Spectatorship and the Technologies of Performance*, Cambridge: Cambridge University Press.

Alfreds, M. (2009), *Different Every Night: Freeing the Actor*, London: Nick Hern Books.

Allred, G. K. (2021), 'Review of *The Tempest*', *Shakespeare Bulletin*, 38 (3): 536–9.

Auslander, P. (2012), 'Digital Liveness: A Historico-Philosophical Perspective', *PAJ: A Journal of Performance and Art*, 34 (3): 3–11.

Barker, M. (2013), *Live to Your Local Cinema: The Remarkable Rise of Livecasting*, Basingstoke: Palgrave Macmillan.

Bucknall, J. and K. Sedgman (2017), 'Documenting Audience Experience: Social Media as Lively Stratification', in T. Sant (ed.), *Documenting Performance: The Context and Process of Digital Curation and Archiving*, 113–30, London: Bloomsbury.

Collins-Hughes, L. (2020), 'Digital Theater Isn't Theater. It's a Way to Mourn Its Absence', *New York Times*, 7 August. Available online: https://www.nytimes.com/2020/07/08/theater/live-theater-absence.html (accessed 28 November 2021).

Doing Shakespeare (2020), [Zoom] Northern Comedy Theatre, June. Available online: https://youtu.be/kvj6zrmih8k (accessed 28 November 2021).

The First Folio series (2020), [Zoom-to-YouTube] *The Show Must Go Online*, March–November. Available online: https://www.youtube.com/playlist?list=PLBFO-wpdFFypTYtKyK7CEBCBgFZtRmL0z (accessed 28 November 2021).

Fischer-Lichte, E. ([2004] 2008), *The Transformative Power of Performance: A New Aesthetics*, trans. S. I. Jane, London: Routledge.

Fresh Life Theatre Company (2020), Twitter. Available online: https://twitter.com/freshlifetheatr/status/1329024832705585153 (accessed 28 November 2021).

Henry V Take 2 (2020), [Zoom-to-YouTube] Cross-Stitch Theatre Company, 20 November. Available online: https://youtu.be/FI374ZYU18g (accessed 28 November 2021).

Kirwan, P. (2021), '*Romeo & Juliet* (Metcalfe Gordon Productions)', *The Bardathon*, 14 February. Available online: https://blogs.nottingham.ac.uk/bardathon/2021/02/14/romeo-juliet-metcalfe-gordon-productions/ (accessed 28 November 2021).

Macbeth (2020), [Zoom] Big Telly Theatre Company, October.

Metcalfe, R. and S. Gordon (2021), 'Two Households…', in *Romeo & Juliet* [programme], 2.

Midsummer Night Stream (2020), [Zoom-to-YouTube] CtrlAltRepeat, 11 April. Available online: https://youtu.be/iEls9I4tSLs (accessed 28 November 2021).

Mortal Fools (2020), [YouTube] Fresh Life Theatre, 20 November. Available Online: https://youtu.be/bcPi8TL3fs8 (accessed 28 November 2021).

'Our Story'. Available online: https://robmyles.co.uk/theshowmustgoonline/ (accessed 28 November 2021).

Phelan, P. ([1993] 2005), *Unmarked: The Politics of Performance*, London: Routledge.

Phelan, P. (2003), 'Performance, Live Culture and Things of the Heart', *Journal of Visual Culture*, 2 (3): 291–302.

Pye, V. C. (2021), 'Zoom Shakespeare: The Show Must Go Online and "Read for the Globe"', *PARtake: The Journal of Performance as Research*, 3 (2). Available online: https://doi.org/10.33011/partake.v3i2.549 (accessed 28 November 2021).

Romeo & Juliet (2021), [Film] dir. Nick Evans, UK: Metcalfe Gordon Productions.

Sedgman, K. (2018), *The Reasonable Audience: Theatre Etiquette, Behaviour Policing, and the Live Performance Experience*, Cham: Palgrave Macmillan.

Serratore, N. (2021), 'Review: *This American Wife*', *Exeunt Magazine NYC*. Available online: http://exeuntnyc.com/reviews/review-this-american-wife/ (accessed 28 November 2021).

Sullivan, E. (2018a), 'The Audience Is Present: Aliveness, Social Media, and the Theatre Broadcast Experience', in P. Aebischer, S. Greenhalgh and L. E. Osborne (eds), *Shakespeare and the 'Live' Theatre Broadcast Experience*, 59–75, London: Bloomsbury.

Sullivan, E. (2018b), 'The Role of the Arts in the History of Emotions: Aesthetic Experience and Emotion as Method', *Emotions: History, Culture, Society* 2 (1): 113–31.

The Tempest (2020), [Zoom] Creation Theatre Company and Big Telly Theatre Company April-May.

This American Wife (2021), [Live-stream] Fake Friends, May.

'This American Wife', Available online: https://www.thisamericanwife.live (accessed 28 November 2021).

Viper Squad (Remastered) (2021), [Zoom] CtrlAltRepeat, January–April.

4

Creation Theatre and Big Telly's *The Tempest*: Digital Theatre and the Performing Audience

Pascale Aebischer and Rachael Nicholas

In April 2020, Creation Theatre, a producing company known for staging performances of classic texts in unusual locations in and around Oxford, was one of the first professional theatre companies in the UK to reimagine a Shakespeare play for performance on the Zoom platform in a co-production with Northern Irish theatre company Big Telly, which specializes in site-responsive touring performances and participation projects. *The Tempest*, directed by Big Telly's Zoë Seaton for Creation Theatre, became an international hit which, following word-of-mouth recommendations via social media and reviews in the UK from *The Guardian* and BBC Radio 4 and New York's *Time Out* and *The New York Times*, enjoyed a run that was extended into May 2020.

In June, our work began on *Digital Theatre Transformation: A Case Study and Digital Toolkit*, a rapid-response Covid-19 project funded by AHRC/UKRI that focused on Creation Theatre and Big Telly's creatives and their audiences. The aim of our project was to understand how Creation Theatre was able to transform its backstage operations and its production as comprehensively as it did, allowing the company to continue to produce new work and employ freelance creatives at a time when many freelancers in the creative industries were unable to access the UK Chancellor's bespoke Covid-19 support packages and theatres were under existential threat. We also wanted to find out how audiences responded to the production's interactivity and its pricing, given that Creation Theatre was, at that point in the first UK lockdown, an outlier in charging £20 per device for ticketed performances. The 177 survey responses and twenty-two in-depth audience interviews we carried out revealed that in key areas such as perceived value for money, quality of made-for-digital content and perceptions regarding digital theatre as a community-building environment, our findings diverged from those of cultural sector consultants Indigo, who carried out nationwide surveys of cultural sector audiences between April and July 2020 (Raines 2020). Our research enabled us to offer a differentiated understanding of a company and audience community who have successfully adapted to digital modes of making and watching theatre. Our industry reports (preliminary report published in August 2020; final full report in October 2020) therefore shed light on how high quality made-for-digital theatre could be a route to commercial success and continued employment for freelance creatives and non-building-based companies such as Creation Theatre and Big Telly.

Here, we revisit the research we did in 2020 in order to draw out the trajectory of the production from its initial analogue version in 2019 to its recasting for Zoom in April 2020. Our focus, in the context of this collection, is on the role of Shakespeare as an entry point into digital performance and a facilitator, for both the production company and its audience, of the transition from analogue to digital. Key to that transition in this production, we argue, was the liminal character of Ariel (played by Itxaso Moreno), who inhabited an imaginary space that was poised on the border between the analogue and the digital, the audience and the performance. It is Ariel, more than any other character in the production, who was able to move between the fictional world of the performance and the real world of the audience members in their individual homes, and who was able to generate a virtual theatrical community characterized by a sense of shared experience and synchrony, participation and an intense feeling of liveness. In the final part of this essay, we examine in more detail how the Zoom production invited participation from audiences and consider how audiences responded to those invitations. Focusing on how such participation generated liveness, a sense of community and emotive responses, we argue that audience participation was key to audiences experiencing this digital Shakespeare production as a unique and specifically theatrical event.

'What's past is prologue': *The Tempest* in 2019

Between 19 July and 15 August 2019, Osney Mead, a small island surrounded by tributaries to the Thames on the outskirts of Oxford, hosted Creation Theatre's production of *The Tempest* as a site-specific, immersive and participatory production described by its director Zoë Seaton as a 'live game' that moved between twelve indoor and outdoor locations. In an interview, Simon Spencer-Hyde, the production's Prospero, spoke of how Seaton had 'edited the script of *The Tempest* ... to make it flexible, more of a movable feast that we can tweak and move around', in a quest 'to try and empower the audience as much as possible so they make the choices and it's a game for them' (Mitchell 2019).

The production began in a large hall in a conference venue decked out as the restaurant of the Creation Cruises cruise ship. Once the audience had settled down in groups seated around round tables, they were welcomed by the Ship Captain, who was played by Production Manager Giles Stoakley. For the arrival of the royal party consisting of King Alonso of Naples (Al Barclay), his sister the Archduchess Sebastian (Madeleine MacMahon), Antonio, the usurping Duke of Milan (Chris Robinson), and young Prince Ferdinand of Naples (Ryan Duncan), who were joining the cruise on their return journey from Tunis to Milan, the Ship Captain asked the audience to stand up for the guests of honour, who swanned through the room to enthusiastic applause. As the ship's entertainer, Trinculo (Keith Singleton) began to belt out Bobby Darin's 'Beyond the Sea' as a sing-along with the audience, a sudden storm brought about by the incursion of Itxaso Moreno's electrifying punk-inspired Ariel caused him, along with the ship's crew and royal party, to sway and be tossed from side to side to the sound of thunderous crashing, until the Ship Captain ordered the table-by-table evacuation of the now shipwrecked audience to the pavement outside.

Thereafter, each audience group followed a different trajectory along a 3 km-long route through the interiors of the industrial estate on the island and its wild river paths, to encounter characters and piece together the story of Shakespeare's *Tempest*. The experience involved what Jeremy Dennis described as 'Part escape room, part scavenger hunt, part promenade, part urban exploration, where audience, extras and crew twitch between surveillance dystopias, coffee shop dramas and royal intrigues, alliances shifting and sympathies twisting' (2019). Audiences were asked to blend in with their surroundings by assuming the shape of trees and objects whenever a 'zombie' (any passing cyclist) approached; they were invited to 'hack' into the surveillance apparatus of Simon Spencer-Hyde's Prospero; they helped the disconsolate King of Naples pull muddy objects out of the river in his search for his drowned son and were knighted in recompense; they were sent to find Caliban (PK Taylor) 'ooz[ing] out of the reeds' and watch him be inebriated by Trinculo; or got to spend time in a coffee shop where they were able to observe Annabelle Terry's Miranda fall for Ferdinand in 'a coffee-bar romance' that rapidly evolved into a stag party (Lafferty 2019). Each of the locations, therefore, represented an episode in the overall plot of *The Tempest*, with audiences becoming part of the storytelling until the whole cast and audience were reunited at Miranda and Ferdinand's wedding party.

The element of the production that emerges from reviews and surviving Facebook Live-streams as the force that tied the production together with its energy seems to have been Moreno's Ariel. Dennis explains: 'As the audience is steadily divided and conquered on the scramble through the scenes, the soft reality of a summer evening becomes augmented and enhanced by irrepressible stories and unsurpressable [sic] spirits, the very best of which is Itxaso Moreno, thrillingly demonic/elfin, exquisitely elusive, the ghost that haunts the production, Ariel' (2019). Esther Lafferty's review, too, describes Moreno's 'bright-eyed energy' (2019). Moreno emerges here as a figure of energetic if nervous disruption, intense moments of confrontation and surprise, and most of all of the ephemerality of a performance that resists being captured. In her elusiveness, she comes to embody the energy of live performance as defined by Peggy Phelan as that which 'cannot be saved, recorded, documented'; as that which 'becomes itself through disappearance' (1993: 146).

The 2020 Zoom *Tempest*: 'Experiencing Shakespeare in a different format'

When, at the start of the March 2020 Covid-19 lockdown, the company reunited to revive the previous year's immersive production for the digital medium of Zoom, the principal challenge was how to adapt participatory theatre and site-specificity to become a form of participatory platform-specificity that would retain a sense of theatricality and the barmy energy of the analogue production. The Zoom production used green-screened set designs that enabled the cast to act together on a virtual stage. Exhilaratingly, at a time when audiences and actors alike were in lockdown and starved of social contact, the production allowed for direct interaction between the cast and the audience via their respective webcams, with prompts to the audience to participate in interviewing the courtiers, rub their hands together to co-create the soundscape of the rising tempest, and show their pets to the disconsolate King of Naples. What helped the transformation was the fact that the 2019 script had already restructured Shakespeare's play so as to create twelve distinct episodes focusing on separate character groupings. These scenes were now pared down further to bring the running time down to an hour.

That this was feasible at all without losing a sense of the overall plot and the individual trajectories of the characters is why Giles Stoakley thinks that Shakespeare's plays lend themselves particularly well to adaptation to Zoom: 'Shakespeare ... we have found is the strongest thing to do on Zoom because it has really, really clear stories and really, really clear emotional journeys for the actors' (2020b). Shakespeare's clarity of storytelling and the previous production's episodic edit of the script made it relatively easy to reconstruct the two-handers of Antonio and Sebastian, Miranda and Ferdinand, or Caliban and Trinculo as dialogues set against matching Virtual Backgrounds that were slightly adjusted to offer two separate viewpoints onto the same scene.

As this suggests, throwing the 2020 Zoom show together in just two weeks was, in many ways, a salvage operation in which whatever elements of the 2019 production that could be saved were either straightforwardly redeployed or hastily reassembled into something that could work on the digital platform. This involved actors wherever possible reprising their former roles and combining pieces of costume they or the company still owned with items from their own wardrobes that would give their characters a similar 'look' to the one they had had the previous year. Having the same designer, Ryan Dawson Laight, work on costumes and set designs for both productions certainly helped establish a continuity of visual style.

Some actors, such as Chris Robinson and Keith Singleton (Antonio and Trinculo respectively) were not available for the Zoom show, leading to the reduction in the number of roles from eleven to nine and the loss of the Ship Captain and the Head of Security who had played a significant part in the Zombie sub-plot of the Osney Mead production. Newcomer to the company Rhodri Lewis stepped into the role of Trinculo and was paired up with PK Taylor's Caliban for scenes that transposed Taylor's wild riverbank creature into the inside of a virtual shack. What remained, however, were Caliban's costume, physicality, and characterization, and with that the quality of his relationship with his scene partner. Giles Stoakley, meanwhile, moved into the role of Antonio, bringing some of the Ship Captain's crowd-corralling functions into the part, along with the character's sartorial style. Another element of Stoakley's 2019 performance that was incorporated into his new 2020 role was the Ship Captain's propensity towards interaction with the audience, which now became part and parcel of the scenes Antonio shared with Sebastian: 'Zoë [Seaton] was keen to get the audience interaction from our scene, largely because in the original show my scene and Chris [Robinson] and Mad[eleine MacMahon]'s scenes were the most interactive, so it made sense to combine the styles of the two scenes' (2020a). The characterization of Stoakley's Antonio therefore bore the imprint of both his own prior performance as the gregarious Ship Captain and Robinson's prior performance in the role of Antonio. Even though Stoakley did not seek to copy that performance, he acknowledges that he had to fit into it sufficiently to not force MacMahon into having to change her characterization of Sebastian in turn.

Stoakley's performance thus became what Rebecca Schneider would describe as 'a kind of archive' of these earlier performances, 'a *different approach to saving* that is not invested in identicality' (2001: 103). These remnants acted like memory traces of the previous production which pervaded the digital performance in the manner of what Marvin Carlson would describe as a haunting characteristic of 'theatre ... as a cultural activity deeply involved with memory and haunted by repetition' (2001: 11). It is certainly significant that our audience research revealed that among the Zoom audience there were several viewers who had seen the analogue version and who were clearly interested in how they might be able to re-experience that production in a new medium.

Some of the memory work that revived traces of the 2019 performances in the 2020 production was not so much an effect of the actors' performances as of the performances of the audience, who played a key role in remembering analogue theatricality through their embodied responses to the digital production. In her reflections about what cognitive science has taught us about mirror neurons, Amy Cook suggests that recognizing how the 'real actions' of the performers 'prompt a co-firing' of mirror neurons 'in the spectator's brain' enables us to appreciate how important the 'coherence of the group created by imitation' is to the theatrical experience. 'Acting in synchrony with others, based on the interplay of social conventions and spontaneous feelings, unites spectator with spectator as it also co-fires mirror neurons' (2009: 113). For Cook, this insight 'shifts focus from the imitation of an action by an actor to the imitation of a performed action by the spectators watching the performance' (114). In this understanding of how theatre works as 'flesh memory', the power of memorializing a prior performance is given not just to the actors but also to the audience, whose embodied responses, whether in the shape of mirror neurons triggered by watching the actors perform, or actual physical movement in synchrony with other audience members and/or the performers, are crucial (Schneider 2001: 105; Cook 2009: 108).

In the Zoom *Tempest* performances, the way spectators visibly participated in the action, performing in almost magical synchrony to shake their screens or dance at Miranda's wedding as their faces were Spotlighted by the invisible stage manager ('Zoom Wizard' Sinéad Owens), thus sharing their excitement with the cast and the rest of the audience, was a crucial component of how the production produced an embodied memory of the shared experience of live participatory theatre as a communal creative act. They performed, in this virtual space, in the synchronous manner which Robert Shaughnessy has observed in audiences and performers in Shakespeare's Globe, where what he identifies as 'entrainment' connects actors and spectators through an experience of synchrony which results in audiences experiencing 'higher levels of engagement with Shakespeare' (2020: 28). The curtain call reinforced that bonding between cast and audience and between audience members, as one performer after another dismantled their green screen set-up, revealing the insides of their homes, and cast and audience came together in Gallery View as a community of individuals in lockdown celebrating through their synchronous applause the successful conclusion of a live theatrical performance.

Not only the moments of explicit audience participation, but all the scenes performed live in 2020 were unpredictable and improvisatory, open to their physical and virtual environments in a manner that marked them as contingent and therefore intensely live despite being performed using a digital medium. This might be because of a glitch-prone internet connection, because a Zoom background would 'swallow up' a piece of costume or property; or because Hex, the live snake who, curled around Al Barclay's head, performed the role of Gonzalo in a two-hander with King Alonso, was misbehaving. But even the production's few pre-recorded sequences, which pushed at the boundaries of both the Zoom set-up and the lockdown situation, partook in the creation of a live embodied response. In one such scene, Miranda pushed her hand 'through' the side of her Zoom frame towards Ferdinand in the adjoining frame, with whom she interlaced her fingers in a moment of magical connection. As Judith Buchanan remarks, this moment 'catches us. ... It plays to something that is a very deep craving. And it also ... emblematises something that is true of [the production] in relation to us' because this moment is 'inviting *us* to try and reach

FIGURE 4 *Ferdinand (Ryan Duncan) and Miranda (Annabelle Terry). The Tempest, dir. Zoë Seaton for Creation Theatre and Big Telly, 2020. Screenshot reproduced courtesy of Creation Theatre and Big Telly.*

out, as well beyond those frames, to make a connection' (Interview with John Wyver 2020).

Reflecting on her approach to integrating pre-recorded material in the production, Seaton recalls how the storm scene in the Zoom show was initially going to be 'a beautiful film of a storm and I was like, no, it's died, the whole thing has died, it's gone.' What might have been similarly 'dead' theatre in the Ferdinand-and-Miranda sequences was experienced as live in part because Seaton was careful not to turn it into 'a dead piece of tied-in finished film' but instead tried to use 'film as a live thing ... full or surprise and potential'. Even more so, it was made live by the audience's collective and contagious response of delight. Heidi Liedke's 2020 review of the Zoom show reveals the extent to which this scene was an effective piece of theatre because of the interactions between audience members as their embodied responses knit them together into a community in synchrony: Miranda and Ferdinand 'touching'

> is an incredibly moving moment to witness what can happen when the technological divide is broken up and bridged. I feel myself wishing to be pulled into the screen as well, an emotional yearning that is only heightened, when I see the other spectators, including the woman who had watched the performance with a neutral facial expression a moment ago, start smiling brightly. To see the faces of my fellow spectators is a new and wonderful addition ... Here, we may be alone in our living rooms, but we are more aware of the actual community of spectators we are part of because we can see them and see their reactions.

What Liedke describes is precisely the operation of mirror neurons firing in the audience, as the performance triggered an embodied response which was shared within the theatrical community. Even for Liedke, who had not experienced the 2019 production, this moment produced a 'flesh memory' of the way in which the audience in Osney Mead had been able to see and feed off each other's reactions in broad daylight.

While in this example, the communal synchrony of audience response was triggered by a piece of digitally manipulated pre-recorded footage, for the most part audience participation and the embodied experience of 'flesh memory' that connected the 2020 production to its predecessor was the result of Itxaso Moreno's investment in live performance and her resistance to documentation. Once again, Moreno emerged as a disruptor and the principal source of analogue energy and embodied, ephemeral, elusive, performativity. Lockdown, it was clear, had forced her Ariel to bend to Prospero's digital rule and have her face reproduced, seemingly infinitely and identically, in the bank of television screens that constituted the Virtual Background of Prospero's cell-as-surveillance-room. However, even as she reluctantly allowed her image to be captured and reproduced, she was the unruly spirit who did so with a profound investment in the analogue that resulted in her being the only character whose body was located not in the virtual environment of a two-dimensional Zoom background, but rooted deeply in the 'real' world of an under-stairs cupboard converted into Ariel's three-dimensional cave.

As Zoë Seaton recalled, it was the performer's profound technophobia that resulted in this adaptation: 'we just started trying to help her to build a space in her house which felt like Ariel's cave and for me that was more beautiful than any virtual background we could have had. ... She was clever and artistic enough to help us make that remotely in her little space.' Seaton contrasts the three-dimensionality of Ariel's cave, and the fact that this was 'a real space', with the 'two-dimensional backdrop' of Zoom environments, which for her have a 'kind of flatness' and 'dullness.' In the end, in fact, it was Moreno's resistance to Zoom that gave the whole production the intense sense of theatricality for which it garnered acclaim: having Moreno's Ariel 'in a real space', with real objects, Seaton acknowledges, 'gave us the key to that playful theatricality of how she was making a storm in a bowl in her room.' Moreno's rootedness in analogue theatrical magic as opposed to the virtual magic made possible by Zoom allowed her to reach out to spectators in their individual homes and involve them in creating the soundscape of the storm, or to torment the shipwrecked lords by becoming harpies who were Spotlighted as they flapped their imaginary wings and screeched at their screens. This, Seaton maintains, is what made Ariel 'a real portal into the world of "we're all going to make a storm by clapping our hands" ... It came from that: the fact that it was going to involve physical things rather than virtual things.' Moreno's technophobia allowed her to become the production's bridge to its previous analogue incarnation, to its audience, and to a 'Shakespearean' mode of participatory theatricality that combines the cultural capital of Shakespeare's verse with community-building and uninhibited playfulness. If Shakespeare's Ariel speaks of his execution of the play's storm 'as though he himself were the very special effects of the theatre' (Davies 2015: 178), Moreno's performance bodied forth the *theatricality* of those special effects, and their dependence on collective acts of imagination that demand a synchronous response for the deep engagement of entrainment to happen.

While cramping Moreno into an under-stairs cupboard and having her image reproduced in a wall of television screens literalized her character's confinement by Prospero and became an apt metaphor for the lockdown situation cast and audiences were painfully aware of, that very restriction also gave additional power to her irrepressibly physical performance, lending her the power to seemingly burst out of the frame as a force of live theatrical performativity that bodied forth both her past and her present Ariels. Schneider speaks of how the performing body, rather than always already in the process of disappearing, can be 'resiliently eruptive, remaining through performance like so many ghosts at the door marked "disappeared".' Indeed, 'performance becomes itself through messy and eruptive reappearance, challenging, via the performative trace, any neat antinomy between appearance and disappearance, or presence and absence' (Schneider 2001: 103). Moreno purposefully propelled the analogue past into the digital present, bursting out of the Zoom frame to bring the audience's own bodies into (the) play to activate their muscle memory of participating in live theatre and being part of a creative community.

'Ariel's accomplices': Audience participation, community and emotion on Zoom

As became clear from the survey responses of *The Tempest*'s Zoom audiences, Moreno's Ariel struck a particular chord: in their answers to the question asking viewers to identify their favourite aspect of the production, Ariel was repeatedly singled out:

- The bits where Ariel instructed the audience as the fairies.
- Ariel involving us all in shouting/barking etc.
- Specifically, Ariel's performance and her role in instructing the audience participation were glorious.
- Ariel in the first performance was brilliant in a slightly sinister way that was especially enjoyable.
- Place where Ariel lived.
- Ariel in her stair cupboard!
- I liked the bits with Ariel best – the 4th wall breaking – I think it was a really great way to interpret Shakespeare/theatre for current climate.[1]

The frequency of the mentions of Ariel in our respondents' answers bears witness to Liedke's insight that Ariel, in the Zoom production, became 'the bridge between fiction and reality, technology and materiality, "us" (the spectators' [sic]) and "them" (the actors and actresses).' Our audience interviewees also felt that Ariel's use of direct address bridged the gap between audience and performer, describing how Ariel 'cast us all as spirits of the island' making them feel like 'Ariel's accomplices' during the performance, reflecting Liedke's observation that 'our emotional connection to Ariel is especially strong – we are part of their team, after all' (2020).

Ariel's popularity among audiences is indicative of how central participation was to the experience of the Zoom *Tempest*. One interviewee explained that she had liked 'the connection that was brought by the actors to the participants directly', while another appreciated that 'the audience was not an afterthought ... we helped move the story', suggesting that direct address was important in making audiences feel part of the performance. Rather than taking audiences out of the narrative, the breaking of the fourth wall brought audiences into it, with audiences recognizing Ariel's role as 'audience-wrangler' and appreciating her instructions for when and how to act in this novel form of performance. Gareth White has argued that considering 'how invitations to participate are made, and how people are able to respond to these invitations' is key to understanding the impact of an interactive performance (2013: 30). According to White's taxonomy of invitations, Ariel's invitations, along with the majority of the invitations made in *The Tempest*, can be considered 'overt' invitations, which 'consist of a performer, in or out of character, addressing spectators directly in a way that makes it clear that they are being asked to respond in some way' (40).

Recordings of the Zoom performances and the responses from our audience interviewees suggest, however, that some invitations were more appealing than others. While the direct invitations from Ariel (and later, from Alonso) were largely a success with audiences, responses to the press conference, which opened the performance, were more mixed. In this scene, the audience were positioned as members of the press; a short invitation with instructions appeared in the chat box at the beginning of the performance alongside some pre-scripted questions. Antonio acted as compère, soliciting questions from the audience and filling with improvised material as he waited for an audience member to be Spotlighted. Despite the instructions provided in the chat box, audiences sometimes misunderstood (or creatively interpreted) what was being asked of them. The recorded performances show various unexpected responses, such as children becoming suddenly shy, audience members being visibly shocked to have appeared on screen, someone asking the same question as a previous audience member, and audience members asking their own questions.

These unintended responses forced the performers to improvise, and the resulting moments were highlights for some audience members. One interviewee, for example, described how, having been picked to ask a question, he went off-script and 'made a very oblique reference to [British TV sitcom] *Blackadder* ... the guy playing Antonio instantly picked up on it and came back ... with a related but different reference to *Blackadder*'. As well as being exciting, this audience member described how this moment of deviation had made him feel 'more involved with the performance'.

As many audience members understood the request and were able to engage, this first invitation to participate was not exactly what White might term a 'failed' invitation, but for some, the invitation was a confusing one. One interviewee explained:

> [T]here was some confusion at the beginning, we weren't quite clear what we should do or whether we should speak ... but actually as we got through the play we realised everybody was clapping, we weren't going to be the only ones clapping or making a noise. It wasn't quite clear at the very beginning, the expectations. They did say audience participation but we weren't quite sure, shall we do it now?

As well as demonstrating initial uncertainty about participation, this comment also illustrates the power of group participation to alleviate this uncertainty. In comparison to the press conference invitation, which asked audience members to speak as individuals on screen, Ariel's subsequent invitations were directed to the audience as a whole (click your fingers for rain, clap your hands for thunder, pretend to be a bird). Participatory theatre, White suggests, 'presents special opportunities of embarrassment, for mis-performance and reputational damage' with audience members making 'conscious and unconscious choices about how and whether to participate' based on their individual perception of risk (77). Crowd or group participation, he explains, can lower the perception of risk for audience members:

> Being in a crowd that participates together can make people feel safe, for a number of reasons. First, simple safety in numbers prevents an individual from either being seen to be choosing to give a performance individually, or even just from being seen while they are participating. Second, we are more likely to associate ourselves positively with an action that we see a number of other people undertaking. Third, the understanding on which we build our assessment of risk is ongoing, and will be influenced by the evidence of the actions and implied risk assessments of others.
> (81)

Although White refers only to in-person participatory performance here, the responses from audiences of the Zoom *Tempest* suggest that even though they were watching alone or in small groups, that participating in synchrony as a group – and crucially, being able to see other audience members participating – was key to lowering the perception of risk and encouraging audience performance. Indeed, some audience members reported feeling more comfortable participating remotely via Zoom than they would have in person. One described, for example, how she had been put off watching the original in-person *Tempest* because she was 'kind of nervous about the amount of audience participation' and another explained that 'if I was in person I'd be apprehensive ... I think I felt more free because I was on the camera away from other people and I didn't know anybody'. Even though there was the chance of being Spotlighted and appearing on screen, these audience members found liberation in distance and anonymity, with the Zoom production providing a low-stakes way of engaging with participatory performance.

Unlike in-person performances, then, the Zoom format gave the audience the option of not being seen (by controlling when their camera was on), but it also provided new opportunities for being seen and, perhaps most significantly, for seeing others. Audience members reported excitement at being chosen to appear on screen, disappointment at not being chosen to appear, and having acted in ways to try and increase their chances of being selected by the stage manager for a fleeting moment of screen 'fame'. While the chance to appear on screen was a huge part of the experience for some, audiences more often mentioned finding joy in witnessing these audience performances. As demonstrated in the audience comment quoted at length earlier, being able to see other audience members participating lowered audiences' perception of risk in the ways that White outlines. However, the low-stakes moments of synchronous group participation facilitated by Ariel's commands, and the visibility of audiences on screen during these moments, also had an impact beyond encouraging further participation. Seventy-five per cent of our questionnaire respondents either agreed or strongly agreed that being able to see other audience members was important, and audience interviewees regularly mentioned seeing other audience members as something they valued about their experience of the production. For these audiences, being able to see others do what they themselves were doing contributed to a sense of connection and community that they felt matched or even exceeded the sense of connection they ordinarily experienced during analogue performance. For some, this was about the greater level of access to the audience that the Zoom production afforded in comparison to 'conventional' theatre:

> [A] big thing that I loved about this performance was how communal it was, how collegiate, how you see not just the cast but your fellow audience members almost more so than in a traditional theatre where you kind of shuffle past them to your seat and see them in profile ... but you're actually right in people's living rooms for moments here and that's really interesting.

Here, it is not only seeing audiences, but seeing audiences in their own homes that contributed to a sense of connection. Like Liedke, audiences reported looking through the gallery of audience members while they watched, with one interviewee explaining that it was 'wonderful to get to see other audience members watching it' and another respondent explaining that the audience became 'part of the spectacle'.

Despite being physically separate, audiences reported that 'the sense of being part of a larger experience was surprisingly similar' to in-person performance, and that watching the show had 'really felt that you were sharing an experience'. Participating in the performance at the same time as the actors and other audience members, and being able to see that audience, was key to the creation of this sense of entrainment and community, and had a powerful and often emotive impact on audience members. Watching live, our research suggested, was important to the audience of the Zoom *Tempest* in large part because doing so created a community of reception, which made them feel connected to other people at a time when physical communities were not possible.

As well as inviting audiences to participate in a live performance of *The Tempest* for our research project, a recording of that production was also made available for audiences to watch the following evening. Audiences who watched this pre-recorded version reported that they had not felt the same sense of community and connection that those watching live had experienced, further emphasizing the importance of liveness and synchrony in shaping audience experience. Interestingly, however, those who watched the pre-recorded production reported that although they were not temporally simultaneous with those on screen, they nevertheless found watching images of the audience emotionally affecting. One audience member described how she had enjoyed watching the audience participation sections of the production even though she was not able to participate herself. Elaborating on why this was, she explained that she found '*montages* of different people doing things quite a powerful thing in art and drama' and that while she 'did not feel so much like part of the community' she still gained enjoyment from the reminder that 'there were really other people watching this'. This comment suggests that *being* one of Ariel's accomplices and *watching* those accomplices from a temporal distance were fundamentally different experiences. Those watching the pre-recorded production were not able to participate in the community of reception in the same way as those watching live; as the identification of the pre-recorded audiences on screen as a '*montage*' suggests, when watched from the outside, the audience were transformed from co-conspiratorial accomplices into *mise-en-scène*.

While highlighting that watching live was key to creating a sense of community, this outside perspective also reveals something new about the emotional impact of the production on audiences. Although the responses from those who watched live demonstrate that seeing other audience members encouraged participation and helped to create a sense of community, the fact that this audience member found the audience '*montages*' emotionally affecting despite not watching live suggests that the very display of audience members may also have contributed to the heightened, and often unexpected, emotional responses that audience respondents regularly described. The ending of the production, when the actors took down their green screens and began to pack their sets away, and after the curtain call, when the audiences were put into Gallery View and unmuted in order to applaud, were moments that elicited particularly strong emotional responses. For some, this mirrored the response they would usually have at an in-person performance: 'I always feel emotional at the end of plays.' Others, meanwhile, felt that this was a particularly special moment: they found being able to see other audience members and the actors in Gallery View after having shared a new kind of experience together profoundly emotional.

The audience of this *Tempest* felt that these emotional responses were heightened by the particular conditions in which they were living at the time. Audiences and actors alike described feeling physically and mentally isolated from other people, with the production enabling a much-missed sense of connection and providing an emotional boost in the context of the first Covid-19 lockdown. Following Martin Welton's work in his 2012 publication *Feeling Theatre*, White describes a shared emotional state among audience members as 'affective weather', which, he argues, can 'shape our mood and incline us to act or refrain from acting, or impel us to act in certain ways' (2013: 166–7). The reception of the Zoom *Tempest* – the way in which audiences responded to invitations to participate, their attitudes to community and liveness, and the emotional responses produced – must be understood as having been contingent on the 'affective weather' of the early days of the Covid-19 pandemic. While audiences may have grown more comfortable with digital performance through time, allowing Creation, Big Telly and other theatre companies to experiment with new material, technologies and types of participation, the success of *The Tempest* can partially be attributed to the way in which it appealed to audiences in that particular moment. As well as lending itself to Zoom adaptation and therefore representing a safe choice for the company, the familiarity of the play also moderated the risk of participating in a new medium for audiences; audiences were able to try out a new medium, safe in the knowledge that, as a Shakespeare play, they would be on tried and tested ground in terms of content and narrative.

Shakespeare, then, offered a safe way into new technological and spectatorial territory for audiences at the start of lockdown, but also provided ways of guiding them through the terrain once they were there. Shakespeare's dramaturgy, which so frequently uses asides and soliloquies to break through the boundary separating the fictional world of the play and the real environment of the playhouse and its audience, provided a scaffold through which Ariel was able to guide and instruct the virtual Zoom audience. This not only created a live connection between actor and audience, but created a community of reception, making the play a particularly successful vehicle for a performance in lockdown in which audiences and actors were suffering from social isolation and lack of interaction. Moreover, Moreno's performance, shaped by her own resistance to the technology, was grounded in both the analogue theatricality of the 2019 production and her own physical environment, allowing her to inhabit the fictional world of the play and the multiple reception spaces of the audience. Through this, Ariel provided space for audiences to be unfamiliar with the medium, giving them permission to feel unsure and awkward within the performance. While Shakespeare's dramaturgy authorized direct interaction that allowed audiences and performers to connect and viewers to become participants in the performance in a manner that was a digital equivalent of 'immersion', Ariel's ability to act as an anchor for feelings of uncertainty meant that this direct interaction was met with trust by the audience; emboldened by their position as her accomplices, the audience were able to step together with the company into the brave new world of interactive Zoom performance.

Note

1   Unless otherwise noted, all interviews with creatives and audiences were recorded and survey responses were collected in July and August 2020. The anonymized survey responses can be accessed at: https://figshare.com/articles/dataset/Digital_Theatre_Transformation_Audience_Questionnaire_anon_xlsx/13076963 (accessed 28 November 2021).

References

Buchanan, J. and J. Wyver (2020), 'The Arts in Lockdown', *TORCH: The Oxford Research Centre in the Humanities*, 9 July. Available online: https://youtu.be/DLw0du1sKQI (accessed 28 November 2021).

Carlson, M. (2001), *The Haunted Stage: The Theatre as Memory Machine*, Ann Arbor: University of Michigan Press.

Cook, A. (2009), 'Wrinkles, Wormholes and *Hamlet*: The Wooster Group's *Hamlet* as a Challenge to Periodicity', *The Drama Review*, 53 (4): 104–19.

Davies, C. (2015), 'Strange Devices on the Jacobean Stage: Image, Spectacle, and the Materialisation of Morality', PhD thesis, University of Exeter.

Dennis, J. (24 July 2019), 'Creation create a hilarious after-dark adventure comedy Tempest where the audience are as shipwrecked as the cast', *Daily Info*. 24 July. Available online: https://www.dailyinfo.co.uk/feature/15426/the-tempest (accessed 28 November 2021).

Lafferty, E. (2019), '*The Tempest*: Creation Theatre Magic Brought to Shakespearean Classic', *Oxford Magazine*, July/August. Available online: https://www.oxmag.co.uk/articles/the-tempest/ (accessed 28 November 2021).

Liedke, H. L. (2020), '*The Tempest* (2020) by Creation Theatre: Live in your Living Room', *Miranda* 21. Available online: https://doi.org/10.4000/miranda.28323 (accessed 28 November 2021).

Mitchell, L. (2019), Interview with Creation Theatre Company. *BBC Radio Oxford*, 13 July. Available online: https://www.facebook.com/watch/?v=443882296448706 (accessed 28 November 2021).

Phelan, P. (1993), *Unmarked: The Politics of Performance*, London: Routledge.

Raines, K. (2020), *Act 2: National Audience Research*, Indigo-Ltd. Available online: http://s3-eu-west-1.amazonaws.com/supercool-indigo/Act-2-Report-wave-2-results.pdf (accessed 28 November 2021).

Schneider, R. (2001), 'Performance Remains', *Performance Research* 6 (2): 100–8.

Shaughnessy, R. (2020), *About Shakespeare*, Cambridge: Cambridge University Press.

Stoakley, G. (2020a), Email to Pascale Aebischer, 30 November.

Stoakley, G. (2020b), Interview with Pascale Aebischer, 16 November.

The Tempest (2020), [Zoom] Creation Theatre Company and Big Telly Theatre Company April-May.

White, G. (2013), *Audience Participation in Theatre: Aesthetics of the Invitation*, Basingstoke: Palgrave Macmillan.

5

Immersion in a Time of Distraction: 'The Under Presents: *Tempest*'

Erin Sullivan

The average length of a video on TikTok is sixteen seconds. The average length of a production of Shakespeare is five hours, twenty minutes and thirty-eight seconds. Or maybe it just feels that way.[1]

This is an essay about paying attention — to Shakespearean performance during a global pandemic, but also, more generally, to life in the twenty-first century. Alongside the extraordinary and often terrifying uncertainty that came with Covid-19 and its widespread lockdowns was a huge increase in opportunities to experience the performing arts online. At the same time, the ability to pay attention to and really appreciate this explosion of creativity was, for many, at an all-time low. In the UK and elsewhere, children were out of school, many people were working from home and anxiety about the future was draining the mental and emotional energy needed to focus. The result was an environment in which concentrating on any long-form, culturally worthy event was at best difficult and at worst unappealing.

In this essay I reflect on my own search for deep, absorbing attention during the chaos of the early months of the pandemic and how I rediscovered it through one of the highest-tech examples of Lockdown Shakespeare: 'The Under Presents: *Tempest*' (2020). Created by the Los Angeles-based gaming studio Tender Claws, and winner of Raindance Immersive's 2020 award for best narrative experience, this loose adaptation of Shakespeare's play plunged spectators into an interactive, virtual reality (VR) environment where they were joined in real-time by a live actor playing Prospero and a handful of other audience members. Drawing on my own experiences of attending the production and interviews with members of its creative team, I explore the way this *Tempest* and its wider gaming world reacquainted me with what it feels like to be profoundly, unconditionally present. In a world so often characterized by the ability to do many things and be many places at once, immersing myself in VR allowed me, somewhat paradoxically, to disconnect from the demands and worries that distracted me in my everyday, digitally networked life. Away from the noise of non-virtual reality, what was left was me, a story and the opportunity to discover both anew.

This distracted globe

Even before the pandemic, the experience of sustained, unbroken attention was becoming an endangered phenomenon. As early as 1971, the economist Herbert A. Simon predicted that the rise of ever-faster communications technologies would bring with it a decline in focused concentration. '[I]n an information-rich world,' he wrote, 'the wealth of information means a dearth of something else: a scarcity of whatever it is that information consumes. What information consumes is rather obvious: it consumes the attention of its recipients' (Simon 1971: 40). Fifty years on, it turns out that Simon was not only right, but prophetic: by the 1990s, scholars were starting to talk about how the world wide web was inaugurating an 'attention economy', and by the twenty-first century the idea that 'Attention is one of the most valuable resources of the digital age' was so widely held as to verge on cliché (Goldhaber 1997; Lanham 2006; Kane 2019). By this time, 'paying' attention had become an ever-more valuable and therefore commodifiable activity — and with so many vendors competing for this precious currency, it had become an increasingly fragmented one too.

Enter 2020: a year of virtually unprecedented global illness, restricted movement and, for many, mental unfocus.[2] In May of that year, just a couple of months into an experience that would last far longer than most people realized, *New Statesman*'s Sarah Mavis reflected on 'one of the few universal problems this pandemic has brought on: that it feels near-impossible to stay focused on anything' (2020). 'Since February,' she continued, 'there has been a 300 per cent increase in people searching "how to get your brain to focus", an 110 per cent increase in "how to focus better", and a 60 per cent rise in "how to increase focus"' (ibid.). As the year wore on, discussions about bandwidth were not limited to fibre optic kind. Mental and emotional bandwidth, and the strain that coronavirus was putting on it, was also making news (Wallace and Patrick 2020). For the most fortunate, digital connectivity meant that work, school, socializing and even theatre could carry on in some guise despite global upheaval, and yet many people's ability to engage meaningfully in these activities was heavily curtailed.

For me, the combination of a depleted ability to focus and a surge in online cultural content made for an interesting, challenging and at times frankly embarrassing situation. As someone with a secure job and relatively good health, I was unspeakably privileged to be untouched by coronavirus's greatest ravages. Beyond that, the fact that I was already researching Shakespeare and digital performance meant that I found myself in the strange position of seeing my field flourish even as the work of so many colleagues, within academia and beyond, ground to a halt. Digital recordings of past productions flooded the internet, while new, born-digital work sprang up within months, weeks and in a few cases even days of lockdown being announced, as this collection amply attests. In the midst of what was irrefutably a catastrophe for the performing arts, digital innovation was opening up new possibilities for audience access and artistic creativity.

And yet, despite the important and even ground-breaking nature of these developments, I found myself struggling to pay attention to the productions I attempted to watch. Some of this mental fuzziness was no doubt due to the stress that comes with being plunged into an unknown and open-ended situation. According to Jennifer Wallace and Vanessa Patrick, if '[mental] bandwidth is the limited store of focused attention we have to expend in any one day,' and every moment of deliberation 'use[s] up that precious mental energy', then 'navigating unfamiliar territory, such as, say, home schooling, housekeeping and working through a pandemic', takes a particularly heavy toll on our ability to remain fixated on just one thing (2020).

But alongside this collective psychological struggle was also a new lack of boundaries when it came to watching theatre. Without the socially imposed demands of in-person theatre-going – for the most part, staying in one place, remaining quiet, not doing other things while watching – engaging with theatrical performance became a different kind of experience. Before the pandemic, I celebrated this broadening of theatrical experience in my research on streamed performances. In a survey that I conducted in 2016 with audience members who watched a live-stream of a theatre production at home, I found that the vast majority (81 per cent) carried out at least one other activity while they spectated, and often more, including cooking and eating, looking after family members, posting on social media or doing emails and housework (Sullivan 2020: 105). Such a model of 'attending' a performance challenged long-held values about deep, unbroken absorption in a work of art, while also creating opportunities for new kinds of engagement and access. 'In accepting a wider range of audience behaviours that might occur alongside a performance,' I argued, 'we implicitly accept a wider range of audience members' (ibid.: 108).

I stand by that argument, and yet when 2020 came and watching at home, surrounded by countless other distractions, became the *only* way of experiencing theatre, my convictions were tested. I found myself recognizing the value of boundaries and longing for the focus that can come with shutting everything else out in order to take just one thing in. Such concentration was something I dearly missed in the suspended everywhere and nowhere of my home, which had swiftly turned into a workplace, social space, nursery and domestic refuge all at once.

In an effort to pay better attention, and to put into practice some of the principles I had previously championed, I started looking for ways to watch with others – and in doing so create a sense of community and social contract – despite being locked down at home. I took part in watch parties with friends, using Twitter and text messaging to connect with others and turn a potentially isolating experience into a collective event. I watched while doing other things, often unrelated to the production at hand, including cooking dinner, folding clothes or sorting through bills and the general detritus of life. At other times I experimented in the opposite direction, watching productions asynchronously in fully focused, half-hour segments – not unlike television episodes – during the quietest and most solitary hours of otherwise very boisterous and child-filled days (i.e. *very* early mornings). In a few cases where productions were only streamed in real-time, meaning that on-demand viewing was not possible, I attempted to generate a sense of theatrical boundedness by going down into the office in our cellar, putting on headphones and doing my best to ignore the shouts and thumps from the rest of the household as it got on with its daily living.

What I didn't know at the time was that, in oscillating between these different arrangements, I was exploring in an inexact manner what it means to engage with theatre as a form of 'soft fascination' versus a 'harder' one. If objects involving hard fascination 'fill the mind, leaving little room for more peripheral mental activity', then those requiring soft fascination 'capture attention more loosely, permitting unrelated thoughts to emerge' (Basu et al. 2019: 1057). While environmental psychologists typically associate soft fascination with experiences based in nature, such as walking in the woods or looking out of a window, more domestic activities like 'taking a long shower' can also produce 'a softly fascinating environment [that] allows for reflection' (ibid.; Damour 2020). The same might be said of listening to music in the background or appreciating a painting in a room while doing other things, but watching theatre in a similarly soft way has, until recently, remained culturally strange if not outright taboo.

Engaging with digital performance in a less intensive way offered a number of benefits: it enabled much-needed connection with others at a time of unprecedented separation, allowed me to keep up with the many practical demands of a suddenly reformulated daily life, and accommodated the reality of a beleaguered attention span. And yet, I also found myself longing for those moments of harder, absorbing, transporting concentration that might temporarily liberate me from other concerns and the ever-present, multilayered world of my home. I wanted to escape everyday life and rediscover what it meant to experience focus — not because hard, all-consuming attentiveness is intrinsically superior to its softer cousin, but because in those first months of the pandemic it had almost entirely disappeared from my life.

Going under

Towards the end of June, about three months into the first UK lockdown, news appeared about an adaptation of Shakespeare's *The Tempest* that would take place not on Zoom – by then the near-universal home for pandemic performance – but in virtual reality. This *Tempest* was a spinoff project from the creative games studio Tender Claws, which in November 2019 had launched a surreal VR experience for Oculus called 'The Under Presents'. Described in one review as 'idiosyncratic', 'reality-bending' and 'one of the most ambitious VR experiences ever made', 'The Under Presents' invited players into a strange, labyrinthine world of moody desert vistas, an old vaudeville theatre and dramatic scenes on a storm-tossed ship (Damiani 2019). Through portals located throughout the virtual world, players could travel between these different environments and 'bask in [their] weirdness'; as they did so, they would learn more about the narrative that connected them and how to cast their own magic spells (Kamel 2019). In gaming parlance, it was both an open world in which multiple players could explore their surroundings and interact with one another with no fixed objective, as well as a single-player, story-driven experience in which participants could work independently to unravel a central mystery.

As soon as 'The Under Presents' debuted, it attracted attention not just for its unconventional aesthetic but also for its use of live actors within the game world. Ten pre-recorded acts could be watched on a loop on the vaudeville stage, but live performers also entered the space and interacted in personalized ways with the players, often to their surprise. For many in the tech community, this blending of automated and live performance represented 'a game-changing innovation in virtual reality entertainment', opening up new possibilities when it came to real-time, embodied human interaction in digital worlds (ibid.). One of those possibilities was 'The Under Presents: *Tempest*', one of the first – and certainly highest profile – attempts to stage live, scripted, ticketed theatre in VR. For Samantha Gorman, co-founder of Tender Claws and director of *Tempest*, creating live theatre in VR was both a long-term goal and a more immediate, practical response to the Covid-19 pandemic. 'It had been something that was creatively interesting to me for some time', she explained to me in an interview; then 'lockdown hit' just as '"The Under" was coming to a close', and her cast of actors suddenly found themselves facing limited opportunities to work.[3] Staging live performance in VR had become one of the few ways of staging live performance full stop.

Practically speaking, theatre and VR had remained relatively uncommon partners until this point, but in theoretical terms they had long shared a history of interconnection. For many, the origins of the phrase 'virtual reality' lie with the legendary director Antonin Artaud, who in his 1938 *The Theatre and Its Double* described theatre-making as a kind of 'reálité virtuelle' (1958: 49). 'Words say little to the mind', he wrote elsewhere in that treatise, whereas 'violent physical images crush and hypnotize the sensibility of the spectator seized by the theatre as by a whirlwind of higher forces' (ibid.: 83, 87). Though Artaud's vision of theatre as a sensory-rich, virtual reality did not involve the kind of high-tech equipment we associate with VR today, it posited an intrinsic connection between transporting oneself to immersive, imagined places and the most daring forms of theatrical creativity. It is a link that theatre-makers and tech developers have often reiterated: 'Theatre is the original virtual reality machine', the director and scholar Mark Reaney has argued, while for the technology writer Howard Rheingold VR is 'an ultimately theatrical medium' (Reaney 1995: 28; Dixon 2006: 23).

It is perhaps surprising, then, that Tender Claws' use of live actors in VR was itself so surprising. But as highly anticipated as VR technology has been for several decades, it was not until the late 2010s that it entered anything resembling the mainstream. In 2012, the twentysomething founders of Oculus made headlines when they launched a crowdfunding campaign to develop the first affordable VR headset for household use, and then again in 2014 when they sold their still-nascent business to Facebook for $2 billion USD (Kumparak 2014). It was another two years before the Oculus Rift finally came to market, by which time two other commercial headsets – the HTC Vive and PlayStation VR – had also emerged. Still, despite a 'boom' in VR use during the pandemic, the technology remains culturally esoteric: according to one survey, 'in the United Kingdom only four per cent of individuals have access to a virtual reality device in their households' (Higginbottom 2020; Alsop 2021).

Among that niche community of VR users, however, a rapidly advancing, often highly experimental world of creativity lies in wait. Indeed, my own experience of going under in 'The Under' was one of startling strangeness, delightful confusion and – at last – hard, engrossing concentration. Generously supplied with a Rift that belonged to a friend-of-a-friend, I descended into my cellar late one August night to buy my tickets, get my VR bearings and start discovering what it felt like to visit somewhere else while still nestled in the privacy and familiarity of my own home.[4] Not being a gamer myself, I was uncertain about how I would manage in a digital environment that presumably required some degree of spatial acuity and bodily coordination — skills I had dismally failed to demonstrate when attempting to play my brother's videogames some twenty years prior. But I was ready for something different and willing to give it my best try, especially if plunging myself into a new world brought with it a refreshed ability to concentrate and attend.

The first thing I saw when I entered 'The Under Presents' were shadowy sand dunes in every direction and flashes of lightning that illuminated a stormy sky. The wind swirled about my ears and, as I held my hands in front of me, two black, rippling shapes – airy spirits of sorts – appeared within my view. As I clicked the different buttons on my hand controllers, the triggers under my index fingers produced snapping noises that were accompanied by visual bursts of energy; after several clicks, the shapes in front of me transformed into elegant, inky, disembodied hands. Moments later, two glowing rings floated towards me, and as I reached out to grasp them they slunk down my hands and onto my wrists. A soft melody began to play on something like a xylophone, while energetic crabs burst from the dunes and scuttled on their way. The virtual world had come to life.

I describe this opening sequence in some detail because it set the scene – visually and experientially – for 'The Under Presents' as a whole. As the VR designer Alex Coulombe has commented, 'The Under Presents' didn't start by telling its players 'what's about to happen' or offering 'any kind of tutorial or instructions' (2019). Rather, it immediately dropped them into an atmospheric, enigmatic world and challenged them to figure out what was going on. If they ran into difficulties, a white outline of their controllers would illuminate in their field of vision, along with arrows showing them how to liberate themselves from the situation in which they were stuck, but otherwise a large part of this game was discovering for oneself what it was all about. In this sense, Coulombe suggested that 'The Under Presents' offered VR adventurers something akin to 'an immersive theatre experience ... something that warrants multiple visits, something that doesn't do too much hand-holding with you, something that feels more like art' (ibid.).

That open-ended, artistic and at times confusing experience continued as I entered the game world proper, courtesy of a portal bearing a golden mask that I grasped and clumsily placed on my face. The dunes around me faded to black, and in their place a vintage-style cinema and old dive bar materialized. Turning up at this scene reminded me of what it felt like, in the days before smartphones, to arrive at an unfamiliar place and timidly, expectantly approach it. If you went to that dive bar on the right, you entered the sprawling landscape of 'The Under Presents', full of rickety doors, seemingly deserted rooms and colourful characters — an environment that did indeed remind me of my own visits to immersive theatre productions and performance art installations. This is where I spent my first-ever hour in an open-ended VR experience, and it calibrated my expectations for what *Tempest* might bring: confusion, captivation and a temporary forgetting of things beyond the fictive here and now.

Something rich and strange

But what about that old cinema on the left – pleasingly named The Decameron – and the *Tempest* that its marquee promised inside? The first night that I visited 'The Under' I also travelled to The Decameron to purchase my tickets for *Tempest* and see what kind of Shakespearean adventure it might offer. As I approached the animated ticket seller sitting in his old-fashioned booth, the screen changed to a two-dimensional display that allowed me to select the dates and times of my tickets and purchase them. At $14.99 USD, they were far cheaper than most in-person, immersive theatre productions, though finding performances that happened during waking hours where I lived posed a greater challenge (most took place in the evening in California, eight time zones away). As I came out of the ticketing interface and prepared to leave, I glanced behind the ticket booth at the glass doors that led into the cinema. Through them I saw another dark, sandy landscape and an abandoned ship run aground — the lonely, haunted wreckage after the storm. The boundaries between game, theatre, cinema and 'real' life continued to blur in a tantalizing and indeed fascinating way.

But if that sombre view through the glass suggested a rather melancholy *Tempest* to come, then my assumptions were swiftly reconfigured when I arrived at the show the following night. Transported into a colourful cinema lobby, I found myself part of an energetic group of six black, ghost-like avatars, who rushed around picking up bottles, casting spells and looking for clues about the show that was about to commence. Like me, these mostly silent figures were audience members, and their silhouetted, cartoon-like appearance matched that of the players I had seen the night before in 'The Under Presents'. Many were clearly experienced players of the game, and it soon transpired that some were repeat visitors to the live show as well. Speaking to Gorman later, I learned that some of 'The Under's' most ardent fans attended *Tempest* repeatedly – in one case fifty times – to the point that the actors could identify them by their body language and behaviour. The closeness of this relationship between creators and players, she commented, proved one of the most 'moving and magical' parts of 'The Under Presents' experience.

As a newcomer to this community, the ease and familiarity with which its members interacted with the environment and one another, largely through enthusiastic bursts of snapping, was at once intimidating and exciting (in both 'The Under Presents' and *Tempest*, players could snap their fingers as a way of communicating with one another but they couldn't speak). Here was a group of people busily carrying on with embodied, social interaction – not to mention deep, fascinated focus – in the midst of extraordinary isolation and uncertainty. I did my best to copy their actions, and at one point an usher from the game world came out to teach me and a fellow novice some basic spells, but it wasn't long before we were all thrust, ready or not, into the live performance. The scene around us faded, a new location appeared and at last the show began.

Shakespeare's *The Tempest* features one of the playwright's smallest casts and shortest scripts, but Tender Claws' production took such concision considerably further. With a running time of around forty-five minutes and a cast of one, it was an extremely pared back adaptation, with the actor playing Prospero calling on audience members to take on additional roles from scene to scene. Gone were Caliban and the insurrection subplot; central was the love story between Miranda and Ferdinand. After arriving at a campfire and being greeted by Prospero – a role shared by a rotating ensemble of eighteen performers – spectators travelled through a selection of scenes, including the opening shipwreck, the meeting of the young lovers, the disrupted banquet and the wedding masque. Prospero's tone was chatty and informal throughout – like a guide for 'a museum tour or a city walking tour' – with the actor who played him flitting in and out of character and improvising commentary with the audience as he went (Savage 2020). Lines from Shakespeare's *The Tempest* appeared in climactic moments, but the aim of this adaptation was not to offer detailed engagement with the language of the source text. Rather, it was to use *The Tempest* as a starting point in an exploration of VR as a kind of 'magic circle', as Gorman put it, in which audiences participated in an imaginative and interactive 'realm of play'.

The importance of playfulness, and the sociability that so often attends it, is immediately clear in the script that Tender Claws

FIGURE 5 *An audience member shining a light on Prospero in the opening scene at the campfire in 'The Under Presents:* Tempest'. *Image reproduced courtesy of Tender Claws.*

released online after *Tempest* closed. 'Make Players feel seen', the document states in its 'Top Level Notes' for actors, just after it highlights the importance of making the show fun: 'At the end of the day, in this context, this is what matters in a performance' (Tender Claws 2020: 2). Silly interludes including a scripted 'pee break' and informal, personal touches such as references to the actor's cats undercut the seriousness often associated with Shakespeare's play, injecting everyday humour into what is, after all, a comedy (ibid.: 6, 17–18). Like Creation Theatre and Big Telly's *The Tempest* on Zoom, the production celebrated the joyful togetherness that could be found in Lockdown Shakespeare and left darker themes for another day (see Aebischer and Nicholas Chapter 4).

Reading through the script, it is also apparent how much this *Tempest* was created with the fans of 'The Under Presents' in mind. Both the suggested dialogue and the notes to the actors stress the value of audience role-play and active participation — activities far more germane to gaming than to theatre. 'Players have shown that they *really* get into being asked to take on roles and act out scenes', the notes in the script explain just before the meeting of Miranda and Ferdinand, which were parts that Prospero asked audience members to perform (ibid.: 19). Likewise, the final page of the script offers a list of activities 'that worked WELL' from 'The Under Presents', and that accordingly would be 'carr[ied] over' into *Tempest* (ibid.: 34). They include 'Contests (especially light hearted)', 'Group spells', 'signaling out individuals', 'Enabling performance opportunities for players' and making space for 'Moments of connectedness and appreciation' among the group (ibid.). Through these actions, the performers helped audiences kindle a sense of togetherness in a space habitually described as 'virtual', but emotionally experienced as very real.

This is not to say that there weren't moments of more meditative, aesthetic wonder. The shipwreck scene at the start took the audience to the ocean floor, where they looked up at the tattered remains of the vessel and listened to the actor, as Ariel, sing an echoey, affecting rendition of 'Full Fathom Five'. Shortly after this 'Evocative interlude', as it is described in the script, the group journeyed to Prospero's cell, where alongside more joking they could collect objects such as a staff, books, coins and a child's shoe (ibid.: 3). Returning the shoe to the actor cued a more poignant mood, along with some of Prospero's most touching lines: 'Miranda, Thou wast that did preserve me. Thou did smile ... ' (ibid.: 14) Though such sequences were relatively brief, they intercut the prevailing levity with a contemplative feel. If Shakespeare's *The Tempest* offers audiences a world that oscillates 'between what is ordinary and ornate', as the Tender Claws script suggests, then such moments produced shifts in tone that lifted the production out of the everyday and into something more delicate and even sublime (ibid.: 32).

As a whole, though, it is fair to say that this *Tempest* was a cheerful one interested in making people laugh, play and feel part of a community. According to Haylee Nichele, one of the actors in the ensemble and my guide the second time I attended, the primary aim of the show was to 'push a bunch of participation and fun into it and make it feel more like an experience and less like traditional theatre where you sit yourself down and you watch something happen in front of you.'[5] Being there with others and taking an active role in proceedings were crucial features, as they are in so many multiplayer gaming experiences. More theatrical and literary values were present too in the form of spectacle and thematic exploration, but they always remained in service to Tender Claws' central goal: having fun. After Miranda and Ferdinand's wedding, Prospero returned the audience to the campfire for a group hug, more snapping of their fingers and a final dance party. The scene faded, and we were swept into a psychedelic swirl of colour and sound where we danced and waved at one another until it was clear that the show had finished. One by one we clicked a button to exit the game, took off our headsets and returned to our everyday, locked-down lives.

Presence majestical

As someone intrigued by and yet not exactly at home in 'The Under Presents', *Tempest*'s invitation to play was at once exciting and unsettling. Being an active player in this production made me step outside of my comfort zone as an academic, theatregoer and gaming novice and offered me the freedom to stop taking myself, and Shakespeare, so seriously. But as valuable as these things were, they did not reconnect me with the experience of all-consuming, mental absorption. If anything, they encouraged a softer but no-less-valuable meta-consciousness, in which I was aware of the many roles I was playing and my positioning both within and outside the gaming world. I was often distracted, but in a good way: my mind was 'draw[n] in different directions', and even 'asunder', as it worked to make sense of a show that for me was at once very familiar and very new (*OED* 2020: 'distract, *v*.', 1.a.).

What *was* entirely absorbing for me about the world of 'The Under Presents', however, was the experience of my own embodied self in VR. Though I had used VR equipment before, I had never done so alone, at home, or for anything more than a few minutes at a time. This go round I was able to enter the 'wild world of VR', as Nichele aptly described it, for about an hour at a time, several days in a row over the course of a long weekend. As I did so, I found myself marvelling at the way my arms, legs, stomach and brain felt as I grappled with both the practical logistics and the phenomenological strangeness of being physically present in two places – the bizarre landscape of 'The Under' and my mundane, cluttered office – at the same time.

Like Rebecca Bushnell, I was captivated by my 'disembodied avatar's hands', which registered as both mine and as having 'a life of their own' — as 'instrumental members of an estranged body' (2018: 5). There I was, both inside and outside of myself, actor and spectator, subject and object, at once. I suddenly had a new appreciation for what Jaron Lanier meant when he described VR as 'A way out of the dull persistence of physicality' (2017: 3). The release was less about escaping to new, exotic places, and more about rediscovering what it means to be present with one's own self — to experience physicality, and the psychology that attends it, afresh.

Whether or not this extraordinary feeling is one that would persist with repeated trips to VR is a question that I cannot answer, at least yet. There's no doubt that some of the wonder I felt was due to the novelty of the experience and the exoticism of the technology. Were VR to become part of my regular, even everyday life, then presumably the experience of using it would eventually fade into what Zara Dinnen has called the 'digital banal', or 'the condition by which we don't notice the affective novelty of becoming-with digital media' (2018: 1).

And yet, there are aspects of VR that resist easy naturalization, at least as the technology currently stands. First and foremost, it doesn't allow the user to multitask in the ways that have become so common since the rise of the smartphone. You can't check your text messages or social media in VR without exiting the virtual experience or relying on apps that patch VR and social media worlds together in inexact ways.[6] You can't fold laundry or cook dinner either, or look after children or keep an eye on work emails. The bulky headset that critics have long pointed to as one of the biggest obstacles to VR's success may also be, in a strange way, what makes it so effective when it comes to experiencing immersive, engrossing presence (Spaull 2019). With a computer strapped to your face and your vision and hearing largely obscured, there's little choice but to focus on what's in front of you and temporarily ignore all the other things swirling through your life, begging for attention.

This is true of VR experiences in general, but I felt it particularly strongly while visiting 'The Under Presents' and its *Tempest*. Perhaps it's because the experience was live – if you stepped away, it kept going without you – or because it required participants to stay in VR, and consequently away from 'real life', for a relatively long period of time. (A 2019 review of a different VR Shakespeare project described an hour as 'extremely long by the standards of virtual reality and extremely short by the standards of [Shakespeare]' (Harris 2019).) But perhaps it was mostly because the creative team behind *Tempest* understood how strange and even rapturous the experience of embodied presence in VR can be and worked hard to conjure this rough magic for its visitors.

Indeed, both Gorman and Nichele stressed the importance of the body in their reflections on the show, noting how the visual limitations of VR challenged them to focus less on the naturalistic representation of shared presence and more on evoking the feeling of it. 'I'm really big on physicality and embodiment and mask work', Gorman commented, adding that 'high realism is not something you want to try to go for in VR.' This emphasis on the expressiveness of the body could be seen and felt in the production's pared-down, dreamlike style and the way that gesture became so central to communication between participants. 'We had to really lean into the aesthetics of limitation in terms of avatars and movement', she explained, and take full advantage of 'the haptic feeling of presence' that comes with VR. Rather than striving for verisimilitude – with its uncanny payoff, at best – Gorman and her team focused on creating an abstract world that came alive through the audience's imaginative and sensory participation.

For Nichele, figuring out the relationship between her body and the avatar's, and the effects of their shared movements in VR, was a crucial part of the rehearsal process. 'You have to spend a lot of time figuring out how to make the avatar work and what makes that avatar look good', she explained; 'the best way to describe it is a very bizarre costume that you need to figure out the parameters for.' Such work was aided by her own training as a dancer and her experiences as a performer in immersive theatre productions such as Punchdrunk's *Sleep No More* and Third Rail Projects' *Then She Fell*. 'Practicing the intimacy of performance definitely helped in VR,' she commented, as did 'really learning how to read body language'. Both skills helped Nichele make 'quick decisions … in the blink of an eye' about how to relate to her audiences and create experiences of shared presence with them.

The result was a *Tempest* that not only made me feel part of the magic in a way I hadn't before, but also made me feel part of myself in a way that was at once estranging and remarkable. In this brave new world, the person who most surprised me was *me*, and the thing that most astonished me was the deep, magnetic focus I felt as I became a spectator both to the show in front of me and my own presence within it. Visiting 'The Under Presents: *Tempest*' reminded me of what it feels like to stop paying attention to everything a little bit and to submit to a single work of art totally and unreservedly. As its script suggests, the production 'telegraph[ed]' the 'value of art now' – or indeed *the art of now* – at a moment in history when so many people found themselves anxious about the future, longing for the past and uneasy about an increasingly unpredictable present (Tender Claws 2020: 3).

Of course, this *Tempest* didn't make all the difficulties of living through a pandemic go away, though it did provide temporary relief from them. Far longer than a video on TikTok and far shorter than most stagings of Shakespeare, it immersed audiences in an artistic experience that was accessible and engrossing during a time of unprecedented distraction. Like Artaud's vision for a more urgent, radical theatre, it offered visitors 'something to get us out of our marasmus, instead of continuing to complain about it, and about the boredom, inertia, and stupidity of everything' (1958: 83). Living life differently, even for an hour, renewed my ability to appreciate the present – and the forms of presence that exist within it – as polyvalent and deeply fascinating. Most importantly, it reminded me that there are worlds elsewhere that await us through dark, uncertain times — worlds in the future, worlds in art, worlds in ourselves.

Notes

1. Actually, neither of these things is true. One blogger has suggested that the *optimum* length of a TikTok video is 15.6 seconds, a figure he reached by timing the top 100 videos of 2019 (Slee 2020). As far as productions of Shakespeare go, the better part of three hours, including an interval, is common at many UK theatres.
2. Of course, there have been other global pandemics with even direr consequences than Covid-19, but no one living in 2020 has memories of those earlier, more severe catastrophes, so in that sense this one was indeed unprecedented.
3. All quotations from Gorman are from an interview conducted on 21 October 2020. I'm deeply grateful to Gorman for the time she took to speak to me.
4. Enormous thanks are due to Elizabeth Jeffery and Steven Richards for helping me find an Oculus Rift in Stratford-upon-Avon, and to Michael Anderson for letting a total if well-meaning stranger borrow his equipment. None of this would have been possible without them.
5. All quotations from Nichele are from an interview conducted on 25 November 2020. I'm deeply grateful to Nichele for the time she took to speak to me.
6. A quick trawl through VR message boards suggests that more expert players have found ways of joining up their social media and VR lives, and I have no doubt that further integration is on the horizon. But for novices like me, right now entering VR means cutting oneself off from other, more mundane realities.

References

Alsop, T. (2021), 'Access to a VR Device in Households Worldwide 2020', *Statistica*, 4 January. Available online: https://www.statista.com/statistics/1107878/access-to-virtual-reality-device-in-households-worldwide/#statisticContainer (accessed 28 November 2021).

Artaud, A. (1958), *The Theater and Its Double*, trans. M. C. Richards, New York: Grove Press.

Basu, A., J. Duvall and R. Kaplan (2019), 'Attention Restoration Theory: Exploring the Role of Soft Fascination and Mental Bandwidth', *Environment and Behavior*, 51 (9–10): 1055–81.

Bushnell, R. (2018), 'Gesture and Performance in Virtual Reality', Shakespeare Association of America, unpublished seminar paper.

Coulombe, A. (2019), 'Let's Experience The Under Presents VR – Pt 1 (with Commentary)', YouTube, 19 November. Available online: https://youtu.be/MnxFU0aRUTM (accessed 28 November 2021).

Damiani, J. (2019), '"The Under Presents" Is a Novel Exploration of VR and Live Immersive Theatre', *Forbes*, 19 November. Available online: https://www.forbes.com/sites/jessedamiani/2019/11/19/the-under-presents-is-a-novel-exploration-of-vr-and-live-immersive-theatre/?sh=1acb7af67455 (accessed 28 November 2021).

Damour, L. (2020), 'How Teens Use Downtime to Connect, Distract or Reflect', *New York Times*, 3 December. Available online: https://www.nytimes.com/2020/12/03/well/family/teenagers-downtime-free-time-choices.html (accessed 28 November 2021).

Dinnen, Z. (2018), *The Digital Banal: New Media and American Literature and Culture*, New York: Columbia University Press.

Dixon, S. (2006), 'A History of Virtual Reality in Performance', *International Journal of Performance Arts and Digital Media*, 2 (1): 23–54.

Goldhaber, M. H. (1997), 'The Attention Economy and the Net', *First Monday*, 2 (4–7). Available online: https://firstmonday.org/ojs/index.php/fm/article/view/519/440 (accessed 28 November 2021).

Harris, E. A. (2019), '*Hamlet* in Virtual Reality Casts the Viewer in the Play', *The New York Times*, 25 January. Available online: https://www.nytimes.com/2019/01/25/theater/hamlet-virtual-reality-google.html (accessed 28 November 2021).

Higginbottom, J. (2020), 'Virtual Reality Is Booming in the Workplace amid the Pandemic', *CNBC*, 4 July. Available online: https://www.cnbc.com/2020/07/04/virtual-reality-usage-booms-in-the-workplace-amid-the-pandemic.html (accessed 28 November 2021).

Kamel, O. (2019), 'The Under Presents Review', *6DOF*, 25 November. Available online: https://6dofreviews.com/reviews/games/the-under-presents/ (accessed 28 November 2021).

Kane, L. (2019), 'The Attention Economy', Nielsen Norman Group, 30 June. Available online: https://www.nngroup.com/articles/attention-economy/ (accessed 28 November 2021).

Kumparak, G. (2014), 'A Brief History of Oculus', *TechCrunch*, 26 March. Available online: https://techcrunch.com/2014/03/26/a-brief-history-of-oculus/?guccounter=1 (accessed 28 November 2021).

Lanham, R. (2006), *The Economics of Attention: Style and Substance in the Age of Information*, Chicago: University of Chicago Press.

Lanier, J. (2017), *Dawn of the New Everything: A Journey through Virtual Reality*, London: Bodley Head.

Mavis, S. (2020), 'Why Can't We Focus during This Pandemic?', *New Statesman*, 6 May. Available online: https://www.newstatesman.com/science-tech/coronavirus/2020/05/how-focus-concentration-pandemic-brain-motivation-apps-pomodoro (accessed 28 November 2021).

OED (*Oxford English Dictionary*) (2020), Oxford: Oxford University Press. Available online: https://www.oed.com/ (accessed 28 November 2021).

Reaney, M. (1995), 'Virtual Reality on Stage', *VR World*, 3 (3): 28–31.

Savage, A. (2020), 'VR Immersive Theater in The Under Presents: Tempest!', YouTube, 10 July. Available online: https://youtu.be/fSQD8DBLODE (accessed 28 November 2021).

Simon, H. A., et al. (1971), 'Designing Organizations for an Information-Rich World', in M. Greenberger (ed.), *Computers, Communications and the Public Interest*, 37–72, Baltimore: Johns Hopkins Press.

Slee, D. (2020), 'I Watched the 100 Best TikTok Videos to Find the Optimum Length', 21 January. Available online: https://danslee.co.uk/2020/01/21/clipped-i-watched-the-100-best-tiktok-videos-to-find-the-optimum-length-of-a-clip/ (accessed 28 November 2021).

Spaull, S. (2019), 'Four Reasons VR Gaming Still Isn't Mainstream', *Minutehack*, 24 July. Available online: https://minutehack.com/opinions/four-reasons-vr-gaming-still-isnt-mainstream (accessed 28 November 2021).

Sullivan, E. (2020), 'Live to Your Living Room: Streamed Theatre, Audience Experience and The Globe's *A Midsummer Night's Dream*', *Participations*, 17 (1). Available online: https://www.participations.org/Volume%2017/Issue%201/7.pdf (accessed 28 November 2021).

Tender Claws (2020), *Tempest* (final script). Available online: https://drive.google.com/file/d/15oI7Py4ELjAG2ZKH8KMgX8BLijgTEunz/view (accessed 28 November 2021).

'The Under Presents: *Tempest*' (2020), [Oculus VR] Tender Claws, July–September.

Wallace, J. and V. Patrick (2020), 'Life in Lockdown Is Testing Parents' Bandwidth', *Washington Post*, 27 April. Available online: https://www.washingtonpost.com/lifestyle/2020/04/27/life-lockdown-is-testing-parents-bandwidth-heres-how-protect-your-mental-energy/ (accessed 28 November 2021).

6

What You Will in the Time of Covid-19: Exploring the Digital Arts, Race and Flexible Resistance

David Sterling Brown and Ben Crystal

In 2020, uncertainty and fear generated by the pandemic forced virtually all countries into lockdown, and theatre practitioners around the world had to confront a new reality.

For the Shakespeare Ensemble, an international collective of multidisciplinary artists, lockdown led to the August 2020 production of What You Will, a 'virtual theatrical promenade' that used Shakespeare as a springboard for reflection on the increasingly universal feeling of isolation felt during the early months of the pandemic.

In this conversation, Ben Crystal – actor, author, creative producer – and Dr David Sterling Brown – a Shakespeare and premodern critical race studies scholar – reflect on how the challenges created by the pandemic facilitated artistic innovation. Touching on such *subjects as the 'digital arts', Twelfth Night, access, agency, race and whiteness, they explore the tensions between resistance and flexibility: two types of responses to the pandemic that have, in distinct ways, led to inventive creations like* What You Will.

DAVID STERLING BROWN (DSB): The age of Covid-19 has forced theatre practitioners to become artistically resistant to the unexpected limitations created because of shutdowns, social distancing, etc. What did artistic resistance look like for you, particularly with respect to *What You Will* (*WYW*)?

BEN CRYSTAL (BC): Artistic resistance is a good phrase, and makes me realize how often I think of artistic flexibility. There were an awful lot of reasons not to create in 2020. There was shock, isolation, fatigue and bafflement: even if you *did* create, would anybody see or engage with it? And if they did, would they feel anything from that little black dot that is the webcam? Being a creative has never been easy. It's often poorly paid, unless you're very lucky, and yet so many creatives create, despite ever-difficult circumstances. If you've got that fire that burns to make [art], you don't feel you have much choice. The pandemic just made it a lot harder.

DSB: That's where I'm going when I think about resistance: resist the urge to give up, to succumb to negative feelings, low motivation. However, I also understand the need to be flexible.

You had to be flexible in response to the pandemic and with respect to working on your craft. Given that, how did the idea for *WYW* originate?

BC: In March 2020, the Shakespeare Ensemble met virtually when we would have gathered physically together from around the world for a Research & Development project. Anirudh Nair, in Delhi, said, 'We're an international ensemble. To come together, it's expensive both financially, and in terms of the climate. Irrespective of the pandemic, what does distance collaboration look like for us?'

So we met online every week and talked. The first thing that came out of these meetings was a virtual birthday cake for 23 April 2020, a collection of Shakespeare lines recorded in pockets of nature all around the world, edited into a film, dipping a toe into the creative waters of digital arts.

Then we started talking about things we liked about Zoom, and, importantly, things that we *didn't* like: sound going in and out, the continual question of 'Am I muted?', family members walking past in the background, the lag, not knowing if you're being listened to or not, all of the natural occurrences in this medium.

We saw a lot of theatre projects being filmed – projects designed for one medium being squeezed into another. And also theatrical projects that had been adapted towards this 'Zoom' medium, with actors using Virtual Backgrounds, pretending to talk to each other, with a lot of pre- or post-production work smoothing things out. We wanted to do something that was designed *for* the medium, and *with* the medium, that really interrogated what the medium *can* do. We found ourselves asking, 'What are the advantages of this new art platform that neither regular theatre nor film/TV could do well, but this could do brilliantly?'

We talked about isolation, about the idea of showing our audiences a window into India, Japan, America. We talked about isolated characters in Shakespeare, and then the first idea: 'Wouldn't it be great to spend time with Malvolio in his cell? What would forty-five minutes of *that* look like?'

We knew there were lots of people sitting at home slumped in front of their desks, working, and they would flip a channel, in a sense, and watch more. But how do we take advantage of the medium in our isolation, and provoke more agency and engagement? Together with feeling a growing resonance towards *Twelfth Night*, we organically found the four corners of *WYW*: the medium, characters in isolation, audience agency / congregation / entertainment, and *Twelfth Night*.

DSB: That's fascinating. I hear the importance of resistance and flexibility, which is clearly becoming a through line here.

The pandemic began and it sounds like you and the Ensemble, instead of just diving into the new waters, you stood on the shore and watched first.

That patience is evident in the rich texture and innovation of *WYW*. And to your last point about engaging the audience, who was, who is, your envisioned audience?

BC: When curating, co-creating or collaborating we don't have an age demographic in mind. Apart from safeguarding younger minds, the audience is the world, everyone in it and every demographic, and especially those that feel that Shakespeare is out of reach. That said, the audience that we failed was the audience without internet access.

DSB: So, standing on the shore at the beginning and observing paid off. It sounds like an enlightening and enriching creative process. On the website, *WYW* is referred to as a 'virtual theatrical promenade', one that facilitated distance collaboration. Can you explain that term?

BC: When the Ensemble goes somewhere, we listen. When we toured Japan in 2019 we prepared three sets of parts for three plays and built them all in Japan, in response to the environments we visited. It's important to us to design responsively, to allow projects to resonate with the places where we play.

DSB: Listening in and to the environment, that's an interesting exercise.

BC: And listening to this digital medium, the conversations that kept coming up were about Punchdrunk's *Sleep No More* and *The Drowned Man* and how much ownership, congregation and entertainment came from these open-world, promenade theatre pieces.

Everyone was going crazy wondering when they were going to perform, act or practice again, and keening for an opportunity to spread their creative wings as widely as possible. We were missing being together, and missing theatre, and we heard that audiences were too. So, how do we provide something that offers congregation as well as entertainment, that togetherness of, 'I went to see that show, so did I', or, 'I saw it in the front row, I was at the back, I saw a different show', that wildly different engagement with the same piece of art? Our answer was to gift them something to freely explore in the digital world.

Out of the reflections of agency, ownership and freedom we started to ponder this idea of a virtual promenade piece. The characters would be connected by the play, linked together online through a house of rooms, or a treasure map (we went for a map, using artist Patrice Moor's collages).

If the actors are devising in isolation, they need guidance to keep them all in the same 'world', so a storyboard would bring everyone together at particular points, and Feste (Folk artist Hazel Askew) would play music that each actor could hear, through an earpiece, while they were performing. The combination of storyboard and music provided a skeleton structure to work with, and paths for an audience to follow.

The original idea was much bigger on the performance end and post-production. The core was to build something live that allows the audience to fully control what they see and hear. The idea felt positively disruptively different in aesthetic from visiting a static Zoom screen of rectangles.

But we hit a wall with the technology. I reached out to ModStreaming, a company I'd worked with before, but what we were looking for wasn't technologically possible. Most home computers and broadband providers don't have the processing or broadband speed to simultaneously run the equivalent of two dozen YouTube live-stream windows. ModStreaming suggested that we trial the idea with eight live-streams instead of twenty-five.

DSB: Did you push back and say, 'Well, what about nine to ten?'

BC: Absolutely, I did!

DSB: See, resistance! You forced the live-stream company to be flexible – there seems to be synergy with resistance and flexibility here: you pushed them to reconsider what the technology *could* do.

BC: One hundred percent. We compromised with nine live-streams, two of which were different takes on Maria. It was a loss for some of the actors who wanted to play, but we focused on our original cornerstone: audience agency.

DSB: How did you finance this project?

BC: It was profit share with an open-book accounting model. The shows were Free For All or Donate What You Will, to open up accessibility. The Ensemble were invited to opt into or out of the pool received; then proceeds were split between opt-ins. About four months' work – the last eight weeks of that were full-time – was just the love of the craft. The web designers and ModStreaming kindly gifted their time.

DSB: So you got them to donate their time and energy – that's awesome.

BC: We were so grateful. They were excited by the innovation, the experimentation, the scale of the idea and the global reach. One of the best lessons I learned about producing – especially producing big, wild dreams – is 'don't ask, don't get'.

DSB: I've learned the importance of asking for what you want, too. The worst that you will get is a 'no', but you might end up getting more than you wanted.

The goals for *WYW* were huge. In a way, you were still standing on the shore with your original idea since you had to wait for the technology to develop. Nevertheless, it sounds like your intention was to create something enduring. Shakespeare endures as well, as evidenced by *WYW*'s engagement with *Twelfth Night*. It's not a linear Shakespeare adaptation, and it's not a production that follows what the more mainstream, trendier productions were doing at the pandemic's start. Why did you choose that route? And what's gained or lost for the audience, or even in relationship to the play, by going the non-linear route?

BC: We knew we wanted it to be live, and also to persist after the live event. A lot of big theatres shared their archives last year. It's interesting how many people saw those shows and said, 'I was there in real life and I've seen the stream, and it doesn't … ' There's a feeling that there's something missing. Cameras filming theatre struggle to convey atmosphere and empathy.

DSB: And the energy, too.

BC: Absolutely. Film is film, theatre is theatre. Personally, being up in the back row of a theatre is infinitely better than having a ringside seat at a filmed piece of theatre. The human energy that's expelled, the dynamic quality that emanates from the stage as passion is expended, it's an incredibly intimate experience, whether you're in the yard at the Globe or in the nosebleed seats on Broadway. The living quality, the life force is somehow absent when it's filmed. That said, filmed theatre has brought experiences to people who would never normally get to see it, which is fantastic. Still, the question for us was, how can something endure in a different way, having been live?

DSB: I see, again, the importance of flexibility.

BC: We could have easily done a linear *Twelfth Night*. It would have been edited, it would have been cool, but it would either be a screen of rectangles with people sort of talking to each other, like the incredible *The Show Must Go Online* project, or it could go the Speaker View route like Creation Theatre, where they're cutting between speakers much like TV and film. What was more exciting to us was to sit with these characters in the shipwreck of their own lives, to be able to revisit them again and again after the live event, and see different things.

With our global membership we had to prepare for people from different cultures coming to this with varying degrees of awareness of Shakespeare. By using the play as a starting point and having everyone devise in their own worlds, there would hopefully be something in the final piece for everyone, whether you knew Shakespeare well or not.

We wanted *WYW*'s non-linear-ness to be a springboard to a linear *Twelfth Night* production, or to reading the text. If *WYW* endures, it will be because the singular approach to the play was married with the singular approach to the medium. We were looking to interrogate so many aspects of this new digital medium, so perhaps a more linear approach to the play – a storytelling narrative – would get in the way.

Some actors devised their streams using lots of Shakespeare, some used hardly any; some moved around outside a lot, some stayed stock still in their space. So you could absolutely just visit Feste for the forty-five minutes if you wanted, or you could hop around until you found the character with the most Shakespeare, if that's what you were there for. If you loved *Twelfth Night*, you'd get some insight into the internal machinations of these characters. And if you knew nothing about Shakespeare, and you didn't really get what one of the characters was doing, chances are, you would stumble across *something* that caught you, that resonated.

DSB: That's great to hear! As an audience member, I didn't feel stuck. I think audience agency is also key in considering how *WYW* was innovative. When you say the audience is essentially people globally who have internet access, and that you feel *WYW* offered something for everyone, that gestures in the contentious 'Shakespeare as universal' direction. But I understand here you're talking more about universal, or easily identifiable, themes. Take Keith Hamilton Cobb's *American Moor*: I don't think somebody needs to be familiar with *Othello* to fully understand what's going on there or to take something away from it, but knowing the play helps.

In that respect, Shakespeare serves as a useful springboard. You mentioned the different performers devising their approaches to *WYW* in varied ways. How were the characters chosen? And can you speak to the casting choices?

BC: The number of characters we could have was restricted by the tech, and we whittled the characters down again when we considered actor availability. Do we have two Violas or two Marias? Can we make this work without Sebastian? – yes. Andrew Aguecheek? – no. Then casting was based on a number of factors: we're an international ensemble and I have personal feelings about what a modern Shakespeare company should look like, demographically, so it might reflect a breadth of the human condition. The Black Lives Matter (BLM) movement in 2020 provoked some theatre companies to make statements about the importance of inclusivity, antiracism and diversity; we wanted to make our statement through the work, and especially the casting.

Arian Karp, a director and actor in California, started working on the mood boards and character packs we gifted each performer – art and words that the devisers could sink their teeth into. The artist Helen Foan began responsive design work – listening to the Ensemble's conversations and sketching out the unifying aesthetics each deviser might use in their backgrounds to tie everyone together.

As the project started to build steam, I gave a workshop at a high school in Long Island, New York, and one of the students, Renee Rose, was terrific. I spoke with her teacher over the next few weeks and we invited her to play Olivia. Meanwhile, a dancer and choreographer, Xdzunúm Danae, got in touch at the beginning of lockdown, having graduated from university. I had given a workshop in Stratford, Ontario four years earlier and at the end of that session said, 'When you finish training, give me a call.' So she did, and she ended up exploring one of the two Marias.

So, some of the casting happened organically, and the rest was sketched out with the actor and Artistic Director of Seven Stages Shakespeare, Dan Beaulieu, who explored Belch. We were very conscious of the fact that we were white men doing this first casting sketch: attempting to represent the beliefs of the

Ensemble at large, and this idea of what an international modern Shakespeare Ensemble should look like today. So we made sure that it was a non-male identifying majority with predominantly Global Majority actors.

DSB: In organizing *WYW*, in the collaborative process, you faced trials and tribulations, and I was struck when you mentioned to me how, at times, members of the Ensemble would drop in and out of communication, disappearing and then reappearing. And that's the reality of the difficult pandemic situation we're all in; people are exhausted and sometimes, without warning, need space. Another challenge of this pandemic is the forced reframing of audience experience and reconsideration of what theatre can do. Is *WYW* supposed to be an escape? A reflection of life? An accompaniment to life? I want to understand how it differs from theatre, even 'Zoom theatre'?

BC: The modern audience experience invites us to sit in a theatre, slumped in a seat in the dark, while entertainment is flooded onto us. There's a degree of activity that comes when you visit a theatre like the modern reconstruction of the Globe, though. When you're standing as a groundling around the stage, or even sitting on the benches, your core is engaged, and you're active in a way that a proscenium arch audience isn't. Accessing that activity and taking our audience away from the slump is what theatre is for us – a life-slump-taker-away-er. And what Shakespeare is.

DSB: Yes, absolutely!

BC: Active listening, between audience and actors, that's what Shakespeare and his players were so good at: lulling their audience into a sense of vulnerability and then gently inviting reflection and identification. That's what makes us laugh, and cry.

We offered audiences a window into these characters' private lives. Each devising actor worked with a member of the Ensemble as their 'outside eyes'. Not as a director, but to say, 'This is what I see in what you're devising.' The Scots director Alasdair Hunter then worked as a satellite Ensemble member, 'outside-eyes-ing' each of those groups and keeping a check on whether everyone was either within the same playing field, or if they were going outside it, that they were doing so in a useful way.

DSB: Interesting, so this process required a lot of trust given the challenges presented by Covid-19.

BC: Yes, and especially as the mirror was challenging at times. I think Dan's look at Belch with the lens (or 'engine') of 'addiction' was one of them. And there were moments when the mirror was more softly angled, with Colin Hurley's Malvolio, working with the engine of 'madness' – that first idea we had, of spending all forty-five minutes in prison, this man going mad by himself in his little black Zoom box.

We got to see a searingly contemplative exploration of Viola, devised by Em Thane. They're non-binary and their exploration of Viola felt necessary; they started their stream with a different kind of gender transformation, washing one version of themselves away, before journeying out of the house, down a country lane, leaving the camera behind, only to return drenched (thanks to a local Welsh pond), all the while slowly working out the speech they're preparing to give when they visit Olivia.

We offered glimpses into someone else's world, with Hiroaki Kurata's Aguecheek, a stationary camera in a traditional Japanese *tatami* room, stylized props, a man trapped and frustrated in melancholic unrequited love. Amba Suhasini Katoch Jhala's Maria (with the engine of 'ambition'), travelling through an endless sequence of palatial Indian rooms, slowly revealing the painful wish to be the Madam, not the Maid. The sister piece was Xdzunúm's Maria (with the engine of 'opportunism'), an incredible journey through the mind and heart of the character, above- and below-stairs. Anirudh's Orsino was filmed at three different times of day. When he stepped out onto the streets of Delhi dressed as a woman there was a radically different feeling between the daytime and night-time performances. With each stream there was a different mirror being held up to a different human condition. You don't get such variety in a regular theatre experience.

DSB: Did you say you *don't* get those things in regular theatre?

BC: Ha, ok, yes, of course you do, but you get them served to you in a tailored order and if you don't like an actor or a particular character and you're in the theatre – or you realize that you're in a theatre with folx that don't look like you or speak to your world – you're there until the interval at the least, unless you bust out.

FIGURE 6 *Andrew (Hiroaki Kurata), Olivia (Renee Rose) and Maria (Amba Suhasini Katoch Jhala) in* What You Will. *Image collage created and reproduced courtesy of The Shakespeare Ensemble.*

We leaned into the agency that Netflix and YouTube have opened up. No matter where you are in the *WYW* site, whichever character's stream you're visiting, you always have the opportunity to tune into Feste's audio: music, song and the play of a clown were everywhere you went, if you wanted them. A reflection of life, on life, and with all these elements combined we felt we were just starting to answer questions about what the digital arts can do that makes them so different from regular theatre experiences.

I consciously don't say Zoom theatre. The digital arts are beyond one particular platform, especially a platform that was built for corporate conferencing. Between theatre and the screen, somewhere in the middle is this unusual new art form. All of us in this last year are scratching at the surface of its potential.

DSB: That's what's so exciting about this because it's being born right now. It's developing. When I consider this pandemic moment, I don't even know if two or three years will be enough time for me personally to reflect and provide answers to, 'What the heck happened during this time?' It's fascinating that we're having this conversation right now, in this moment, especially because we don't know when this chaotic, uncertain time is going to end; and we don't know what additional innovations it will lead to before it's over.

BC: Anirudh's original prompt was, 'Irrespective of the pandemic, how can we collaborate at distance?' I was a consultant creative producer on *The Show Must Go Online,* and curated the introductions; one of the beautiful things that came out of it was we got reports from folx who have always lived in isolation, who are disabled, in palliative care, in hospital, who *never* have access to Shakespeare, or theatre in general, and were getting to see Shakespeare for the first time in their life, and in some cases, the last. Whether or not the world goes back to normal, that audience is not going away; even when the pandemic becomes a memory, the digital arts are staying.

DSB: True – this pandemic moment has offered an opportunity to build a better future for different audiences, especially as it pertains to access.

BC: Now the digital arts have gained more legitimacy, the exciting slice will be what they can offer that theatre or the screen can't.

DSB: Literally and figuratively, the world is being rocked right now. Once we get an opportunity to stabilize ourselves, that's when we'll begin to understand what'll come from this challenging time. Speaking of challenges, there was a relatable emotional, psychological darkness to *WYW*, which has a content advisory that includes mention of topics like racism, mental health, addiction, suicide, drug use and self-isolation. Isolation is a key term because when the world shut down in 2020, most everyone felt isolated, and many people still do (though some people enjoyed the shutdown!). Can you speak to how *WYW* addresses the content advisory issues?

BC: *Twelfth Night* is a stunning blend of comedy and tragedy. Those two theatre masks touch each other in most drawings, and Shakespeare seemed to know that if you want to make the audience cry, you have to make them laugh first; *Twelfth Night* is so funny, though grief runs through the play.

DSB: Yes. That's so right what you say about that symbiotic emotional aspect of the work. I mean, *Hamlet* is very dark. It's grief, but you also laugh through those particular moments, and throughout that play as well.

BC: We laugh in the darkest moments… It's what helps us get through difficult times. We get grit from the darkness, to push off into moments of jubilation.

In *WYW*, Dan's Belch was arguably the darkest piece. Much of his stream took place in a familiar setting, a twenty-first-century bathroom, and his Belch had really recognizable traits: you've either experienced what you see him do, or you've heard about it: alcohol and drugs are familiar, even if hiding vodka under a bathroom sink might not be. But if you've had experience with alcoholics, there'll be moments in Belch's stream that resonate.

DSB: As someone who is deeply invested in mental health advocacy, and as someone who understands the dynamics of addiction, those moments certainly resonated with me.

BC: That's terrific to hear. Resonance is good, though no one wants to go to the theatre and be lectured. Drama is not therapy. But it can be therapeutic. So there was a very careful lightness of touch that bubbled throughout, and a party scene in the middle of the show when everyone could dance around together, the audiences too.

One of the tones of the Ensemble's work is a visceral and emotional deep dive. We often get to that place from looking at original practices and exploring modern versions of them. There's something about adapting the original practice rehearsal and performance methodologies that seems to be very 'roll your sleeves up and get dirty' rather than keeping the poetry pristine. We wanted *WYW* to be challenging and to resonate, but we didn't want to upset folx and push them away. Shakespeare wrote the qualities of humanity that were challenging and upsetting to his time, and we tried to do the same.

This is back to the cornerstones of congregation and entertainment in a time of pandemic. We didn't attend to that congregation cornerstone as well as we might have, but we tried. We offered a Zoom room which was the virtual lobby for the audience to gather in before and after the show, and we kept a chat going throughout as an anchoring meeting place.

DSB: Gathering people virtually to create a sense of live, shared community is challenging.

BC: Very, though we didn't want folx to be cut adrift as soon as the show was over, with no one to decompress with, having been through a bunch of grit.

DSB: Speaking about the challenging qualities of humanity, you mentioned BLM earlier. As someone who's engaged with race all the time from a professional standpoint, I want to turn in that direction and consider how *WYW*, and your practitioner work, addresses race and racism. One of the things that's so interesting about race is that we are born into it, and so it covers our lives in ways that other aspects of our identities don't because they have to develop over time. Race is with us from the start. How does race matter in *WYW*? And how does addressing racism matter in and to this project?

BC: While we were creating, we were listening very keenly to the state of the world. The pandemic, the racist state violence in America… the reaches towards equality and inclusivity, and a more humane acceptance of diversity.

When we thought about Renee, she didn't know *Twelfth Night* at all. Olivia's engine was 'grief'; having lost her brother, the character was in a mourning space. Dan said, 'What hasn't a young Black woman got to do with the engine of grief today?' So very carefully, with her teacher and a few Ensemble members, we invited Renee to share with us – if she wanted to – her perspective on that. She set up a camera in her back garden and sat and talked about grief for forty-five minutes, three times that day… we couldn't even hear her some of the time…

DSB: You couldn't hear her because of the grief, or…

BC: Right, or because the mic dropped out, or because there were times that the grief was just hers. It was a moment performed, not heard by anyone watching, a natural echo of all the moments of dropped calls and lag and phantom muting, of not being heard, of having your voice silenced.

Hopefully, we created a piece of art that was accessible to as wide a demographic as we could make it, and we cast it so as many people that went to see it would find someone in there that looked like them. Or rather, someone who reminded them of themselves.

DSB: Agreed. I don't know that I identified with Olivia as much as I did with Belch – perhaps I identify with both. The emphasis on looks is important but also superficial. Belch doesn't look like a woman but his actions, dilemma and behaviour may very well remind a woman of herself.

BC: Completely. At the time, I was the curator of the Ensemble. It's a multi-ethnic membership, but Global Majority members were only a third of the demographic. I'm a white man, and I recognize that over the years I've had an unconscious bias in the people that I was inviting.

DSB: Do you mean your unconscious bias led you to limit the types of people you were inviting?

BC: Ah no. Let me try again. I set no limits to who could be a member, nor where they might be from, but I didn't think to seek white-Global Majority parity in the demographic. Last year was illuminating, and I saw the imbalanced membership as an unconscious bias.

It was shocking to see the demographic on paper: male and white majority, despite its internationality. The revelation made me work harder. It made us all carefully consider who steps forward to play and how often a room is led by folx who look like me.

DSB: So BLM, and racial diversity, was on your mind while devising *WYW*. When I think about BLM and what it stands for and what it came out of… it started in 2013, after the 2012 killing of Trayvon Martin in the United States. Because it is *Black* Lives Matter and because of how it developed, it's also specifically meant to get people thinking about anti-Blackness, and state and police violence and how, as we saw last year and witnessed around the world, it's not just a US matter. It's a global matter. There's BLMUK, for instance; and there were protests happening in South America as well.

I heard you say that, with respect to world matters, the Ensemble was trying to be conscious about race(ism) and not simply reflect whiteness back to whiteness in the ways we are so used to seeing theatre companies do, in ways that some would actually consider a form of racial erasure or even racial violence. Am I hearing you right?

BC: Yes, conscious, careful, mindful of racial inequities, of the reach white Shakespeare has, and how his works can encourage reflection for all if they're well produced.

DSB: Now, this might be a tough question, but I want you to answer it. With *WYW*, how were you forced, particularly in the context of BLM, which is ongoing, to think about whiteness: your own, the Ensemble's, the *WYW* characters', Shakespeare's, the actors'?

In an interview I conducted with Ayanna Thompson and Farah Karim-Cooper for a *Shakespeare Bulletin* special issue I co-edited with Sandra Young, Thompson highlighted how the theatre world is overrun with charismatic white male leaders (Brown 2022).

I think this is a particularly important moment in our conversation, given what you just said about how once you became aware of something, it stayed with you. And it's not a matter of doing a service to anybody, as attention to equity should be inherent, natural. How and why is that important to you? I'm not asking you to speak *for* charismatic white men, but I am asking you to speak *to* them.

BC: I recognize I have been perceived as a charismatic white male. I founded the Ensemble, curated its first years, and have been stepping back from leading it. It does not sit well with me to have a white male at the centre of an international, diverse, inclusive Ensemble.

I recognize, too, that in the early days of its formation there were invitations from predominantly white-led institutions, and from those places I gathered folx that I thought would enjoy this work. Those folx are from all over the world, and very different types of white in terms of cultural backgrounds, but they still outnumber the Global Majority members. Since *WYW* streamed in 2020, we've been redressing the imbalance of the membership.

A lot of folx say they struggle to diversify their company or board because they live in a 96% white population – very similar to my hometown in Wales. I appreciate that that makes it hard. Then the pandemic hit, and we became even more isolated. Personally speaking, much as I've been working to consult with institutions that are more racially diverse, in those first few weeks in 2020 when travel shut down I wasn't sure how to find a more heterogeneous crowd. But then, we all moved to embrace the virtual world.

DSB: Resistance and flexibility again!

BC: Right? It's become easier to reach out to someone on the other side of the planet and explore playing together.

DSB: Has it become easier? It seems the option was always there; folx just didn't take advantage of it.

BC: Getting funding for an international artistic trip isn't easy, and can take a colossal amount of time and energy to produce. Before Covid-19, if a virtual show was produced, no one would watch it; there wasn't an audience. The medium wasn't deemed legitimate.

DSB: To say this seems to erase the digital arts' long history, whereas I think you are referring to a specific facet of the digital arts.

BC: True – though the option was always there, during Covid-19 actors said 'Yes' to virtual gigs that previously their agent would never have let them hear about. Now, suddenly, neither geography nor medium matters.

It matters that the people I work with and our audience aren't just my demographic. I seek a space that is widely, freely accessible, as diverse as the human race itself. Theatre that speaks to and for every part of the world, where we share in each other's stories, everyone seen, heard, and welcome. A place where you might see a glimmer of yourself, a slice of your life. Theatre is the beacon for diversity and inclusivity, equity, a place to come and tell your story. While there's nothing I can do about my own demographic, I can certainly work harder: I can recognize the parts of unconscious or institutional bias I've been party to or subject to, and address it.

Charismatic white folx in leadership positions hopefully know it's time for folx that don't look like us to step forward. Decentralizing ourselves doesn't have to mean deactivating. It can mean charting a similar course with a different engine. Everyone benefits from the wisdom of the crowd, by gaining perspectives different from the ones we grew up with, by surrounding ourselves with folx who don't look like us, or feel the way we feel.

DSB: Yes! One of the key things I heard was resistance again. Resisting the racial/cultural norm that you were born into – not just where you were born in Wales, but it's the UK, it's global. And also resisting the status quo. Most importantly for folx in the art world, particularly white folx, is resisting the pervasive invisibility of whiteness that society upholds and the desire to centre whiteness. You mentioned decentring yourself, which is important... because if no one who's in positions of power steps aside, then how can we diversify leadership representation?

Shakespeare, when we look at his oeuvre collectively and in nuanced ways, was good about putting in front of his audience, something for me, something for you, something for people of different class statuses, something for people who are disabled, etc. He didn't seem interested in just reflecting back to the world what was familiar to him all the time.

On a different note, there have been contemporary plays that have used the Zoom format. I'm thinking, about *Keene* by the Thai-Australian playwright Anchuli Felicia King. *Keene* was picked up by the American Shakespeare Center, whose Zoom reading in 2020 starred actors like Paul Gross and Grantham Coleman. *Keene*, a riff on *Othello*, as King calls it, is not a Shakespeare adaptation, but it was presented via the digital format. What's the difference between something like that and *WYW*?

BC: I think the distinguishing feature is that *WYW* was made for the digital arts and *Keene* was – I don't mean this derogatorily – squeezed into it.

DSB: Yes, it was not made for but forced into that format, which allowed greater audience access. As a result, myriad people got access to a social-justice-oriented play that touches on race and racism, and calls into question the very definition of whiteness. As I mention social justice and consider issues pertaining to marginalized people as related to racial injustice in the case of *Keene*, I'm wondering how might theatre practitioners conscientiously develop offerings for audiences with atypical access or no access (a demographic of folx that is marginalized) or how might theatre practitioners work to solve such problems?

BC: We can work a lot harder and be more imaginative. There's a great young actor I worked with from Graeae, Jamal Ajala. He's a deaf actor: his profound British Sign Language 'To be, or not to be... ', is available on YouTube. We invited him to explore Orsino for *WYW*, but he couldn't do it. We had no budget, we were scattered across the world, and we were building the engine as we were racing the car – qualities of the final production were being dreamt up days before it went live. But these restrictions mustn't stop us reaching towards greater inclusivity.

There are some incredible theatre companies out there doing work where accessibility is not bolted on at the end of the production. Accessibility needs to ripple through every aspect of what we're doing and making: it isn't just about whether or not there's a ramp outside your brick and mortar building, and it isn't just about whether or not the performance is audio-described, sign language interpreted or captioned.

The pandemic meant that going to the theatre became an inaccessible luxury even for the able-bodied. If we don't work to redress the balance, soon it'll again be a luxury surrounded by obstacles for the disabled, the visually impaired, the hearing impaired, the isolated. We can consider their needs more, with these folx part of the conversation. How does an audio describer sensitively and acutely describe an international and diverse ensemble? How do we reach folx without the internet? What is it to no longer be able to remember your lines and to need, if you're going to continue to perform, to have the script in your hand? To be in a theatre and be blind and not be able to see where the exit sign is? Or to be autistic, and you feel you can't react the way that you need to? Or to be new to the theatre, and not know whether you're allowed to go to the bathroom? We need to help everyone feel truly welcome from beginning to end, and make sure art is available to everyone that wants in.

DSB: That's very true. As you were talking, I thought about something else that distinguishes *WYW*: audience members can individualize their experience as opposed to having a collective experience. When folx are in the theatre they get trained to laugh at particular moments, or they join the chorus of laughter because it's the moment to laugh, so to speak. But maybe there are a hundred different such moments. But a laugh when everyone else is quiet... then *you* become the centre of attention.

With *WYW*, I had total control over my responses to the production, and it wasn't about what everyone else was doing; it was about my engagement with the virtual theatrical promenade. This is why I think *WYW* can, and perhaps should, be the entrance into Shakespeare for some people, as opposed to the other way around.

BC: I hope it's a springboard. It was notable that folx who complained about the lack of Shakespeare in *WYW* were predominantly very familiar with Shakespeare. The Ensemble's response was along the lines of, 'Well, you can go almost anywhere else and see as much Shakespeare as you like... '

DSB: He's definitely not suffering from an attention deficit. I deal with that in my work, too. Some people exhibit fear around decentring Shakespeare. You're pushing people outside their comfort zones when you do that. And what do they do? These people who are deeply familiar with and loyal to Shakespeare, they become resistant to your work and tension arises. They resist being flexible.

BC: Then I know we're onto a sure thing...

DSB: Yes, absolutely.

BC: If we're pushing folx out of their comfort zones, then we're on a great path.

References

Brown, D. S. (2022) '"Unicorns and Fairy Dust": Talking Shakespeare, Performance and Social (In)Justice with Ayanna Thompson and Farah Karim-Cooper', *Shakespeare Bulletin*, 39 (4).

What You Will is still freely available for virtual promenade via www.theShakespeareEnsemble.com

PART TWO

Case Studies

7

'Shakespeare for everyone'

The Show Must Go Online *in conversation with Gemma Kate Allred and Benjamin Broadribb*

Dominic Brewer	Cast member
Lisa Hill-Corley	Cast member
Ben Crystal	Guest Speaker Curation, Consultant Creative Producer, Cast Member
Adam Gibson	Sound Design
Emily Ingram	Stage Manager, Master of Props
Robert Myles (Rob)	Creator, Artistic Director, Cast Member
Andrew Pawarroo	Cast Member
Sarah Peachey	Producer, Cast Member
Matthew Rhodes	Associate Producer, Cast Member

Prologue

The Show Must Go Online (*TSMGO*), created by UK-based Robert Myles and Sarah Peachey, live-streamed weekly performances of the thirty-six First Folio Shakespeare plays from March to November 2020. Myles and Peachey ran a tight schedule of rehearsals each week from Sunday to Wednesday, in the afternoons and evenings UK time, to take account of the globally dispersed cast. A Tuesday technical run focused on scene changes and set pieces, and the only full run was the final Zoom-to-YouTube performance on Wednesday. Myles describes the project as 'a global movement and a cultural export, committed to making Shakespeare for everyone, for free, forever' ('Our Story'). The shows attracted over a quarter of a million views from sixty countries on six continents over the initial nine-month run. *TSMGO* became appointment viewing for its core fanbase, the self-named 'digital groundlings', who became as much a part of the weekly *TSMGO* experience as the shows themselves. The groundlings offered instant feedback as well as lively on- and off-topic conversations alongside each production through YouTube's Live Chat feature, which became a safe and inclusive space online for both regulars and newcomers throughout lockdown. *TSMGO* has continued to evolve to provide a platform for under-represented and early career directors to approach early modern work through unique lenses, while providing an ongoing source of financial support through a hardship fund paid into by Patrons. The company won two OnComm Commendations awards and an OffWestEnd 'One-Off' Award.

We spoke to nine members of the cast and crew in January 2021 to look back over the First Folio Series.

Act 1: What is *The Show Must Go Online*?

[Enter Dominic, Lisa, Ben, Adam, Emily, Rob, Andrew, Sarah and Matthew...]

ROB
> *The Show Must Go Online* was initially going to be a reading group, and that lasted one week. We realized that you can't *do* the plays without *doing* the plays. In wanting to serve the audience, we naturally found ourselves having to embody the text.

DOMINIC
From the very beginning, there were several days of rehearsal leading up to the performance. Even if that was a limited amount of rehearsal time, it was still more than a reading. *TSMGO* was always trying to make something fun for people to watch to get the audience, the actors, all of us out of our heads in that weird first couple of weeks of lockdown. I watched [the first show] *The Two Gentlemen of Verona* with great interest to see what the format was going to be and if it would even work, and I thought: 'These are my people, there's too much enjoyment to be had here!'

ROB
That's why it was nice to start with *Two Gents*, because a lot of Shakespeare devices are there in an embryonic stage. The letter pass, for example: we had to devise that because the play demanded it in order to tell the story to the audience. We were always conscious of wanting to be imaginative with how we dealt with the challenges that the text dealt us.

LISA
What I really appreciated is that *TSMGO* adapted to Zoom. We ditched the idea that this replaces in-person theatre. Zoom is a venue all of its own, and everything was geared towards the format. I remember for *Antony & Cleopatra* there were a lot of moving parts and tech rehearsal was long, just like a 'real' production. At one point, Rob asked: 'Okay, are we taking this seriously? Or are we just screwing around in bed sheets?' For me, that's what sets *TSMGO* apart.

ROB
Exactly: the difference between this being 'faffing around in bed sheets' and being a play is the force of collective belief. If we're all throwing our imaginary force at believing the situations we're in and the characters we're speaking to are real, the audience will buy it. If not, it does get exposed really easily; there's a fragility there that takes everyone to hold it together.

ANDREW
TSMGO has a global cast, which I wouldn't have gotten anywhere else. It was a group doing theatre over Zoom, taking the medium and adapting it so that it looks like theatre, film, a collection of people coming together on a stage. It was this boundary-pushing idea, and I was so drawn to that. Shakespeare is this text that can

be worked into all kinds of situations. Being in lockdown, it was interesting to explore that, and explore different ways of casting or performing Shakespeare.

ROB

We all treated it like an *actual* show every week and wanted it to be the best it could be. The macro was 'Hollywood scale, Poundland budget', and we would always land somewhere in between those two. Some things would naturally have to be lost along the way because of the intense nature of the process, but the ambition was certainly always there.

Act 2: Community

BEN

The most regular, solid thing in my life last year was Wednesday nights, knowing I could tune into some Shakespeare. Within the craziness of last year, that was a nice thing to be able to hold on to, like a banister. I wonder whether that's why *TSMGO*'s got such profound reach. You don't get that kind of audience reach unless it's like a soap opera, and you know when it's on. I think that structure was very attractive, both for the audience and creatives – that congregation, entertainment and togetherness – that's just so necessary.

DOMINIC

The sense that *TSMGO* brought all the Shakespeare nerds to the Yard was important – not only as an actor, but also as an audience member. As Ben pointed out, the consistency of a Wednesday evening was really important. It meant that whenever I wasn't acting in a show, I was happily involved in the groundling chat. Some people were there just to watch the play and not get involved, not get chatting; some people were there *just* to chat, because they needed something to do or they wanted to communicate with people. It grew as its own community, like any acting company grows as a community.

SARAH

Being able to get live feedback on the shows really drove us. Realizing that we had to keep innovating – not only because we wanted to for our own creativity's sake, but because we had that urge to surprise and delight the audience.

ROB

Getting the actors to sing 'Bohemian Rhapsody' in *The Tempest* was a direct response to the digital groundlings 'singing' 'Bohemian Rhapsody' in the Live Chat during *The Winter's Tale*. That was our way of showing that we're listening and we're responding. There is a responsiveness in our approach: it is dialogic. In an early modern environment, there would be no filter between actor and audience. It's long been my belief that heckling should be a thing if you're doing it properly, because the audience feel enfranchised.

Act 3: For everyone, for free, forever

LISA

As an actor of colour, I came to classical theatre because in almost every other theatre, at least here in the United States, you have to be a certain type. Shakespeare is one of the first places where people say, 'What difference does it make if the mom is black and her nephew is blonde? It doesn't matter.' We just expanded on that, and it didn't matter – let's all play.

I remember one of the ensemble for *Titus Andronicus* saying that the most exciting part for them was knowing at the top of the show that there were people all around the world in their own rooms with their own cameras waiting to start. We were all doing the same thing together in different time zones. I just thought that was amazing!

MATTHEW

When we did *Measure for Measure*, we really wanted to do everything justice, not only the central plot point of the attempted sexual assault. I remember having conversations about making sure that this is a sex-worker-positive production; that we didn't want to be in any way sidelining or excluding marginalized communities. We say Shakespeare is for everyone, but that means it can't be for people who want to gatekeep.

DOMINIC

It shouldn't be understated how important Rob and Sarah's commitment to diversity and inclusivity was from the very beginning. The sheer number of people they asked opinions of, to get those things right. I don't know many directors who would have gone to as much effort or cared as much about their community, particularly the marginalized voices, than Rob and Sarah.

ROB

We set up a series of guidelines for our casting – inclusive of gender, age, ability, experience and so on, which *TSMGO* casting director Sydney Aldridge and others championed. They understood what this stood for, and they wanted to actively progress that vision. As the shows went on, more familiar faces started to return, but there would still always be new people getting involved, and that was because we wanted to make sure that as many people got a shot as possible.

FIGURE 7 *Iras (Rebecca Brough), First Guardsman (Neelaksh Sadhoo), Charmian (Maya Cohen), Diomedes (Andrew Pawarroo), Cleopatra (Debra Ann Byrd), Third Guardsman (Alec Stephens III), Mark Antony (Mark Holden) and Second Guardsman (Lois Abdemalek) in TSMGO's Zoom-to-YouTube production of* Antony & Cleopatra. *Screenshot reproduced courtesy of* The Show Must Go Online.

SARAH

Our approach definitely evolved over time in response to what we were capable of doing. Unlike a professional company that can incentivize applications through money, we had to do all of our incentivization through culture – we had to make and keep and continually reaffirm a commitment to inclusivity so people from under-represented backgrounds could see, week after week, that this is a place they could feel welcome.

ROB

We were having to manually unpick the threads of exclusion that have been so tightly woven by cultural imperialists who have weaponized Shakespeare for generations, and that takes time.

SARAH

As more people started to apply we were able to evolve and expand our approach from gender-blind and race-blind to more race-conscious and then identity-conscious casting – we had collaborators from under-represented backgrounds to help steer us. Dr David Sterling Brown gave incredible support to us in our casting of *Othello*.

ROB

We wanted to preserve Othello's exceptional nature in the play without casting exclusively white people in all the other roles. We were conscious about who we placed where in the ensemble to serve Othello's character, while also serving the wider story and offering unique angles on the experiences of those with varied ethnicities navigating a white supremacist world. Similarly, *Antony & Cleopatra* is often told through a racist lens as the emasculation of the 'noble', 'white' Roman Antony, caused by his 'going native' in 'exotic', 'sensual', 'dark' Egypt. Racists and misogynists frequently point to this as an example, as if it proves some point.

SARAH

We wanted to make sure they couldn't do that with our version. We wanted to reinforce our very different interpretation of the text by having as many voices and perspectives involved in the collaboration as possible, to disrupt that sensibility.

Act 4: World creation

EMILY

My background is in object theatre. It's all to do with prop work and actors imbuing fairly mundane objects with transformative qualities. One of the things I have always talked to the actors about with props is: if you believe it's not cardboard and tinfoil, then the audience will believe as well. I think *TSMGO* is in some ways object theatre on a large, digital stage. We still went for a homespun aesthetic once people could get out to shops. I think that was important to us for a lot of different reasons, partly financial – actors have lost so much work over the course of the pandemic, so we were encouraging people to use what they had. But also because if you start mixing and matching – this person has a real sword, but this person has a tinfoil sword – the grammar of the world you've created starts to break down. If everyone's doing the homespun thing, it's an aesthetic and the audience don't question it, particularly if you're imbuing these objects with weight and significance in your performance.

ROB

But you can break the rules, if you do it deliberately. For instance, Sarah played Reagan in *King Lear*, and she owns a real sword, so it's quite shocking to see Reagan pull out a 'legit' sword when everyone else has been using tinfoil! There's a dramaturgical effect that you're trying to extract out of it. On the opposite side of that scale is Robbie Capaldi [as Antipholus of Syracuse] in *The Comedy of Errors* with a sword that's eight feet long made out of cardboard, which is so preposterously unusable that it goes all the way around and becomes awesome again in a different way.

EMILY

Being creative is important in lockdown – people taking up knitting, making sourdough – these are all very physical, tangible things at a time when so much of our lives are very digital and intangible.

ANDREW

That's something I experienced going through the prop-making process: doing something tactile, as opposed to just logging onto a computer and reading a script. That's true of the whole experience, not just the prop making – dragging my computer around, or pulling my own beard and falling against a cupboard – it was those physical aspects of the show and the process that were so awesome.

DOMINIC

For me, the entire experience fulfils that need to have done something tangible in 2020. That fed into the choice not to use Virtual Backgrounds – the 'we're all in our own spaces' aesthetic. That became part of the charm: you really got to know the actors not only from what they were performing, but where they were. I enjoyed the fact that you'd see people returning, and they'd be back in their recognizable 'space' again.

ROB

That being the closest version of the idea of shared space you could establish in this time: the audience are in their living rooms, so you're seeing us in ours.

ADAM

It's always been a bit like that in theatre, hasn't it? Black box theatres, playing stages in the round – you add little touchstones to feed off, and that builds the entire world without there needing to be an entire world already there. When it came to the sound design specifically, it was always just there to enhance and build. Adding a little bit of battle atmosphere if you're on a battlefield, for example.

ROB

For the witches in *Macbeth* Act 4 Scene 1, the music was literally catalectic trochaic tetrameter on a massive drum. It allowed actors to pick up on that rhythm, and then speak together. It's a click track, just done on an epic scale. As the actors were on three different continents, the only prayer we had of syncing them was some kind of unifying device.

ADAM

I've had a ball with being allowed to be creative, feeding off so many wonderful ideas, interesting things, whatever Shakespeare had in his text. The core production team were putting in as much work as we would over a four-month show in one week, and I was in my element.

Act 5: The future of digital performance

ANDREW
   Digital theatre offers things that you just can't do on a stage. I wouldn't have been able to act with people on the other side of the pond simultaneously, I wouldn't have gotten this opportunity to work with these people. It just offers so much on a personal level and a connectivity level.

LISA
   As much as I really miss being on stage and can't wait to get back there, everything that Andrew said about being able to work with and be part of a global community, that was something that I've cherished this past year, in this insane world that we're living in. When people can move around and spend more money, I'm excited to see where Zoom shows will go. Although, I will miss the DIY approach we all had when we were in our living rooms – we will never be able to get that back.

BEN
   It may not have bricks and mortar, but Rob, Sarah and the whole team have created one of the first digital arts spaces. We have to work harder to acknowledge that as being as valid as bricks and mortar in this new world. I think that's really exciting.

DOMINIC
   That push for legitimacy has been very hard, it's true.

MATTHEW
   I sincerely hope that digital theatre continues, because it's genuinely changed my life. I cannot say enough good things about this group of people, all 500 of them. But if digital theatre succeeds post-pandemic it will be one hundred per cent because of individual artists and artists collectives, like *TSMGO* and other groups that have done Zoom Shakespeare, that kept innovating and said, 'This does have legitimacy, and we're the early adopters'. I believe that this has a lot of power.

ADAM
   Digital theatre is an incredible resource. Whether we stay on Zoom or not, the whole point of it is innovation into this new art form. It's taken decades to get certain other art forms built – we're literally just at the start. There's so many ways it can evolve.

SARAH
Something that is really beneficial with digital theatre is just being able to make things so much more accessible for people in different circumstances, such as people who can't physically travel. Childcare is also a massive issue in the industry. In the UK, there are so many brilliant regional theatres, but getting actors and creative teams to them has presented challenges. Audiences too are limited in what regional work they're exposed to, but now they don't have to be. Digital theatre gives the opportunity to open up to anyone, wherever they are, whatever their time or location restrictions are. It means you get to work with so many more brilliantly talented people as a result of it.

ROB
There are serious questions around how funding works, and the limitations that places on creating work, that will need to be answered differently in response to this new medium. The biggest cause for concern is that 'things go back to normal' post-pandemic, and all of the hopeful progress made by artist-led initiatives is lost. We need to protect that, and build upon it, and to do so we need funding and institutional support.

We've proven that there is an audience, and an exciting Wild West to be explored – there's an incredible opportunity here, and the most exciting version of how this story plays out is that the opportunity gets seized in a different way, by different people than have traditionally dominated Shakespeare.

[Exeunt.]

References

'Our Story'. Available online: https://robmyles.co.uk/theshowmustgoonline/ (accessed 28 November 2021).

All *TSMGO* productions are available to stream online free via Rob Myles's YouTube channel: https://youtube.com/c/RobMyles.

8

Ricardo II: una producción bilingüe de Merced Shakespearefest

William Wolfgang and Erin Sullivan

Featuring Claudia Boehm, Cathryn Flores, Alejandro Gutiérrez, Heike Hambley and Ángel Nuñez

In 2020, Merced Shakespearefest, a community-based Shakespeare performance organization, produced its nineteenth year of theatre in Merced, California. In this small agrarian city of 80,000, 46 per cent of the population speaks a language other than English and 52 per cent is Latinx (United States Census Bureau 2019). This year was to feature the organization's first-ever bilingual theatrical production; instead, the pandemic transformed an original English/Spanish adaptation of *Richard II* into the group's first-ever web series. While the medium of the performance had to change in response to lockdown, the mission of providing performing arts opportunities to a larger and more representative section of the community in Merced remained the same.

Merced Shakespearefest's founding artistic director, Heike Hambley, began developing a bilingual theatrical performance of *Richard II* with guest director William Wolfgang, a grassroots Shakespeare practitioner and PhD candidate from the University of Warwick, in the summer of 2019. Due to the geographic distance between William and a team of University of California, Merced students who joined as co-adapters and directors, a six-month, collaborative script adaptation process was conducted through Zoom.

Their adaptation would set the play in 1840s California, during the political and cultural turmoil that occurred between the state's transition from Mexican to American control. Ricardo and his court would speak primarily in Spanish, while Bolingbroke and his faction would speak mostly English. Several characters were written to be fully bilingual, switching between the two languages every few lines and sometimes even every few words. This methodology enabled the ensemble to reiterate specific moments of the text and support monolingual comprehension.

The production team concluded the script design for *Ricardo II* in December 2019 and continued edits via video conferencing. However, the group was not prepared for how drastically the document would have to be altered. In March 2020, the auditions for the production concluded after extensive efforts to secure a bilingual cast yielded an enthusiastic group of local actor-participants, but the worsening health crisis made clear that production would not be able to move forward immediately. William and the other collaborators realized the video conference method of communication used throughout the prior months of script adaptation had foreshadowed what was to come. Co-director and translator Ángel Nuñez recalled the confusion that followed:

> That week, right after we wrapped with auditions and callbacks, the governor of California had just issued the stay at home orders. So, we had just gotten through being able to be in person, before all that changed. After that, in the few weeks that followed, it was kind of a limbo, not knowing if the situation was going to worsen or not. ... We still had the hopes of putting on a live theatre production ... Somewhere along the lines we realised, as Covid got worse, that gears were shifting.[1]

Within days, William and his team decided that rehearsals would have to take place online throughout April, but the hope remained that the production would still go ahead in person. Midway through the month, planning began to stage it outside, but that possibility soon had to be abandoned too. In consultation with Heike and the Merced Shakespearefest board, William made the decision to turn the project into a web series. Following strict physical distancing and safety rules, *Ricardo II* would be filmed on-site at outdoor locations across Merced and then distributed online at the end of the summer. Reflecting on his feelings at the time about the switch, Ángel remembered thinking to himself, 'Well, given that we're locked down and not being as creative, this is an alternative option and I thought it was great ... and somehow we pulled it off.'

Rehearsals carried on through April and May for a total of forty-five days. For many members of the team, participating in *Ricardo II* offered a sense of purpose during a confusing time. Living through the pandemic as it was unfolding, with no certainty about how long it would last or how devastating its ravages would be, left many feeling isolated and anxious about what the future might bring. Political unrest and racial violence in the United States in 2020 was also worsening social divisions and making marginalized communities feel even more vulnerable. *Ricardo II* offered its cast and crew a reason to come together and express themselves creatively. After the production concluded, Alejandro Gutiérrez, who played the titular role, reflected on creating theatrical work in such unusual circumstances:

> You put on top of these dark times even additional darkness because of the pandemic, everybody is locked in their homes and it's very difficult [to create], although not impossible as we collectively demonstrated. I think that we are sort of going through the mini Dark Ages of our times. Just like in the real Dark Ages, there were these little places where beautiful things were created. I think that we are a little bit like that. We are some monastery on some hill that created this one beautiful poem.

Like many other post-production reflections, Alejandro described an experience that inseparably linked the challenges of daily life to the creation of *Ricardo II*. 'It seemed to make an absolutely dreary time, with far fewer opportunities to do art and to meet people ... into what Billy called a theatre of hope,' Heike recalled. 'It was a project to work on and that's what we theatre people love – we want a project to work on.'

A commitment to maintaining hope in a better future informed the development of *Ricardo II* from start to finish, but that didn't mean that adjusting to new ways of working always came easily. When faced with the decision to cancel the production or continue working on Zoom, Heike and William agreed that the feeling of 'human connection' was uniquely valuable in the midst of the developing crisis. While Ángel welcomed this way of staying active during lockdown, he also remembered struggling with online meetings:

> I like being on the move, and the idea of going to a meeting in-person, meeting to collaborate. Being in lockdown just really took that all away. It's an energy you have, especially for theatre, being in a space and working together. Having to change over to Zoom dialled the energy down to 20-30 per cent. But you know, we made it work.

During meetings, cast members cited the challenges inherent to rehearsing theatre without the natural physicality central to the art form. Naturally, members of the company experienced 'Zoom Fatigue' at times along with all the other challenges that came with living in quarantine. Ángel recalled how the team responded to these changing circumstances by 'adapting the script constantly, adapting scenes, and adapting characters'.

Ultimately, the group's resiliency led to the successful completion of six days of physically distant filming in June that took place in identifiable locations around the community. The entire production was filmed, from Ricardo's banishment of Bolingbroke, to Bolingbroke's return from exile, and finally to the deposition and demise of the ordained king. The group reorganized the setting of the production to be during the pandemic, with actors wearing masks and very much embodying John of Gaunt's lines, 'suppose/ Devouring pestilence hangs in our air/ And thou art flying to a fresher clime' ('pretende/ Que aquí hay una pestilencia devoradora,/ Y estás buscando un clima más saludable') (1.3.283–5).

At the same time, aspects of the originally planned 1840s California setting – in particular those relating to political turmoil and regime change – were retained, and with great contemporary resonance. Specifically, the emphasis placed on displacement, a motif that has a stronger resonance for the Latinx community in America than it does for its white population, was a constant in all iterations of the *Ricardo II* script. While this theme makes appearances throughout the text, William, Ángel and their collaborator, Maria Nguyen-Cruz, centred the production's thesis around Thomas Mowbray's speech after Richard banishes him from England. In *Ricardo II*, Mowbray is renamed 'Tomás Mercedes' and speaks solely in Spanish. Ángel's translation, along with the change of the language from 'my native English' to 'mi español nativo', makes an eloquent case for the plight of the immigrant or the exiled: 'La lengua que yo he aprendido estos cuarenta años,/ Mi español nativo, ahora lo dejaré' ('The language I have learned these forty years,/ My native English, now I must forgo') (1.3.159-60).

Ángel hoped that viewers would make the connection that Mercedes is 'essentially being deported for a crime he did not commit'. In some ways, the switch to the web series de-localized this climactic moment, which had particular meaning for the community of performers that staged it. At the same time, presenting this moment online amplified its message by disseminating it to new audiences. The fact that the web series could also be subtitled meant that Spanish and English really did remain side-by-side throughout, with monolingual audiences gaining further assistance in their comprehension of both the play and the project's mission.

Alongside these amplifications of meaning, the new format created opportunities for artistic experimentation. As musical director, Cathryn Flores initially intended to write a score for live performance, but the switch to a web series led her to explore studio-based, electronic approaches. 'We were able to get different sounds that we might not have been able to get in an in-person, live performance', she explained. 'English horns, violins, cellos – I was able to incorporate those using just my keyboard and different synthesizers that I had at my home studio.' Through more prominent underscoring – a technique common in film and television, but used more sparingly in theatre – Cathryn emphasized the emotional dynamics of the bilingual dialogue and made its meaning clearer for those who struggled with one or both

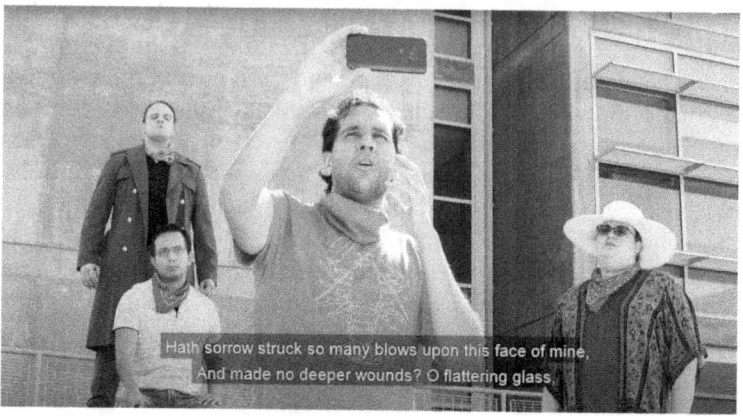

FIGURE 8 *Northumberland (Harker Hale), Henry Bolingbroke (Greg Ruelas), Ricardo II (Alejandro Gutiérrez) and Bagot (Katie Sylvester) in* Ricardo II, *'Ep. 10: Rey de la nieve'. Screenshot reproduced courtesy of Merced Shakespearefest.*

of its languages. 'I found the musical underscoring to be weighted a lot more than it would be in a live setting', she said. 'I think for our monolingual audience members, it was the driving force of the plotline.'

Cathryn also composed a theme song that featured at the start and end of every episode, providing a musical framing that further aided comprehension and spoke to theatre audiences in new ways. Inspired by Spanish-language telenovelas, she combined upbeat, poppy dance sounds with her own melodic voice, singing lyrics that served as a contemporary prologue to Shakespeare's play:

> Two voices, one story, a land divided,
> Misfortune, deception, country misguided.
> Battle for the crown, pride leading the way, Can you survive this reign?
> Ricardo, el segundo, the throne is slipping away.

Cathryn noted that her focus when writing the song had been on distilling the plot and themes of *Ricardo II*, while also creating a catchy refrain that would linger in audience members' minds. At the same time, she observed how the resulting lyrics about a warring kingdom echoed tensions present in a modern-day, divided America. The song resonated with viewers: 'I still get comments about it today from people singing the theme song and wanting it as a ringtone', Cathryn commented. 'You don't really see that in today's Shakespeare. I've never really thought about a Shakespearean theme song. Being able to make a new fusion of Shakespeare and Latin pop or Shakespeare and pop music: I think that's a really great area.' Ángel added that the song helped him think through the bilingualism of the production, clarifying his desire to make the Spanish and English lines tell a shared tale – 'two voices, one story'. 'That theme song is pretty great', he said with a smile. 'I think I would want a theme song for every Shakespeare play just so that I could have a good comprehension of it.'

Cathryn's involvement in the project had her working in her studio for most of the summer, including in June when other members of the cast and crew were meeting in person to film. But once filming had finished, William, Heike, Ángel and others also went to their computers for a stretch of work unfamiliar to most theatre-makers: post-production. For the better part of four months, the creative team, led by videographer Shawn Overton, edited, mixed and subtitled the twelve-part web series, which altogether ran to just under three hours. With the first episode debuting on 4 September 2020 and new episodes following every week, the team completed each episode one at a time, with a week or two to spare before its release date. 'We had a Zoom meeting every Friday,' Heike recalled, 'where we just checked in – did everybody get the music? how do the subtitles look? – and that was very, very helpful, I thought. Just the connection'. Constant communication – even more than would happen for a typical live production – was central to their method, helping ensure that the team remained connected and aware of how everything was coming together.

The result, everyone agreed, was something that was not quite theatre and not quite film, but its own hybrid form. 'It follows the format of a serialised, short-form TV series', Ángel commented, though he noted that the development of *Ricardo II* from live to filmed performance meant that its blocking followed more theatrical conventions. Performed in outdoor spaces across Merced, the web series features long, fluid takes and mid-to-wide shots, creating a sense of site-specific theatre captured on film. True to its grassroots origins, *Ricardo II* showcases the people and places that make up its community, even as it shares them with audiences that extend far beyond the usual remit of local theatre productions.

For Heike, the ability of this mixed art form to reach new audiences and build new skills proved especially appealing, and this is something she's keen to include in future Merced Shakespearefest planning:

> It's definitely a hybrid: it's a hybrid I enjoyed more than I thought I would. On the board we're talking about every year we should do one of these things because we learned that it has ways to reach people in different ways and helps different skills and talents for us. Once a season? That's not a bad idea to do that. I wonder what will happen.

One of the major benefits of the web series, of course, is the scale of its potential reach. As of April 2021, the twelve episodes of *Ricardo II* have viewing figures on YouTube that range from 100 to 1,000 hits each, plus further views on the video channel on Merced Shakespearefest's Facebook page. For a small, community-focused organization these are substantial numbers, and a further benefit of the web platform is that the videos remain available for audience access and classroom use long after the project has officially concluded.

This is particularly important for projects like *Ricardo II* that are committed to widening perceptions about what Shakespearean performance can sound and look like. From the beginning, Heike, William and the team wanted to make sure that *Ricardo II* reflected the diversity of the Merced community and challenged preconceptions about who Shakespeare is for. Claudia Boehm, who played Queen Isabella, discussed how she previously had to leave behind her 'español nativo' when engaging with theatre in California's Central Valley, and how oftentimes she felt that being Latina led to her not receiving roles. 'I always thought the characters [in Shakespeare] were more for white people', Claudia commented, adding that 'it has just been a dream come true to be able to perform in my own language here in California with such amazing people.' For Boehm, and for many people involved in *Ricardo II*, the result has been a much-needed infusion of hope:

Hope right now is something that is very great, not only for this type of thing, but hope right now is everything. Hope that all this passes soon, hope that we return to a normal, not like before but a new normal with more knowledge of how we should treat other people.

For her part, Heike (who is a bilingual German and English speaker) indicated that the production has had a deep impact on how she looks at the plays, even after two decades of directing Shakespeare. She was not alone: the majority of participants asked for more translated texts, and more bilingual opportunities. The positive experience that participants took away from *Ricardo II* was clear, and the medium on which it exists means that the experience is not entirely an ephemeral one.

Merced Shakespearefest is a relatively small organization, but it seems to be at the forefront of a wider turn towards bilingual Shakespeare. On 18 March 2021, The Public Theater in New York debuted its bilingual audio play, *Romeo y Julieta*, adapted by Saheem Ali and Ricardo Pérez González and starring Lupita Nyong'o and Juan Castano. Like *Ricardo II*, that project intertwined Spanish and English lines in a way that made it accessible to speakers of either language. In Merced, Heike, Ángel, William and Cathryn have begun work on a bilingual, filmed adaptation of *Don Quixote*, which they see as a companion piece to *Ricardo II*. The work of grassroots theatre continues, bringing communities together through artistic expression at a time when they need it most. To other companies interested in creating inclusive, innovative, non-traditional work, Cathryn offered this piece of advice: 'Don't be afraid to bend the rules'.

Note

1 This case study draws on interviews conducted by William Wolfgang in English and Spanish with the *Ricardo II* cast and crew on 20, 24 and 28 July 2020 in Merced, and a further interview conducted by Wolfgang and Erin Sullivan in English with production team members on 8 February 2021 on Zoom.

References

United States Census Bureau (2019), 'Quick Facts; Merced, California, United States'. Available online: https://www.census.gov/ (accessed 28 November 2021).

All episodes of *Ricardo II* are available to stream free online via Merced Shakespearefest's YouTube channel: https://youtube.com/channel/UCqwa5-ftfWJhhm_NKxT5W1A.

9

'Your play needs no excuse'

CtrlAltRepeat in conversation with Gemma Kate Allred and Benjamin Broadribb

David Alwyn	Actor, Director and Zoom Technician
James Dillon	Actor and Writer
Rebekah Finch (Bex)	Actor and Artwork & Branding
Suzanne Knight (Suzie)	Costume Coordinator
Sid Phoenix	Artistic Director, Actor, Director and Writer
Rachel Waring	Actor, Director and Composer

It started with a phone call…

CtrlAltRepeat are a digital repertory company founded in March 2020 by Sid Phoenix from a group of creatives faced with having no work as the pandemic took hold. They wanted to perform, so they did, turning Zoom into a performance space. Their first Zoom-to-YouTube production, *Midsummer Night Stream* (dir. Phoenix) streamed for free in April 2020. We spoke to six members of the company in January 2021 to reflect on their experiences of moving to performing on Zoom in the early days of the pandemic, and asked them why they turned to Shakespeare.

RACHEL

James, Bex, Suzie, David and I had all just come off the immersive Secret Cinema production of *Stranger Things* [in London, UK], so we were already working as quite a well-oiled crew. Sid called us and said: 'I've got a really ambitious idea. I don't want this to be an online reading. I want to do tricks, it's going to be completely rehearsed'.

SID

Immediately following the announcement of lockdown, there was that heyday of the first couple of weeks where everyone was just producing digital content. It was a response to an incredibly traumatic thing, an entire industry shutting down, and, for me, saying, 'I don't want to do a table read, I want to do something more'. Shakespeare is a touchstone for any time of crisis – so I reached out to some friends to put on a Shakespeare play and see if it was possible to do it over Zoom. We gave ourselves two weeks to put it together.

SUZIE

It's funny that you said two weeks because I don't remember it being that short, but obviously it had to be! It's that old adage of finding that limitations breed creativity, because we couldn't have a set, proper costumes, things like that.

JAMES

When I got the call from Sid, I was very polite, but privately I didn't want to do it! I was just struggling day to day staring at the news. There was no way I *wasn't* going to do it, it was just difficult. There was a sense of not letting the industry, what we do and what we care about, just go away. Doing Shakespeare was something almost comforting.

SID

I had this pipe dream to create a repertory theatre company, but in the digital age. I was determined that people who had been in supporting roles in *Midsummer* were leads in *The Importance of BCC'ing Ernest* [the company's second production, a Zoom-to-YouTube adaptation of Oscar Wilde's 1895 play] and vice versa, because I wanted to create that sense of camaraderie and familial approach to art.

Sid Phoenix is inviting you to a scheduled Zoom meeting...

In contrast to other Zoom-to-YouTube Shakespeare adaptations, such as those of *The Show Must Go Online*, Phoenix set *Stream* in 2020, with the opening moments taking place from the perspective of Peter Quince (Tom Black) viewing his computer screen. Quince logged in, then headed to 'TheGlobe.com' to read news of Theseus (Adam Blake) and Hippolyta (Anna Sambrooks), 'founders of the world's largest entertainment agency, A10', planning to marry 'despite the lockdown measures'. Quince then initiated a Zoom-style meeting with the mechanicals to rehearse their performance for the upcoming online nuptials. Rather than performing in front of Virtual Backgrounds, the actors' homes doubled as those of their characters. It is an adaptive choice which underpins CtrlAltRepeat's body of work. Whilst *Stream* was overtly set in the present day, Shakespeare's language was maintained throughout.

The company spoke about the challenges of Zoom as a performance medium, and how Shakespeare helped them to navigate the software early in lockdown.

DAVID

> The reason why Zoom as a medium works well with Shakespeare is because it is so dialogue and communication heavy. The language leaps off the page and is beautiful, so we could get away with having Zoom windows as our set. We were able to focus on the performance and the communication between people. Shakespeare has been done for hundreds of years in however many different permutations, so I was fairly confident that it would slot quite nicely into this medium.

SID

> I feel very strongly that no matter what story you're telling, it's important that you utilize the medium as well as possible. I want to know why I'm seeing something on screen as opposed

to on stage. I wanted to make sure that we weren't just doing *A Midsummer Night's Dream* – it had to be a version of Shakespeare that embraced what Zoom is and didn't try to apologize or hide it. It had to use the medium as the vehicle for this telling.

JAMES

One of the first obstacles we had to overcome was trying to navigate the balance of Zoom performance. It's somewhere between film and in-person performance: because we're doing it live, it's very stage-like; but also, we have to be aware of camera angles. Distance from your camera is a serious part of the blocking, like downstage and upstage – it was all changed, it was really tricky.

BEX

We never wanted to pretend that we weren't on Zoom. It was very important that the characters were figuring Zoom out as well. All of a sudden you're having to convey certain things in a different way, having to work out 'Can they see me? Can they hear me?'

SID

It's very hard to think of something that's more of today than Zoom. So many tiny details placed it in the Zoom universe – Snug's ever-changing screen names, from 'Snug Fit Joiners Ltd' at the start to 'Mr. Lion' during *Pyramus and Thisbe* at the end. The more that we can ground it in everyone else's experience, the more resonance we're going to find in these words.

JAMES

I think acknowledging Zoom worked with the humour of the mechanicals. We were hitting it just as everyone had downloaded Zoom and we were playing with everything that will go wrong with a Zoom call, like messing with the setting so the camera was upside down, or moving lights because you haven't quite got that right. It ended up becoming massively endearing.

SID

During the table read James showed up with a puppet show and just did *Pyramus and Thisbe* with stickman puppets in front of the camera. He realized we needed an extra analogue element in this digital medium. It's one of my favourite moments of any show we've done!

FIGURE 9 *Rob Starveling (James Dillon), Nic Bottom (Joanna Brown), Frances Flute (Olivia Caley) and Peter Quince (Tom Black) perform* Pyramus and Thisbe *in CtrlAltRepeat's Zoom-to-YouTube production* Midsummer Night Stream. *Screenshot reproduced courtesy of CtrlAltRepeat.*

Pikachu onesies and pizza box towers...

In May 2020, CtrlAltRepeat returned to Shakespeare for their third Zoom-to-YouTube production, *As You Like It*. Once again locating the action in a recognizable version of the socially distanced world of 2020, director Rachel Waring set her production within the gaming industry and transformed Arden from forest to 'the world's first immersive social platforming game'. Whilst the initial science-fiction parallels with films and TV series such as *Ready Player One* (dir. Spielberg 2018) and Charlie Brooker's *Black Mirror* (2011–) potentially offered dystopian echoes, true to the play's comedic genre Arden ultimately functioned as a place of positivity. With people around the world connecting through life-sim video games such as *Animal Crossing: New Horizons* (released in March 2020) while unable to physically be together, Arden as a safe place online resonated strongly with the world of 2020.

The company spoke about how, with *As You Like It*, they pushed the boundaries of digital performance spaces further.

SID

With Rachel's vision of a gamer Arden in *As You Like It*, David took the tech reins to see what was possible on Zoom. But I was clear that if the show doesn't work without the tech, then it doesn't work. The story must work without pre-recorded game cutaways. If they enhance it, that's fantastic, but we can't be reliant on them.

RACHEL

That's why we grew technologically so quickly as a company. We knew it had to work without it, but David and I wanted to push what Zoom could do. And prove that it can work.

SID

It spurred us into the more technically ambitious and the more emotionally ambitious.

RACHEL

Watching avatars and a voiceover can be very entertaining, but real life people are the thing that we're missing. So although we wanted to integrate video games I didn't want it to be all about that. As a director, you need to work out why you're putting this on and what you're trying to achieve. People during lockdown are either eating, working at a screen or playing video games. I wanted to address the different coping mechanisms. The angle was 'Court Games', who had got rid of the old Duke, their artistic director, because he took too long to create his art. The banished Duke talks about how he's influenced by the elements – the wood enables people to become relaxed. However, if you get lost in that world, how much connection are you actually achieving? Celia ultimately said 'I can't do it anymore, this isn't what I need'.

SID

What Rachel pioneered was bringing in that darkness and going 'Where is the edge? How dark can you make something on Zoom?' Whether or not people died and how explicit we are, for example with Orlando's phone conversation about Adam's illness. You need to be careful about how you play in moments of darkness like that, while leaving the audience with an uplifting feeling.

RACHEL

    David always says that I can find tragedy in the funniest play. We wanted to acknowledge the incredible sense of loss in the Covid world, so we looked closely at Adam and his disappearance at the end of Act 2. So many people have received news of death or illness over the phone and we wanted to reflect the pain of distance from loved ones. But it was very important to both Sid and me that we never wanted a character to die and someone laugh because of the limitations of Zoom.

    I made a conscious decision to create a connection for the audience to their current situation, to access sense memories of that weird schlubby feeling of lockdown, progressively losing any sense of rigidity.

BEX

    As Celia, I started in her proper attire, and you see the progression of her going from sitting upright at her laptop to then changing into a different outfit that's a bit more casual. Eventually she's realized she doesn't have to be this person with makeup on all the time, feeling okay about her friends knowing that she's relaxing in a Pikachu onesie with pizza on her face, surrounded by leftover takeaway boxes. I think lockdown made you think more about how to look after yourself and what is okay to you.

SID

    Setting it during a pandemic, as opposed to being born out of the fact that we are in a pandemic – it's all well and good to escape to something completely different, but it's also nice to have the reassurance that other people are going through it too, even if those other people are fictional. There's an element of escapism and catharsis, no matter the story you're being told, to having that shared experience. Art can be therapeutic, but it should never be therapy, and I didn't want to wind up doing something dark and heavy because we were feeling dark and heavy.

At what point is a dream a plan... ?

Waring's world-building in *As You Like It* also marked an important step in CtrlAltRepeat's wider development of lockdown performance. In June 2020, as theatres remained closed, the company turned to their pre-pandemic experience of immersive theatre. Their fourth production moved away from Zoom-to-YouTube to offer CtrlAltRepeat's first Virtual Theatre production, *Sherlock Holmes and the Case of the Symmetric Mailshot* (dir. Alwyn). A modern-day adaptation of Arthur Conan Doyle's characters in an interactive 'whodunnit', *Sherlock* tasked audiences with gathering evidence and interrogating suspects as they accompanied Watson (Dillon), Mrs. Hudson (Waring), Irene Adler (Finch) and other familiar Doyle characters to different Breakout Rooms, then reconvened on the main Zoom call to share what they had learned. Having previously put on one-off performances available for free, *Symmetric Mailshot* was the point at which CtrlAltRepeat sought to monetize, with multiple performances and paying audience members.

The company reflected on the move from Zoom-to-YouTube to Virtual Theatre, and from free-to-view to paid ticketing.

JAMES

Zoom and the way things are working currently have presented an opportunity. If we had a conversation a year ago about putting on Shakespeare with a bunch of really talented actors, a black box theatre over a pub would be a couple of hundred pounds bare minimum, before you even start looking at the actual things you'd need. We basically now have this electric movable space that we can use, and as time goes on, we are getting stronger at using it – finding ways to do better lighting, tech, costumes and backgrounds.

SID

You look at it right now, and it is the Wild West again – if you have a really good idea and go do it, people might find you this time. That hasn't been the case for a very long time, because even people who really love theatre are going to go see what's on at the 'big guns'. Having that dialled down evens out the industry a bit more and gives us more of a level playing field. What's going to be interesting is whether or not the theatre industry pays attention to the innovators during this time, whether they say, 'Hey, you actually made something work, and we liked those ideas'.

DAVID
We're not creating these things in a vacuum; other people are doing stuff as well. We were right there up front, watching other things that were also being created. [CtrlAltRepeat cast member] Tom Black doing *Jury Duty* [discussed in Part Three] made me believe that we could do an immersive show.

JAMES
When it came to ticketing it was out of necessity: the show we wanted to do needed to have a limited audience – to actually do a run of shows, not just a one-off.

SID
David wanted to do a Sherlock Holmes story, but the only way he could think to make it work over Zoom was to make it immersive. I said we'd have to limit the audience size, which means they have to log into the Zoom call – that's a ticket. But how do you monetize that? When your bar for success is the show broke even, that's not a business plan. To be completely honest, from a business perspective I don't feel that I've gotten that balance exactly right. I am still working on the economics of it.

DAVID
We don't have to pay venue costs, we are still dealing with the fact that we are in a pandemic, and we have a group of people who are willing to put in their free time to make this thing work. But the free time is starting to slowly disappear to the point where you have to start tipping that seesaw of having to make this worth people's time, because their time is now no longer a commodity of which there is an infinite amount.

SID
And also just on a moral level I don't feel comfortable telling my friends to do work for free – you have to fix that, right? A rising tide lifts all boats. Everyone's looking out for each other to the best of their ability, and I think everyone's learning from each other. Not to get too philosophical about it, but one of the things about the current approach to capitalism is this constant sense that there isn't enough to go around, and I fundamentally believe that that is untrue. I don't think that one person's success necessitates another person's failure, and I think that that has been borne out very clearly in the community of online theatre work that has been done since the beginning of the pandemic.

The audience needs a win, no matter what...

In October 2020, CtrlAltRepeat opened their second pay-per-view Virtual Theatre production, *Viper Squad* (dirs. Alwyn and Phoenix), which invited audiences to play the stereotypical action hero in a 1980s blockbuster where they could influence the outcome. It was, as Phoenix affectionately says, 'a big, loud, dumb, fun show with a huge amount of very intelligent hard work behind the scenes'. Offering two hours of escapist fun set outside of 2020, the production felt like an antidote to the ongoing pandemic and proved popular: *Viper Squad* won the 2021 Off West End Theatre OnComm Award for Best Interactive/Immersive Performance, and was revived with enhanced technical features as *Viper Squad: Remastered* from January to April 2021. The company's third Virtual Theatre production, *The Temporal Society* (dir. Phoenix), ran from March to May 2021 and offered an original Victorian steampunk time-travel adventure reminiscent of the work of H.G. Wells and Jules Verne.

CtrlAltRepeat spoke about their exploration of the possibilities of immersive theatre through digital technology, and the benefits to both performers and audience members.

JAMES
The original concept of *Viper Squad* was darker. It was going to be based on actually dealing with real life terrorist situations. I spoke to Suzie and she said 'That's a terrible idea, it's miserable, no one wants to do that!' The wind left my sails quite swiftly!

SUZIE
No one is going to want to put themselves in a hostage situation during a pandemic!

JAMES
She was absolutely right. No one wants to have that sense of realism. So I set it in the 1980s – just big, loud, ridiculous and completely out there.

SUZIE
Sid has a phrase which I love: 'Dumb as rocks!'

JAMES

It just made all the choices and what we wanted to do with the audience a lot more engaging. Any time you tell the audience you want them to do something, it's very important to give them a character. You tell them that they're a badass '80s cop, they'll act like it!

SID

It's play. In the midst of all of this you're allowed to have fun, and fun for fun's sake has value.

DAVID

If we are going to convince people to take time out of their day in what is a really difficult time and do anything it better make them smile, because there's enough stuff out there that's not making people smile.

SID

Bex and David are touchstones for 'But is it fun, though? Will this actually elevate people?' James and I can say there has to be a way for the audience to screw it up, and David and Bex will say 'Fine, if you can still leave them feeling better'. If people leave feeling better than when they came to you, you've done something good.

BEX

The audience needs a win, no matter what. Even if something bad happens, they still need a win, which is so important in immersive theatre.

DAVID

What is lovely about being immersive and having the audience on Zoom is we can actually look in the eyes of our audience.

JAMES

What's really important and really great about this opportunity is accessibility. People are comfortable at home, but you're still entering someone's personal space so it actually can be more intrusive than you think to have access to someone's Zoom screen. We have shows where not a single camera turns on. Our intro video for *Viper Squad* is very important because it gets everyone on the same page and accessible: telling you how to change your name, mute and unmute – basic Zoom functions if you don't know how to do that, because some people don't. All of the joy comes through letting people be comfortable and interact on their own terms. That's the wonderful thing about the Chat function: we've had people save the day in different shows by typing the answer. I've never seen this person's face, I've never heard them speak, but I know they had a good time. You get people who are not involved until an hour in and suddenly they turn the camera on. That's how it works, especially with Zoom. We say, if you don't want to, you don't have to turn your camera on. We give the audience the space to have that freedom to not be Spotlighted on screen, so by the time they're going to say anything, they know they're in good hands. That takes a bit of work, but that's the rewarding part.

BEX

As part of the finale of *Symmetric Mailshot*, I (as Irene Adler) would ask people to dress up as if they were going to a show. Having that one person that's had their camera off the whole time turn it on to show they're wearing a hat, just to show that they are there and joining in, and then turning their camera off again – it was just wonderful!

RACHEL

I was passionate about making sure that at no point were we potentially going to trigger someone who was neurodiverse. Is it accessible for people who don't want to be on screen? Are we sure that we're being acceptable and accessible for everybody? It was incredible to create an environment that is safe enough to feel okay to come together in this format.

SID

The internationality of the audience that you can have in this medium is wonderful too. The fact that you can have someone in the United States, and someone in Australia. What makes this medium a boon as opposed to a burden – you can have a shared experience with people thousands of miles away. That's meaningful, and I think when you do that in an immersive capacity, you can almost feel the show become incidental as people share being the audience. To be the medium via which people are connecting with each other, as well as telling a story – that's wonderful.

All of CtrlAltRepeat's Zoom-to-YouTube productions are available to stream online free via the company's website: https://www.ctrlaltrepeat.com/past-productions.

10

'Are we all met?': Responding to Shakespeare's Canon through Online Community Performance

Jennifer Moss Waghorn, Katrin Bauer, Sarah Hodgson, Diane Lowman, Kathryn Twigg and Martin Wiggins

Introduction

From 4 May to 26 June 2020, fifty readers took part in an online play-reading marathon of Shakespeare's complete dramatic canon. The marathon, led by Dr Martin Wiggins, was held in association with The Shakespeare Institute in Stratford-upon-Avon, but performed entirely online during the first UK lockdown. Performers and audience members included academics, from students to senior scholars, as well as non-academic participants including professional actors and directors – most with an existing connection to the Institute. The marathon was intended to bring together a community of people interested in reading, performing and listening to Shakespeare's works during a period of personal isolation and cancelled in-person theatrical performance. Readers and audiences participated from all over the world, including Brazil, Canada, Germany, India, Italy, the United States and the UK. The readings, which were not rehearsed beforehand, were cast by Wiggins; anybody could perform and roles were not assigned based on professional performance experience or academic seniority. A parallel Chat discussion about the plays during each reading was open to all participants. Both performance experiences and research conversations were deliberately democratized.

What follows is a collection of responses from six participants in the play-reading marathon; reflecting on various facets of the experience from perspectives of academic interest, personal and emotional connection, response to the digital medium, early modern and modern-day parallels, past play-reading experiences, and the continuing developments of the project beyond Shakespeare and the lockdown experience.

Martin Wiggins (Fellow of The Shakespeare Institute, 1990–2020)

We always did it with everyone in the room.

In 2013, I developed a new application of the popular play-readings I had run successfully on Thursday evenings at the Institute since 1993: instead of reading aloud, enjoying and learning about a single play in isolation, we began to explore bodies of related plays by reading them in juxtaposition during a concentrated three-week period in June, between the end of the students' taught assessments and the start of work on their dissertations. At first, we concentrated on large authorial canons (Beaumont and Fletcher, Heywood, Shirley), discovering distinctive individual voices and habits; later on, we also read groups that were thematically related, such as the complete commercial corpus from the decade before Shakespeare, or the plays that defined the imaginative world surrounding the canon of Webster. Some years we ran the marathons as 'gifts' to scholarly projects, such as the Oxford edition of Shirley or Helen Moore's biography of Webster.

But we always did it with everyone in the room.

That's not strictly true. In 2015, the poet and academic Richard O'Brien couldn't get to the reading of Shirley's *The Court Secret*, and endeavoured to read in his part from afar using a then cutting-edge video system, until eventually the drop outs got so bad that somebody else had to take over. Technology had come on exponentially when, in 2020, I was asked if there was any way I could avoid cancelling the planned June reading of the Globe repertory from the period before the opening of the Blackfriars.

That was to be another 'gift' marathon, to myself: I had been devising techniques for extrapolating early actors' careers from the limited surviving evidence of their known parts, and wanted to try it out in practice. But in lockdown, few readers would have easy access to copies of all the plays (which in previous years were supplied by the Institute Library), so the subject had to be the one dramatist we could rely on everyone having on their shelves at home. And though we would be unable to 'play the room' in person, the more sophisticated technology meant that people could take part from different time zones across the world, from late-night Australia to early-morning Uruguay. The exercise completely changed our understanding of Shakespeare and his acting company; and, no less important, it also 'kept us sane' – or in antiseptic modern parlance, 'offered mental health benefits' – during a lonely and difficult time.

When we reached *The Two Noble Kinsmen* at the end of June, the message came through from the participants with a clarity born of unanimity: 'Please don't stop.' So we didn't.

Sarah Hodgson (MA Shakespeare Studies, 2020)

After finding ourselves in similar circumstances to *Romeo and Juliet*'s Friar John, a man forced into quarantine by officers who suspected he had visited a house 'where the infectious pestilence did reign', reading Shakespeare's plays in lockdown gave marathon participants an enhanced understanding of, and a greater empathy towards, early modern anxieties concerning the transmission of the plague (5.2.10). From the fourteenth century, outbreaks of the plague devastated the lives of millions of people around the globe; for example, during a prominent time in Shakespeare's career, the 1592–3 epidemic 'claimed the lives of at least 10,000 Londoners' (Harkup 2020: 15).

Adapting to the prolonged period of theatre closures in London during the 1593 outbreak, Shakespeare's theatre company sought to turn a profit by performing in provincial English towns with considerably lower infection rates. During the summer of 2020, the Institute community similarly adapted to institutional closures by using Zoom to host the annual play-reading marathon, in compliance with national lockdown measures. Rather than lamenting the 'unworthy scaffold' of our stage, participants found innovative methods to transform their homes into performance spaces (*Henry V*, Prologue.10). Marathon readers adapted household items to function as impromptu stage props; for example, many historical battle scenes were amusingly recreated with office stationery, used to imitate swords, daggers and other weaponry, in a manner not dissimilar to the 'homespun aesthetic' employed in other virtual performances of Shakespeare's plays, such as *The Show Must Go Online* (Chapter 7: 156). Contrarily, some performers constructed elaborate visual aids; for example, one reader created King Lear's flower crown from an array of fresh, seasonal flowers.

Participants also utilized the technological features of Zoom to replicate the experience of in-person theatre. In particular, we altered our Virtual Backgrounds to indicate scene transitions and changes to the play's setting, such as the move from Venice to Cyprus at the beginning of Act 2 in *Othello*. Readers also opted to switch their webcams and microphones on and off to indicate stage entrances and exits. In contrast to Friar John's problematic quarantine experience, which ultimately contributed to the play's tragic denouement, the enforcement of lockdown measures actually improved our communal interaction with Shakespeare's plays. The online format offered participation in the marathon to a global audience, forging new academic partnerships and formulating an international social and scholarly community.

Katrin Bauer (Visiting Doctoral Researcher at The Shakespeare Institute, 2018–19)

What surprised me was how well the experience of shared community translated to the online medium. I had attended several of the Thursday evening play-readings during my research visit at the Institute and always enjoyed the cordial atmosphere. The online readings, which I attended from home in Germany, managed to recreate much of that despite the seeming limitations of not being in a physical room together. The atmosphere in the digital space felt as welcoming and energetic to me as it had during my time at the Institute. The readings, in addition to offering fascinating research insights, were also social events that were fun to be a part of, just as the Thursday play-readings had been.

The Chat function, in particular, proved an asset to the marathon. It was used extensively by participants to post comments and questions as they came up during the readings. This immediate nature of the contributions allowed for more spontaneous and topical discussions than would have been possible in the traditional format, where any exchange of ideas would necessarily have had to take place before and after each session so as to not disturb the ongoing reading. Above all, the Chat was an extraordinarily welcoming space that allowed not only input from various fields related to Shakespeare studies but also for more personal interactions. Participants were able to post questions and comments as they arose and work off each other's ideas, whether those were thematic connections to plays we had already read, interesting details about early modern theatre practice, or in-jokes about certain actors that would develop as the marathon progressed.

No matter where participants were physically located, they all had the opportunity to share the same digital space every weekday for a couple of hours. This possibility of connecting people regardless of geographical distances highlighted the immense potential that can be unlocked by modern technology. While for many of us, it was not possible to see our neighbours, friends or even family members, the marathon managed to bridge different fields of study, continents and time zones. It created connections in our digital space while the global pandemic was limiting them severely in real life.

Kathryn Twigg (MA Shakespeare and Education, 2013; PhD Shakespeare Studies candidate)

As a teacher, participating in the marathon made me think about how online play-readings could benefit younger students. Supporting the enjoyment of Shakespeare and promoting learning through a communal experience would be especially useful during any future instances of prolonged school closure, when facilitating engagement with education is notoriously difficult.

During the pandemic, 'loneliness has been a challenge' for young people and mental health has declined (Public Health England 2020). Giving students a space to interact through online, marathon-style readings of plays that they are studying could help reduce the impact of social isolation during school closures. The Chat could be used to facilitate understanding of Shakespeare's works with students who might need to ask for clarification throughout a reading. The added sense of community and peer support engendered through the informal discussion was something I was particularly grateful for during the Institute marathon.

As well as supporting wellbeing, marathon-style readings could be used to support curriculum goals. This would be helpful in maintaining curriculum engagement and reducing educational disparity upon students' return to school. For example, the format of the readings supports the requirement that GCSE students study whole texts, whilst performing and hearing original language would 'give pupils opportunities to discuss language, including vocabulary,' and 'support their understanding of the meaning [of words] ... so feeding into comprehension' (Department for Education 2014). Plays could be read in one session or could be divided into smaller chunks and spread across multiple lessons.

Over the course of the Institute marathon, participants developed notable performance techniques including the use of props and costumes and the signalling of entrances and exits through physical movement and turning the camera on or off. These conventions could enable less-confident students to participate in the shared experience without feeling self-conscious. Sourcing props and costumes could also be employed with young students to promote enjoyment, provide an outlet for creativity, and enhance understanding of the text they are studying. Marathon-like activities for students could present a useful method of maintaining learning during pandemic-related absence and sustaining age-appropriate, social-emotional development.

Diane Lowman (MA Shakespeare Studies, 2018)

To PhD or not to PhD? Many students face this question as they complete an MA at the Institute. I hated to leave the intellectually stimulating environment behind in my adopted home of Stratford-upon-Avon. How, then, to remain engaged with Shakespeare academically if not pursuing a PhD, and from across the pond? When the coronavirus emerged, it changed most things for the worst, but it revealed a few silver linings in its rampaging wake. The Institute, like so many other organizations, shuttered. The marathon would go virtual and I could join in from my home in Connecticut.

The 2.30 pm GMT start time allowed me to start my day in the United States with Shakespeare and a familiar cohort. We enjoyed virtuoso performances and had robust and enlightening conversation in the Chat. This unique, pandemic-fuelled experience provided a new way to stay engaged, not only for me, but for us as a group. Rather than sitting in an academic environment, we were all at home in casual clothes, many of us with pets or children making periodic appearances. Some chose not to appear on screen at all. It felt very inclusive and egalitarian and provided many benefits.

We all know that Shakespeare wrote these plays for the stage. Watching one reveals the deliciously complex nuances that vary from production to production. Listening to them, however, provided an entirely different, focused, concentrated experience. This format made me listen intently to the 'words, words, words' in a novel way (*Hamlet* 2.2.189). It allowed us to reacquaint ourselves with characters very intimately. I watched many recordings of theatre productions during the pandemic, but voicing a character, or listening to people I knew read and participate in the Chat, made me engage much more actively.

This opportunity lifted many of us out of the quarantine doldrums by reconnecting us with former colleagues and introducing us to new ones. It showed us how academics of every level can stay connected and engaged beyond an institute's ivy-covered walls. This virtual marathon breached that physical boundary as an effective Shakespearean aside breaks the fourth wall.

Jennifer Moss Waghorn (MA Shakespeare, Stratford-upon-Avon and the Cultural History of Renaissance England, 2012; PhD Shakespeare Studies candidate)

At the centre of the marathon's aims was the desire to foster a community of people with a shared interest in Shakespeare. But a further focus formed a major academic experiment: reading Shakespeare's plays in chronological order according to Wiggins's and Catherine Richardson's *British Drama 1533–1642: A Catalogue* (2012–forthcoming) to gain a stronger sense of the plays in their original creation and performance context. A second aim was to see if it was possible to trace potential role strings for the original performers from the Chamberlain's and King's Men. Grounded in rigorous, document-based research outside the plays, and consistent analysis of recurring role markers within them, explorations into casting grew in complexity and generated collaborative research deductions through Chat discussions as the marathon progressed.

Within the broader marathon community, a smaller, more intense research group formed. Working with Wiggins, five doctoral researchers – Meryl Faiers, Lucy Holehouse, Héloïse Sénéchal, Jodie Smith and me – developed discussions of the role strings, career paths and offstage lives of early modern actors in more depth. Communication spread from marathon Chats, to WhatsApp messaging, email threads, synced Cloud documents and further Zoom calls. This communication, crucially, developed casually and encouraged us to share not only detailed and carefully considered evidence and theories, but also half-formed ideas, palaeography conundrums and tangential questions. The group also provided an intellectual haven through difficult aspects of home life during lockdown. Above all, we came to appreciate the equal, leaderless working relationship of five female early career researchers, each with their own research strengths and experiences. The five of us have worked through the original records of hundreds of interconnected early modern lives so far.

As the marathon ended, it was clear that there was a sustained interest from many participants in continuing to read and discuss the Chamberlain's and King's Men repertory beyond Shakespeare's work. A sister project, *Reading Early Plays* (*REP*), began; its aim being to read the company's entire extant repertory in chronological order. By Easter 2021, seventy-five further play-readings had taken place, covering the company's repertory from 1594–1626 with a community of seventy-five readers. *REP* reached the final King's Men play from 1642 by the end of 2021, moving onto other company repertories in 2022. A project that started with a shared interest in Shakespeare has continued to expand outwards, growing an ever-broader community to explore the wider world of early modern theatre.

Conclusion

The 2020 play-reading marathon began as a digital substitute for an annual in-person event. As Wiggins mentions, Shakespeare was chosen primarily for convenience, eschewing less familiar early modern works in favour of greater accessibility of playtexts. This accessibility became the key feature of the readings, and in various ways surpassed the in-person marathons of previous years, the clearest being that participants were no longer restricted by their ability to travel to Stratford-upon-Avon. Previous marathons had featured live-tweeting, requiring a separation of focus for those tweeting short-form thoughts, images and GIFs on separate devices. This live Twitter feed was projected at one end of the room, sometimes drawing the group's attention away from the reading with visual distractions. In 2020, readers and audiences could choose to engage with video performances, the written playtext and Chat discussions as they wished – often within the same screen space – without shifting focus or causing distractions. Community conversations flourished in the Chat, allowing for longer-form research discussions as well as mutual well-wishes and in-jokes. Anybody could contribute without interrupting the performance, and everybody had equal space to speak. While earlier marathons were performative in nature, the act of 'reading' was always the focus; text in hand, at a desk, with few other resources. With more frequent use of hands-free, on-screen texts and greatly expanded potential for costumes, props or music in performers' play-reading spaces (often their homes), physical performative elements heightened the communal experience of the plays, evoking greater shared pathos, surprise and (most often) mirth.

The play-readings have continued beyond Shakespeare; *REP* continues to incorporate greater numbers of non-Institute theatre practitioners, researchers and enthusiasts. The 2020 lockdown necessitated the creation of a new digital space for reading, performing, researching and enjoying Shakespeare's works in a non-professional performance setting, but it became more than just a substitute experience. Above all, it allowed participants to take collective possession of the texts and gain confidence in performing and sharing them; a model which could be adapted for a range of other communities to engage with Shakespeare. For the marathon community created in 2020, this approach has become the optimal way to do all of these things as a group, lockdown or no lockdown.

References

Department for Education (2014), 'National Curriculum in England', GOV.UK. Available online: https://www.gov.uk/government/publications/national-curriculum-in-england-english-programmes-of-study/national-curriculum-in-england-english-programmes-of-study (accessed 28 November 2021).

Harkup, K. (2020), *Death by Shakespeare: Snakebites, Stabbings and Broken Hearts*, London: Bloomsbury.

Public Health England (2020), 'Children and Young People', *gov.uk*, 8 September. Available online: https://www.gov.uk/government/publications/covid-19-mental-health-and-wellbeing-surveillance-report/7-children-and-young-people (accessed 28 November 2021).

Wiggins, M. and C. Richardson (2012–forthcoming), *British Drama 1533–1642: A Catalogue*, 11 vols., Oxford: Oxford University Press.

For more information about *Reading Early Plays*, please visit www.readingearlyplays.com.

11

'Present fears are less than horrible imaginings'

Big Telly Theatre Company in conversation with Gemma Kate Allred and Benjamin Broadribb

Nicky Harley	Lady Macbeth
Dennis Herdman	Macbeth
Aonghus Óg McAnally	Witch/King Duncan/Macduff
Lucia McAnespie	Witch/Lady Macduff/Malcolm
Crissy O'Donovan	Producer
Dharmesh Patel	Witch/Banquo
Zoë Seaton	Director

In October 2020, Big Telly Theatre Company opened its fifth pandemic production, *Macbeth*. The show premiered at the Belfast Theatre Festival from 14–17 October, followed by a ten-day run hosted by Creation Theatre which aptly concluded on Hallowe'en night. *Macbeth* was Big Telly's most technically ambitious lockdown project, building on the company's experiences creating digital theatre throughout 2020. Their first Shakespeare production, *The Tempest*, performed in April 2020 in collaboration with Creation

Theatre, had taken a previously in-person production and recreated it for a Virtual Theatre space: Zoom (see Allred Chapter 3; Aebischer and Nicholas Chapter 4). Producer Crissy O'Donovan recalls:

> The reason why *The Tempest* [on Zoom] was so brilliant was the liveness for the audience. The audience came together, and saw themselves coming together. That sense of community is what Big Telly always did before lockdown – the audience were always at the forefront of our work. Coming into this new format, nothing has shifted on that front. Even though it's massively transformed how we tell the story, who we tell the story to and for is still the same.

Whereas *The Tempest* was a digital immigrant, *Macbeth* was digitally native: devised for the new Virtual Theatre space. Performed via Zoom, the production merged live action with pre-recorded footage to offer a hybridity of mediums. Seemingly conjured from within a closed theatre, where the witches have gone to create mischief, the loss of in-person theatre was at the core of the production – as director Zoë Seaton notes:

> This is a love song to theatre. We were always interested in this idea that, while theatres were closed, there was a Ghost Light on, and where else would witches go if they wanted to create illusion? Where better to go to try and manipulate the world than a closed theatre?

Framed in a 2020 narrative, the production opened with a 'Daily Briefing' based on the UK government Covid-19 briefings – albeit the threat was witchcraft rather than a virus. By writing their location down and holding it up to their webcam, audience members could be Spotlighted on Zoom to take part in a 'screening process' to see if they had been in contact with a witch. 'Safe' viewers received a green tick; those with a 'positive result' had a cartoon witch hat projected above their head through a camera filter. Following pre-recorded footage heading backstage at the closed Theatre Royal Brighton, the 'government officials' were then revealed to be the witches in disguise – changing their costumes as they prepared to meet Macbeth and Banquo in Act 1 Scene 3. With a surreal aesthetic – distorted perspectives, glitching Virtual Backgrounds – it was never quite clear what was real and what was illusion. Audience members were added, virtually, to the Macbeths' dinner party in Act 3 Scene 4, and placed in theatre boxes alongside Macbeth to experience the witches' Act 4 Scene 1 prophecy performed in the empty theatre. For Seaton, the scene

> very much became about the joy of making theatre, about the stresses and the complexity, but also about the craic of putting on a show – the witches trying to scare Macbeth while they're backstage doing other things!

Other scenes saw the witches creating the world of the play: unfurling green fabric and painting in green paint to craft the screens upon which the virtual world of the play would be projected.

This case study draws on conversations with the Big Telly *Macbeth* company towards the end of the initial run of *Macbeth* in October 2020; and in January 2021, ahead of Big Telly's next digital theatre production, *Recipe for Disaster* – an interactive cook-along show centred around an '80s-themed Zoom wedding featuring Northern Irish TV chef Paula McIntyre.

[*Enter Macbeth*]: Rehearsal process

ZOË
> We arrived at *Macbeth* as a production team ready to tackle this play in a way that we wouldn't have been six months earlier – technically, emotionally or conceptually. I wouldn't have put *Macbeth* on in March, because people needed joy not darkness. What I love about Zoom theatre is it feels like you can just decide 'I'm going to do this story, because this story is about now'. For example, *The Machine Stops* [an earlier Big Telly project based on E.M. Forster's 1909 short story] was about people emerging out of isolation, and it needed to be done just then, in June 2020, when we were coming out of lockdown – and not necessarily ever again. It feels very Zeitgeisty. At some shows some of the audience went outside and showed us their worlds, and that just felt really emotional.

LUCIA
> I think that's why the choice of play and the casting of it are so important, as they are with regular theatre.

DHARMESH
> Something that I love about theatre: as soon as you walk into the rehearsal room, that is your family for the next eight weeks. Regardless of it being on Zoom or not, I still feel that connection and I would do anything for these people. In this time, this weird moment, this is my family and I love them.

ZOË
> There's something about the individual bravery of actors in this format. There's such a keen sense of the loneliness of the actor and the importance of the ensemble as an antidote to that. It's much more important in some ways in this format that when you step into this Zoom room, it feels like joy and being part of a family. That's more important, I think, than in any other context, particularly when people are in lockdown.

LUCIA
> In traditional theatre, usually the designers show you a model box, so you have a clear idea of what the production is going to look like. That feeds into the work that you do for the next six weeks. The technical rehearsal doesn't start until a couple of days before the performance. From day one on Zoom, every day was a tech day!

ZOË
> There was a much steeper technical learning curve for this cast – rehearsals for this project were probably the most technical we've done. We concentrated a lot on the tech because we had the luxury of people who understood the language and the scenes and the characters from the get-go. This process is particularly rewarding for people who are interested in being theatre makers, as well as actors. That's something we look for in the casting process as well. Some people love that and some people don't, and that's fine. They just shouldn't be in *this* process.

AONGHUS
> Every time you come to a new show there's a degree of learning new skills – you're always embracing something new with each individual production. With this it just happened to be the tech

elements and the possibilities of the platform. I love jumping between mediums as an actor anyway. One of the most important things for me is to fully embrace the nature of the medium. Rather than it being an onerous burden for you to carry as an actor, it's a great opportunity to have new tools in the toolkit.

[*A cavern. In the middle, a boiling cauldron.*]: Enter the audience

NICKY
Always on the first audience member Spotlight during the government briefing, I go into Gallery View and more audience members turn their cameras on than off. I just love that moment because you can see them getting ready to be involved and be part of the show. That's my favourite thing to do every evening!

LUCIA
In a conventional theatre, the audience is really good at being an audience. But in this show the audience were nervous because they're not quite sure, or they're a bit embarrassed – are they on screen, are they not? Maybe there is a lack of cynicism sometimes because it's a new thing to the audience and they get extra excited by it because they genuinely don't know what to expect.

CRISSY
At the start of the show we advise the audience to watch in Speaker View. But we have had audience members that watched the entire show in Gallery View, and they said, 'I was really fascinated, I got to see them changing costumes and doing [Virtual] Backgrounds'. We don't have that control of the audience in the same way as we do in a theatre – they're much more liberated, they can do what they want. We have to work harder.

ZOË
I love that, though. We did talk about whether actors should have their cameras off when they're prepping, but for me the joy of this medium is that people can choose to watch somebody who's just sitting!

DHARMESH
> Before the start of the show, I am like a hawk, making sure that every prop is in the exact position I need it because if it isn't I'm going to panic. Normally in theatre you say, 'I'll just run this scene in my head', but actually rather than running the scene I'm doing a checklist, mapping it out.

ZOË
> Dennis made a time lapse video of one of his performances showing what happens backstage in *Macbeth*, and it absolutely alerts you to that sense of the bravery of somebody on their own in a bedroom and delivering this incredible piece of art to the world. There's something about that which will always feel incredibly special to me.

LUCIA
> No one gets a break in this show. Even when we're 'off', we've got the script up on our screen because we know we might have to cover somebody else's lines – their internet might go down. This is an ensemble piece by its nature, through the way it's been edited and the way Zoë's put it together, but it's a *real* ensemble piece because there is no 'dressing room' time. You're either setting up your next thing or you're keeping an eye on everybody else, just to make sure that everybody's okay and you don't have to jump in.

[Editors' note: as Lady Macbeth's final act, Nicky was seen in a pre-recorded sequence walking into the sea while, in voice over, Dennis, as Macbeth, performed 'Tomorrow, and tomorrow, and tomorrow' (5.3.17–27)]

DENNIS
> When you're in a theatre in front of an audience and you can see and feel and hear them, all your senses are engaged in a heightened way – it's about each and every moment. It's great when you feel that as a performer and it's a wonderful thing to allow it to be different each time. It always is, but to have an *awareness* of that and to use the fact that it's different each time. That's liveness. There are lots of bits of *Macbeth* we could have recorded, but what would be the point in doing a recorded performance? That would be like television but it wouldn't look as snazzy. For example, the speech 'Tomorrow, and tomorrow, and tomorrow', hopefully it will be different each time. There's

FIGURE 10 *A witch (Dharmesh Patel) prepares to deliver the theatrical prophecies during Big Telly's Virtual Theatre production of* Macbeth. *Image reproduced courtesy of Big Telly.*

a certain roughness to the live element of it as well, which I think is useful to embrace with this medium. You see sort of disembodied heads at a banquet, and that's a bit weird – but good, and intriguing – then you're in Nicky's bedroom, then you're somewhere else. So it's a very sort of 'cut and paste' world and that's a nice thing to embrace. So somehow recording too many elements I think would rob one of that live feeling.

LUCIA

The little girl in *Macbeth* is my daughter. When she asks where her daddy is in the Macduff scene – there's just no way that we could do that live every night, my nerves just couldn't take it! Choosing to film something like that just makes sense. The effect of Nicky walking into the sea is so dramatic, but obviously we can't do that live every night – there's no point in sacrificing those amazing bits.

NICKY

Theatre's my love; I've never been totally drawn to film or TV. At the start, when I did my first Zoom show, I didn't know who I was – it was an absolute nightmare! Something about it felt really familiar, but it felt half a millimetre off where my brain usually feels. But I think you start appreciating that. You start placing it in a different place, so that sense of liveness returns and that sense of working with an audience returns as well.

AONGHUS

The word I keep coming back to is 'hybrid'. We can fuse the live and the pre-record to become greater than the sum of their parts. This is the thing that I'm learning most about fully embracing the nature of the digital medium. Rather than say, 'We can't have the audience in the room, the smell of the greasepaint, the roar of the crowd' – don't worry about what you're losing, embrace what you're gaining: opening up new avenues, new stories, new voices, and that's where the revelations can go.

ZOË

There are several times in this where we could have achieved naturalism, but is that worth fighting for? Is that what we're trying to get? That point where you go, 'Are we just making crap TV?' Let's not do that! Let's try and expose the process more. For Act 2 Scene 3, we needed everyone in the Macbeths' hallway – we had many different attempts at how to make that work. We had so many photos of people's homes we 'auditioned', so many front doors and driveways. And then we said, 'Well, what we actually need from that is a sense of place, but we don't need to be brutally hoisted by our own petard'. We don't need to be killed by our own rules, we can break these rules, and I like breaking rules. The breaking of conventions is part of the craic.

'Posters of the Sea and Land': *Macbeth* in India

In November 2020, *Macbeth* was re-staged as part of the online Good The@ter Festival, organized by non-profit organization The Red Curtain International based in Kolkata, India. The production was lauded with multiple awards: Best Individual Performance for Harley as Lady Macbeth; Most Innovative Use of Technology; and Seaton receiving an honourable mention for her direction.

ZOË
We jumped at the chance to revisit the show at the Red Curtain Festival. We were all still very much attached to it.

CRISSY
India was lovely because it felt like there was a whole host of not only different digital theatre but different cultures – how they've managed to navigate their way through lockdown, how they've digitally responded to things – and that was really exciting. Both personally and professionally we wanted to make more international connections. Because of our global audiences, we feel we now need global representation in our work.

NICKY
I wasn't ready for it to end, so it was so great to be back and doing it again – like an *au revoir* and then a quick dip back in. Our last night [in October 2020] we did all stay on a Zoom call and we gave a proper send off to the show, and it was quite difficult to hang up. Like every show, if you really enjoy it and really love it, regardless of whether it's on Zoom or whatever, there's a part of you that goes, 'I wonder if this will ever remount again? Maybe it's not really over'. I don't think I'm ever prepared for a show to be done if I love it.

'Contending 'gainst obedience': A new frontier of theatre

ZOË
I think digital performance is an evolving space and art form. It responds to what's happening in the world. I don't think we'll be saying now that we've done *Macbeth*, we'll do three other Shakespeares like that. It's about evolving and working with different artists, who will bring different things to the medium. There's so much potential for how we tell stories. How do we give people joy and connection in these times?

CRISSY
It's accessible too, for people in the industry who have children or who are carers or who have physical restrictions and financial

restrictions which mean they can't afford to take certain jobs. It means we can work with different people from all over the world that will influence our work, our stories and how we make theatre.

ZOË

I've been to a lot of in-person stuff that felt a lot deader than digital stuff I've seen. If we're going to go back to in-person, we need to make sure it's worth people's time and the money to get there. I really think physical theatre is going to have to massively up its game. That's a real challenge for the industry.

AONGHUS

The sense that keeps coming back to me is that idea of a new frontier, like the Wild West. Like early adopters of technology, there's a sense of investment, a sense of buy-in from the audiences. We're constructing our own rule set for how we do this. We are there blazing a trail opening up new possibilities.

DENNIS

But that's the beauty of theatre, isn't it? You can do what you want, and therefore, why shouldn't you do what you want when it's Zoom theatre too? Especially when no one knows the rules.

AONGHUS

I think the genie's out of the bottle. It's just changed too much in terms of audiences where geographic or socioeconomic impediments are in the way, non-neurotypical people or people with physical disabilities. It has opened up theatre to people where there were barriers before and, equally as importantly, for marginalized voices who can't get their work on the main stage in the big houses for whatever reason. The democratization of the technology means there is a global platform for whoever wants to have their voice out there now. I don't see why you would ever go back. The 'original' still exists. One does not negate the other. I think it's just to be embraced – it's an awesome thing.

DHARMESH

Digital theatre is so much in its infancy that you can make up your own rules, which is amazing isn't it? We've flattened it and gone, 'What can we do, if we can start again?' How much money you earn or where you're from, for once, doesn't make a difference. The colour of your skin, your sex, doesn't make a difference. Surely you're not taking away from anything? We've been given a chance to flatten it and start again as an equal – let's move forward. Surely that's a fucking positive?

DENNIS

Definitely, and it makes a refreshing change. Big Telly's leading the way – the National Theatre's not doing this, is it? No one's doing anything particularly interesting. Those big institutions that a lot of the general public think of when you say 'theatre', I feel like they're left behind.

DHARMESH

Simple things like captions. The fact that you can put that on screen for every show has levelled it – that's the difference. Storytelling has been around since humans were around. The platform may be different, but you're still telling a story, and that's all we're doing on an equal basis. That's a nice feeling as a person that wants equality. We're at a place of equality, and we need to drive that surely.

NICKY

Recipe for Disaster is picking up people who haven't experienced anything on Zoom yet because it's something totally different. Some audience members have been ten months 'in training', understand Gallery View and Speaker View. Then there's going to be people coming to a Zoom show for the first time, so it's catering for everybody. It's like a fruit bowl of people again where people really well trained on Zoom are coming to watch this show with people perhaps joining for the first time. I think that's what's great about these projects coming up, it opens it all up again. It says you don't have to be part of this exclusive club of people who go and see Zoom theatre – come on in and have a dance!

[Flourish. Exeunt omnes.]

12

Teaching Shakespearean Performance in Lockdown

Andrew James Hartley, Sarah Hatchuel and Yu Umemiya in conversation with Erin Sullivan

How do you incorporate practical performance work into your teaching, and what adjustments did you have to make because of the pandemic?

ANDREW JAMES HARTLEY
    In my English classes at the University of North Carolina at Charlotte, 'performance' is generally limited to reading aloud and studying extant productions, whereas in my theatre classes the courses are often built around the practical application of performance techniques. In 2020, our shift to online classes midway through the spring semester forced a reliance on reading via Zoom, but the impact was minor. In the fall semester, however, I was scheduled to direct a production of *Julius Caesar* for the theatre department that would open in October.
    As early as March it was clear that a conventional live show in our black box theatre was unlikely to materialize and we began drawing up various contingency plans. We spent some

time exploring video options using green screens, but soon found that – without the ability to put actors in the same space – the result would always look abstract at best. When the university completely banned in-person presence on campus for the first three weeks of the fall semester, the video idea was abandoned. We moved to a radio drama-style approach, all audio, rehearsed and recorded online with every cast member in complete isolation.

SARAH HATCHUEL

In January 2020, I began teaching an MA-level class at the University of Paul Valéry Montpellier 3 titled 'Filming Theatre', with a specific focus on Shakespeare's plays. The aim is to explore the different ways of transforming a play written for the stage into an audiovisual object. This course requires students to create a video of a scene from a Shakespeare play. Students may adapt the text slightly and even adopt a queer perspective if they want to, but Shakespeare's scenes must still be recognized at first sight. If the film's language is French, the video must be subtitled in English; if the performance is in English, it must be subtitled in French. In any case, the video must be submitted with a few written pages explaining the *mise-en-scène* choices.

Then, on March 16, all universities closed down in France due to the Covid-19 pandemic. Teachers could no longer meet their students face to face; collective projects were threatened – especially the Shakespeare video project since students could neither meet to organize their work nor go out to shoot scenes. All their preparatory work that started in February on script writing, casting, location spotting, rehearsals, storyboarding and technical preparations first seemed to have been in vain. My role as a teacher was to reassure students in these difficult times and offer new assessment modalities.

YU UMEMIYA

From 2017 to 2020 I conducted a class called 'Theatre as Entertainment' at Waseda University, where I used to work as an assistant professor. There, lectures and seminars generally focus on the academic side of Shakespeare and not necessarily on theatre practices (although some classes deal with creative writing, translation and film making). My class covered general theatre history and explored various types of representation on stage. We, then, focused on methods of vocal delivery and rhythm in verse lines. The classes were conducted in English, but due to the diverse nationality of the registered students, we also spent time translating lines from a play.

After working on the performability of the text, both by watching examples of previous theatre productions and reading the script with staging in mind, I divided the class into three roles: actor, director and audience. I asked the director to choose a scene from *Macbeth* or *Hamlet,* which would be used to train a group of actors for a performance. For the audience, I distributed the scripts that would be performed and asked students to think about how they would represent these scenes. At the end of the class, each group presented its scene on the stage of Waseda's Tsubouchi Memorial Theatre, which is a replica of the Fortune Theatre.

In 2019, about a dozen students who took this class in the past formed a student society called Waseda Institute Players. This group aims to reconsider how early modern plays might become accessible for a modern Japanese audience. In April 2019, the company began working on *Doctor Faustus* and the final performance took place in October. Then, in January 2020, the company started working on *Twelfth Night,* but the spread of Covid-19 prevented the event from happening. In April, the directorial team shifted the production from a stage performance to Zoom, and it was finally completed at the end of August 2020.

What were some of the challenges you faced as you made these changes to your teaching?

HARTLEY

It was extremely difficult and time consuming to adjust to the audio drama format. We committed to doing nothing in person, so all rehearsal and recording was done with everyone alone in their home. We were able to use budget from costumes and props to buy every cast member a microphone and headset, but had no way of dealing with the variations in their computers, wifi and bleed-in noise. It was impossible to synchronize everyone because of wifi lag, so chanting in unison, for instance, had to be engineered in post-production. I had a student sound designer and her mentor, a faculty engineer, both of whom had signed on for a regular theatre production. The moment we moved to an audio drama, their workload went up tenfold.

Our rehearsal time was significantly abbreviated by the delayed start to the term, so we mostly had one evening to work on each scene before it was recorded the following day. We had to make snap choices and commit to them quickly, then try to build the larger soundscape around what we got. The result was a breakneck pace.

HATCHUEL

To protect themselves and others, I obviously encouraged my students to respect lockdown and to favour communications by phone, email, video calls and collaborative tools such as Framapad (an online text editor). I asked them to hand in either the completed video (if they had managed to shoot their scenes before lockdown) or a very detailed script and storyboard. The script had to be written in both French and English and give a very precise idea of what the final video would have looked like.

Understandably, almost all groups chose to hand in detailed scripts, some going as far as including photos of shooting locations, actors' pictures, precise shooting technical sheets and screen captures taken from well-known films to provide a sense of what their videos would have looked like. Nevertheless, despite the fact that it was forbidden to go out, meet and shoot on location, two groups managed to find alternate ways and produce thought-provoking videos. Coincidently or not, both films were based on *Macbeth*, notably including excerpts from Lady Macbeth's sleepwalking/handwashing scene. This was no doubt inspired by the worldwide prevailing discourse on hygiene to control the virus, but also by the nihilistic, apocalyptic feel of the lockdown situation.

UMEMIYA

First of all, the live event where we had been asked to perform got cancelled and, therefore, our production of *Twelfth Night* went on hold without any prospect of staging. Secondly, there were several members in the group who could not come back from their home country to Japan. Because February is a period of spring break, a lot of students return to their family or use the opportunity to travel around the world. In 2020 this did not work in our favour at all, and we had to lose some of the original cast.

Once we had decided to relocate the production to an internet platform, reconsideration of casting and the script was required. It was also vital to explore effective ways to utilize camera angles and screen presentations on Zoom. In the eavesdropping scene, for instance, we used small objects, such as a bottle or a vase, to imply that Sir Toby, Maria and Feste could not be seen by Malvolio. The rehearsing process was very demanding in terms of time and effort. Since we could not gather in one space, all my directions were given in response to recorded clips or to occasional live tutorials. With some participants based abroad in China and Indonesia, different time zones and the quality of the Internet were also obstacles we had to work around.

In what ways did the adapted teaching and assessment methods affect the dynamics in the classroom, or the work that was produced?

HARTLEY

The timeframe constrained what would normally be a more organic process of discovery over about a month and a half. Without that luxury, I was forced to push actors to interpretive decisions more quickly, and though we had a faculty voice coach and student dramaturg, the whole experience felt more clearly manufactured and driven by a single vision. On the other hand, the shared strangeness of the experience, something none of us had attempted before, created a good working relationship which in some ways mitigated that problem. The medium clarified our roles, and the isolation reinforced a sense that we were each responsible for our corners of the project. The cast were more appreciative of the stage managers, who had to control the recording, and of the sound designer/engineer, who gave the whole show a sense of place. They heard that work in ways that actors on stage generally don't. It was a different kind of community which was formed by the experience, less the group hug that it usually is, but it was a community, and one which was perhaps more clearly about the work and the work alone.

HATCHUEL

What I think the Covid-19 crisis brought to my students is a new kind of inspiration that helped bring out new ideas. One of the finished videos, simply titled *Macbeth Act 5 scene 1*, is the product of the collaboration between two students in theatre studies and three in film studies. They imagined that the sleepwalking scene is taking place during the Covid-19 crisis. In this rewriting, the scene becomes a remote interview between a female journalist (formerly the English doctor of Physic) and a female hospital GP (formerly the waiting gentlewoman). The two characters react with great empathy via video conferencing as they watch Lady Macbeth's recorded breakdown and express their amazement and sorrow over her mental health – a response which can be perceived as a discourse on the current state of the world affected by Covid-19.

The other video, titled *Witches' Wishes*, was made by four theatre students and two film students. Although it is also adapted from *Macbeth*, it offers a very different take on the play. Classic narration and representation here give way to an experimental and expressionist black-and-white montage, mixing speeches from the Witches and Lady Macbeth with images of different kinds that cogently illustrate them – shots of the Yellow Vests demonstrations and vigils across France, shots of downtown Montpellier taken before lockdown, images filmed at home by each student with their own cameras or phones. It also offers stark contrast between the macrocosmic (with regular shots of the Moon and the sky) and the prosaic (water flushed down the toilets). Extreme close-ups of mouths, tongues and meat being sliced up, as well as the slight reverberation of the voice-over and the constant change in image formats (from vertical shots taken by a phone to horizontal taken by a camera), create a nightmarish atmosphere.

In these two instances, the Covid crisis created constraints which have acted as artistic catalysts for students. It provided the inspiration for the themes they broached but also stirred them into trying new formats that respected physical distancing and got around the lockdown situation. These Covid Shakespearean videos (or Shakespearean Covid videos?) are testimonies to the paramount effect this sanitary, economic and social crisis has had on our students – an event that creates a 'before' and an 'after', calling for a complete change in the world policies and equilibriums. I do hope that this generation will be more politically aware and more ready to fight than we were, so that, to put it very simply and brutally, the Anthropocene does not mean ultimately the extinction of our species.

UMEMIYA

With the activity of Waseda Institute Players, the crucial factor for good communication was how much the director interacted with the other members. Nevertheless, I found a negative change in dynamics in my regular teaching when I was conducting a seminar which dealt with Shakespearean adaptation in Japanese theatre. During the class, the students were required to exchange their thoughts on the subject given each week. Alongside their basic knowledge about theatre and their eagerness to learn, the students were always divided into two groups, active and less active ones. In face-to-face sessions, lecturers can maintain the standard of discussion, but with the online breakout system, it was extremely difficult to 'overhear' what all the students were saying and to keep the discussion going.

Did the changes that you made to the assignment affect its reach and reception?

HARTLEY

Night and day. For all the joys of live theatre, if you aren't there, you don't see it, and even those who do only get to keep it in their memories. The podcast has a potential reach far greater than any show we could have done on campus, and an entirely different kind of afterlife. There was some confusion over how to get access initially, so I suspect our local audience was smaller than usual (though that will change), but more striking is the feedback I've had from colleagues around the country and overseas, who would not have seen a regular stage show. This appeals to me, since ours is a production very much of the present moment (it foregrounds the pandemic and the political volatility of the US 2020 election), so it's good to know it is being heard in other places. The format also means that the student cast has, for the first time, something concrete they can attach to their resumes and share when they audition as professionals.

HATCHUEL

For us there was no change in the ways the works were received. The best videos were still posted on the course YouTube channels but they were less seen because they were not presented at an international conference, as they had been the previous year.

UMEMIYA

The change for us was phenomenal. As Andrew mentions, a production somewhat concealed within a university can now be seen by many people around the world. *Doctor Faustus* in 2019 attracted approximately thirty audience members to one limited show. By contrast, *Twelfth Night* on our official YouTube channel has over 450 views. Also, thanks to the mobility of recordings, which can be shared instantly, I was able to send videos of our rehearsals to colleagues based abroad and incorporate their feedback into the final production. Of course, the transitory nature of live theatre can give the audience a unique feeling of privilege, but it is extremely rare for a Japanese student theatre group to be able to reach out internationally to such an extent. This could not have happened without the digital medium.

Are there any changes that you might carry forward into future versions of the course?

HARTLEY

Our department is thinking seriously about more of this kind of work, since the general consensus is that it came out well, but also because it forces the students to use muscles/skills they might not otherwise develop, and which will help them find work in the increasingly digital marketplace. I feel that the audio format allows us to do something with an almost professional feel which we could not achieve in film, but I am now more alert to the demands of doing it well. Were I to try something similar again, I would completely restructure the rehearsal process in an attempt to get more time for character exploration. We would waste less time wrestling with the technology and I'd make bolder sound/text choices now that I understand the medium better. If circumstances permitted, I'd like to see us rehearse and record in a shared space: the result would be better and easier to achieve than what we had to do, but that presupposes a relaxing of the current pandemic protocols. I feel like we found something in 2020 that we could do better in the future if we were less constrained.

HATCHUEL

I think I will encourage students to use video conferencing platforms creatively as an alternative to making usual videos.

UMEMIYA

I would try and come up with a means of combining merits from both live stage and streaming programmes. Due to its flexibility, digital projects can be shared with students in different countries and at different universities. This provides a good opportunity to mix a variety of opinions about Shakespeare and interpretations of his plays. At the same time, in an effort to maintain the intimacy of the auditorium, mixing a live show with recorded or streamed parts might produce a new and interesting style. In 2016, the Royal Shakespeare Company produced *The Tempest* with motion capture technology, which used sensors to process the movement of an actor to create a live, moving avatar. Such grand technology is not accessible to everyone, but the combination of digital and live was already present then and it is interesting to consider how this principle might be reimagined for the classroom.

PART THREE

Lockdown Digital Arts: An Extended Year in Review

Gemma Kate Allred, Benjamin Broadribb and Erin Sullivan

This Extended Year in Review presents a chronological account of the evolution of Lockdown Shakespeare and digital arts more widely from approximately March 2020 to May 2021 – matching the period of theatre closures in the UK. In doing so, our aim is to record and analyse the streamed productions that Big Theatre offered alongside new digital productions created within this cultural moment. Whilst many of these new productions are small-scale and have not enjoyed significant international attention, they are important elements of the global proliferation and evolution of Shakespeare and digital performance in lockdown. They are also essential in establishing the fundamental trends, influences and aesthetic choices identifiable within Lockdown Shakespeare and the digital arts that sprang up organically across cultures and continents.

Our aim is not to provide an exhaustive record of *every* production that happened in lockdown, but to offer a snapshot of this exciting period of evolution. As a result, we have had to be selective, focusing on productions which offer a key example of Lockdown Shakespeare and the progression of digital performance and adaptation during the Covid-19 pandemic. Purely educational projects have therefore not been included, although we acknowledge and applaud the ingenuity of educators around the world in adapting to a new teaching space. We have also for the most part not included amateur play-readings, as the intended audience is the participants and, as a result, they most often take place privately. By the same logic, whilst we have focused primarily upon Shakespearean and early modern productions, these did not take place in a vacuum; we have included non-Shakespearean performances where these marked a new direction or spoke to a particular moment, in order to present a comprehensive narrative of this year of innovation.

Editors' note: whilst the custom is usually to write about live theatre productions in the past tense and recorded screen productions in the present, lockdown performance has disrupted the binaries between these two mediums. In light of this, and in order to maintain consistency of voice throughout this Extended Year in Review, we have opted to write about all productions, whether live or recorded, using the past tense.

Spring: 'The uncertain glory of an April day' (*The Two Gentlemen of Verona*, 1.3.85)

When theatres went dark in March 2020, the light moved from physical spaces to digital ones, illuminating laptops, tablets and smartphones alike. The response from many big names in the theatre industry was to offer recordings of past performances. In the UK, the National Theatre released NTLive recordings for free via YouTube as *NT At Home*. Each week from 2 April, a play was made available for a week; a Thursday night 'premiere' gave those watching 'live' a shared viewing experience. Of the sixteen productions made available over the next four months, four were Shakespearean. Similarly, beginning on 3 April, Andrew Lloyd Webber made recorded versions of his musicals available for free for forty-eight hours through the YouTube channel *The Shows*

Must Go On! Shakespeare's Globe Theatre followed suit, offering a new recording every two weeks, once again for free with a watch party 'premiere', starting on 6 April with Michelle Terry's 2018 *Hamlet*. Around the same time, the RSC made six RSCLive recordings available for UK TV license fee payers to stream via the BBC's iPlayer platform as part of their *Culture in Quarantine* series. Those based outside the UK could access RSC offerings, as well as shows from a number of other theatres, through subscription-based, streaming platforms including Marquee TV, BroadwayHD and BritBox. The pull of these streaming opportunities cannot be ignored – viewing figures for the National Theatre's *One Man, Two Guvnors* on 2 April peaked at around 216,000, approximately 242 sold-out performances at the Lyttleton Theatre which staged the original run. By the end of the week, viewing figures had reached 2.4 million. Invitations to donate appeared alongside the streams, with viewers participating in 'live' watch parties contributing most generously ('Visualised #3' 2020).

Other Shakespeare-focused theatres responded in kind. In Canada, the Stratford Festival hosted *StratFest@Home*, an online festival of freely accessible recordings from its archives. Starting with Antoni Cimolino's 2014 production of *King Lear* on 23 April, the theatre also offered new, live paratexts, including Zoom-to-YouTube interviews with cast and creatives. *StratFest@Home* curated the first twelve streams into four pandemic-inspired themes: 'Social Order and Leadership', 'Isolation', 'Minds Pushed to the Edge' and 'Relationships'. The Folger Theatre in Washington, DC, put its 2008 *Macbeth* co-directed by Teller and Aaron Posner onto YouTube for free, while the American Shakespeare Center in Staunton, Virginia, created its own on-demand, paid-for streaming platform, BlkFrsTV. In the UK, London-based deaf-led theatre company Deafinitely Theatre made four of their past productions available to stream online from 19 April, including their 2012 production of *Love's Labour's Lost* directed by Paula Garfield for Shakespeare's Globe. In addition to these examples, The Wooster Group, Cheek by Jowl and numerous other theatre-makers helped flood the internet with recordings of past Shakespearean performances throughout April and well into May.

This extraordinary outpouring was not limited to Anglophone companies: German theatres, including Thalia Theater and the Berliner Ensemble, made archive recordings available for free, sometimes on a nightly basis. In March, the Schaubühne Berlin launched *Coercive Measures*, an online season which streamed a recording from its repertoire every night for six hours, including Thomas Ostermeier's 2008 *Hamlet* and 2015 *Richard III* on 1 and 3 April respectively. The Craiova Shakespeare Festival in Romania cancelled its annual, in-person gathering and presented an online celebration of past work streamed on the Festival's Facebook page, including recordings of Silviu Purcarete's *Ubu Rex with Scenes from Macbeth* (1990) and Yury Butusov's *Measure for Measure* (2010). Audiences of 4,000–5,000 attended the showings, with many using Facebook's discussion features to create 'a sense of microcommunity' over the course of the two-week festival (Smith, Valls-Russell and Yabut 2020: 160, 168). In Poland, Krzysztof Pastor's 2016 ballet adaptation of *The Tempest* attracted 4,300 viewers to a one-day showing on International Dance Day (29 April); in Ukraine, the Ivan Franko National Academic Drama Theatre presented Serhii Masloboishchikov's 2010 *The Tempest* via YouTube; in Belgium, Thomas Jolly's 2019 opera, *Macbeth Underworld*, streamed on the Théâtre Royal de la Monnaie/De Munt's website; in Greece, Poreia Theatre presented Oskaras Korsunovas's *Miranda*, translated into Greek and performed in Thessaloniki in 2015; in Japan, Takashi Kageyama's 2018 *A Midsummer Night's Dream* streamed on YouTube for a week. Live stage performance also featured amongst these global offerings: on 3 April, the Dae-hak-ro Arts Theatre in Seoul broadcast a live performance of Jae-Hoon Shin's *Othello and Iago* to 10,000 viewers on Korean streaming platform Naver TV, with audio descriptions and subtitles also available (Cho 2021: 9, 12). Sun-Woong Koh's *King Lear* followed on 14 April, which also played before a reduced, in-person audience (Lee 2020).

Alongside the torrent of archive streams, pandemic-born digital performances began to appear. An early Shakespearean example was the international *The Show Must Go Online* (*TSMGO*) (see Introduction; Allred Chapter 3; Chapter 7), which aimed to perform all thirty-six plays of the First Folio in chronological order as Zoom-to-YouTube performances. *TSMGO*'s first production, *The Two Gentlemen of Verona*, was performed on 19 March, days before the UK went into lockdown. Offered as weekly appointment viewing, *TSMGO* placed community at its heart offering both creatives and audiences a weekly dose of Shakespeare. With minimal costuming, little attempt to hide microphones and headsets, and absent the characteristic world-building of the later performances, *Two Gents* had the feel of a rehearsed reading – albeit one that imagined and engaged with an audience.

Perhaps spurred on by *TSMGO,* other regular Shakespeare online performance groups emerged. In the UK, Shake-scene Shakespeare Theatre Company began creating Zoom-to-YouTube scenes performed from cue scripts from 29 March, and went on to stage full cue-script performances of plays. In the United States, Shakespeare Happy Hours, a collaboration between New-York-based Rude Grooms and Seven Stages Shakespeare Company from Portsmouth, New Hampshire, staged their first rehearsed reading, *The Tempest,* on 1 April. The group went on to cover the Shakespearean canon through thrice-weekly readings, as well as returning on Hallowe'en night with Thomas Middleton's *The Witch.* Also coming out of New York, Red Bull Theater organized their first online staged reading on 30 March, John Ford's *'Tis Pity She's A Whore* – only to have to cancel it on the day due to confusion about whether online performances of this kind fell under theatre unions' jurisdiction (Fuchs 2021b: 13). *'Tis Pity* eventually went ahead on 20 April, and the company continued to hold regular staged readings of predominantly non-Shakespearean early modern texts throughout the pandemic.

April was the month of *A Midsummer Night's Dream,* with several versions of the play appearing. Perhaps the earliest was UK-based CtrlAltRepeat's Zoom-to-YouTube *Midsummer Night Stream,* performed live on 11 April (see Wyver Chapter 1; Allred Chapter 3; Chapter 9). Director Sid Phoenix set the production in 2020 with Zoom acting as both a performance space and a narrative setting. This not only created an authentic reason for the characters to appear in different places, it also powerfully tied CtrlAltRepeat's production to the cultural moment of 2020 – reflecting back at the audience their own experiences of connecting online rather than in person.

This was followed by an adaptation of *Dream* by Chicago-based The Back Room Shakespeare Project (BRSP). Not performed live, but filmed and edited in lockdown, the production streamed to YouTube on 20 April. Like CtrlAltRepeat, they set their *Dream* overtly in 2020. The film opened with a phone call between Theseus (Samuel Taylor) and Hippolyta (Courtney Abbott), here recognizably real-world figures. He wearily marked the days on the wall beside him before calling; she jogged alone through an isolated park, stopping to answer by an out-of-use picnic bench (a stark sign reads 'COVID NOTICE: THIS AREA CLOSED'). Theseus told Hippolyta, 'I won thy love *in this time of injury*' rather than 'doing thee injuries' (1.1.17), reframing their love as a pandemic romance. The moments after Theseus and Hippolyta's nuptials, as the couple toasted their union remotely, were presented as a FaceTime call. Here, the film shifted briefly to black and white to nostalgically recall both classic Hollywood romances and traditional wedding photography. Just as their opening conversation was characterized by a literal sign of the pandemic, their wedding also featured a homemade sign: Hippolyta sat next to an empty chair labelled 'Theseus', a visual marker of the fact they could not be together.

To mark 'Shakespeare's Birthday' on 23 April, the Prague Shakespeare Company performed a Zoom-to-YouTube *Dream*. In contrast to CtrlAltRepeat and BRSP's productions, the English-language production was overtly *not* set during the pandemic. Directors Guy Roberts and Amy Huck used Virtual Backgrounds throughout with impressionistic backdrops designed by Marketa Fantova. The opening scene was performed in Gallery View, with each actor in front of the same image – a detail from a cathedral's gothic architecture and gargoyles (reminiscent of Prague's St Vitus Cathedral) blended with a doorway into a mansion house. Puck (Vanessa Gendron) spoke to a host of spirits, expanded from Titania's train mentioned in the play. Each fairy appeared in front of a different ethereal woodland background. Two of the fairies rotated their cameras to create a further supernatural impression, as if appearing on screen from the side or top of the frame. Making intentional use of the Zoom quirk of people 'disappearing' into their Virtual Backgrounds, one fairy's face appeared to be 'made' of the night sky behind her, whilst another seemed to emerge from a glowing white orb. Once the young lovers entered the forest later in the scene, however, each appeared in front of the same woodland background in a manner similar to the court scenes, creating a sense of shared location but not shared space. This distinguished the spirits from the humans, suggesting the supernatural characters were able to break free not only from the monotony of the mortal world, but also from the restrictions of Zoom itself, blurring the lines between the fictional world and the digital medium.

Other companies found ways of immersing lockdown audiences through Virtual Theatre, inviting viewers into the Zoom performance space to interact with the production itself. The progenitor of Shakespearean Virtual Theatre performance was *The Tempest* (dir. Zoë Seaton), a collaborative production performed in April–May 2020 by Big Telly Theatre Company from Portstewart, Northern Ireland, and Oxford-based Creation Theatre Company, which received international press coverage (see Introduction; Allred Chapter 3; Aebischer and Nicholas Chapter 4). This production used Ariel (Itxaso Moreno) as an intermediary guiding the at-home audience to create theatre magic and provided a clear framework within which the audience could work to understand this new performance medium. Both companies subsequently explored the possibilities of Virtual Theatre through non-Shakespearean productions: at the start of May, Big Telly performed *Operation Elsewhere* (dir. Seaton), a production based on Irish folklore; whilst at the end of May, Creation staged a digital version of their production of H. G. Wells's *The Time Machine* (dir. Natasha Rickman). The original immersive production's run at The London Library had been cut short when theatres closed.

Guildford Shakespeare Company's (GSC) *The Shakespeare Solitaire* adapted a previously in-person murder mystery format, utilizing Zoom functions to increase immersion and interactivity. Breakout Rooms were used for smaller groups of participants to interrogate individual suspects, and the audience voted on 'whodunnit' at the end of the show via a Poll. *Solitaire* offered intertextual 'Easter eggs' for participants – an in-joke between the company and those in its audience who knew their Shakespeare – playing with Shakespearean allusions rather than adapting the plays. In a parallel to Big Telly/Creation's Ariel, Solanio (Sarah Gobran) took on the role of compère. Gobran interacted with participants as they entered Solanio's 1920s 'swinging speakeasy' and offered guidance on both the unfolding plot and the technical aspects of Zoom, such as when to switch between Gallery and Speaker View. GSC followed up *Solitaire* with two further Shakespeare-themed murder mysteries – forwards to the 1980s for *All That Glisters* in July, then back to the 1950s for *The Verona Lounge* in February 2021 – and Gobran's Solanio hopped through time to resume her compère role for each. The continuation of the character allowed GSC to playfully echo the way in which lockdown distorted our perception of time. *All That Glisters* offered a blurry timelessness: the 1980s were drenched in nostalgia for a time of perceived affluence and freedom; the 1920s were simultaneously two months ago and six decades in the past; both time periods, and echoes of Shakespeare's characters and words, were framed within the technological together-apartness of 2020.

Creatives also turned to other methods of performing Shakespeare together beyond Zoom. Video-sharing through social media proved popular with micro-videos offering Shakespeare in Pieces. In some cases, these projects involved collaboratively 'staging' a single work; in others, they involved bringing different scenes of Shakespeare together, collage-like, to create a new body of material. An example of the former was California-based actor Julia Giolzetti's *Sofa Shakespeare*. The project started life on 15 March when Giolzetti posted on Facebook asking other local actors who had found themselves suddenly out of work to record themselves reading or performing one-minute sections of *Romeo and Juliet*, which she would then edit together into the full-length play. On 25 March, *Romeo and Juliet* was released on YouTube, and within a month *Twelfth Night* (1 April), *Titus Andronicus* (9 April) and *A Midsummer Night's Dream* (19 April) followed (see Broadribb Chapter 2).

Shakespeare's Globe launched its *Love in Isolation* series of short films in April, which invited actors to record a passage from Shakespeare whilst in lockdown. The first two films, released on 23 April, feature Shubham Saraf performing Richard's prison speech from *Richard II* and Stephen Fry reading Sonnet 29. In Italy, HOMEShakes released the first of its nine episodes on 29 April; these short films, in Italian, adapted scenes from Shakespeare that were placed within a modern-day, domestic setting. In Brazil, Cena IV Shakespeare Sia began '*Projeto A Web é um Palco*' ('All The Web's a Stage Project') on 5 May: a series of Shakespeare monologues performed in Portuguese by actors in isolation and released on YouTube throughout May and June. In South Africa, Shakespeare ZA – a performance and teaching community dedicated to Shakespeare – undertook a similarly ensemble-driven project. On 6 April, the organization invited actors from across the country to create short videos of themselves performing a Shakespearean speech and upload them to social media using the hashtag #lockdownshakespeare. Actors could perform in any language and in any style. Lee Roodt, from Cape Town, performed Marc Antony's 'Cry havoc' speech (3.1.254-275) in English using a single camera take, imbuing the lines with tense foreboding as he plotted in front of a wood-panelled wall. Amanda Seome, in turn, performed Lady Macbeth's 'The raven himself is hoarse' speech (1.5.36–52) in a cavernous room using a mix of English and Zulu; lines in the latter language came from Welcome Msomi's famed adaptation, *uMabatha* (Bell 2021: 38).

#lockdownshakespeare bore similarities to Elliot Barnes-Worrell's UK-based 'Thinking Out Loud: Quarantine Shakespeare'. Hosted principally on Instagram, this six-week project featured twenty-eight videos that located Shakespeare in familiar, house-bound settings. In one, Thea Gajic held a baby and turned Macbeth's 'Tomorrow, and tomorrow, and tomorrow' speech (5.3.17–27) into a weary lament about the monotony of lockdown; in another, Barnes-Worrell stared at a melodramatic show on television and interspersed Hamlet's 'O, what a rogue and peasant slave am I!' speech (2.2.545) into its pauses. Famous faces from British theatre and television occasionally appeared, with Ben Whishaw as Jaques reflecting on the eerily quiet London streets outside his window and Cyril Nri as Henry IV hunched over his laptop in the middle of the night. Like the other projects, 'Quarantine Shakespeare' sought to naturalize, diversify and domesticate Shakespeare's writing, drawing attention to the familiarity and accessibility of its emotional contours while simultaneously exposing the extraordinary quality of everyday life.

Elsewhere, the sonnets proved popular for isolated performers. Sir Patrick Stewart's 'Sonnet a Day' series began on 21 March when the actor tweeted a video of himself reciting Sonnet 116. In response to thousands of grateful replies asking for more, Stewart returned the following day with Sonnet 1. For the next six months, the actor tweeted a daily recording of a sonnet from his home, with the domestic ease of the readings suggesting the idea of a soothing, medicinal Shakespeare for difficult times. In Italy, drama students at the Scuola Teatrale d'Eccellenza in Padua put together their own sonnets project as part of the Teatro Stabile del Veneto's '*Una Stagione sul Sofa*' ('A Season on the Couch'). From late March until Shakespeare's birthday weekend, the students performed sonnets, translated into Italian, to webcams and smartphones.

Emerging into the mainstream during this first period of lockdown was the video-based social media platform TikTok: the app 'hit 53.5 million weekly average users in the U.S. in the first week of September', a 75 per cent increase since the start of that year (Koetsier 2020). With user-generated micro-content, anyone can become a creator. Following closure of the theatres, creatives turned to TikTok as a performance outlet. Playwright Jeremy O. Harris's 'TikTok Theatre' series took on theatre classics starting with Ibsen's *Doll's House* on 4 April; *Titus Andronicus, Othello, Hamlet* and *Lear* swiftly followed. Reducing key scenes of established high culture to pop culture memes with an aesthetic of TikTok filters paired with repurposed domestic items as props, Harris captured the made-at-home spirit of lockdown. Other, less famous users also turned to Shakespeare. In May, under the #ModernShakespeare hashtag, a number of predominantly women creators cosplayed Shakespeare's characters, challenging the inherent gender stereotypes of the canon. Exploiting the Duet function of TikTok, @ahobbitstale and @mythicallrose examined Ophelia and Hamlet's relationship, questioning and reframing Shakespeare, filling in the romantic relationship alluded to in Shakespeare's text, and creating an alternate universe happy ending. In a socially-distanced world, creators' story arcs played out in a series of Duets, such as @mythicallrose's Tybalt against @queerelfclub's Mercutio. The visual aesthetic of Harold Perrineau in Luhrmann's 1996 film was set to Michael Bublé's 'Sway', Mercutio fighting Tybalt in stylized movements. The two halves of the TikToks existed both in isolation and together, side by side, the Duet function placing moments filmed, in advance and in response, both together and apart. Mercutio fights an as-yet unknown, uncast Tybalt, waiting for a Duet.

Three months into lockdown, it was clear that in times of crisis there is solace to be found in the arts, whether in existing material from the archives or through the digital stages of Zoom, YouTube or TikTok. Creatives and audiences alike started to explore the possibilities of together-apart. New voices, faces and identities emerged on these stages, which in many ways proved more egalitarian than traditional, in-person ones. Also emerging in these early months was the homespun aesthetic and unfiltered domesticity which would continue to permeate Lockdown Shakespeare in the months to come.

Summer: 'And summer's lease hath all too short a date' (Sonnet 18, line 4)

The genesis of digital theatre created in lockdown was rapid. In May 2020, little more than two months after the first examples began to appear, New York's Bard College and Theatre for a New Audience opened up their student production of Caryl Churchill's *Mad Forest* to global audiences. This game-changing Zoom production pushed the technology in ways that had not been seen before. 'Hacking' the Zoom interface, through use of Open Broadcast Software (OBS), allowed the production team greater control over where each actor's window appeared on screen. Director Ashley Tata used intricately designed Virtual Backgrounds, carefully planned sightlines and intricate positioning for the isolated performers to create an innovative illusion of shared space. Importantly, *Mad Forest* never attempted to achieve a sense of realism, but embraced the low-definition homemade aesthetic of lockdown. Tata created a world that was impressionistic and at times abstract, but always believably complete, for the narrative to take place in (see Wyver Chapter 1).

The performance possibilities of Zoom continued to expand across the globe. In Russia, Teatr Praktika presented *Gamlet Nachalo* ('*Hamlet. The Beginning*') in late June to an audience of 1,600 people. The charity performance featured 'several high-profile actors and public figures' and used Boris Pasternak's famed translation to explore Act 1 of *Hamlet*, intermixing pre-recorded segments with live Zoom performance (Makarov 2020: 5). In Japan, the Shochiku Company offered the first ever online Kabuki production, presenting *Kanadehon Chūshingura* ('*The Treasury of Loyal Retainers*') across five performances from 27 June to 25 July. Zoom Kabuki '*CHŪSHINGURA*', directed by Matsumoto Kōshirō, was performed live via Zoom with pre-recorded elements. Although access to the stream was limited to domestic viewers only, *Zoom Kabuki* was well attended: the first performance, which offered 'The Great Prologue' to Act III of the play, streamed to 1,100 people ('Report on "Zoom Kabuki"' 2020).

Creatives also began creating new work native to Zoom. In the UK, Exit Productions's *Jury Duty* offered a hybrid theatre performance and escape room experience. Audience members were placed in the role of virtual jurors working through evidence, interviewing witnesses and ultimately voting to determine the outcome of the case. Where *Jury Duty* excelled was in the detail: the production involved witness statements, photographs, police interview transcripts and characters' social media accounts. Audiences were instructed to have their phones on and a second device to hand, and they received illicit phone calls and emails attempting to either subvert or redirect attention. *Jury Duty* ultimately formed the basis of the Jury Games brand, leading to the November 2020 sequel *The Inquest*.

Lockdown Shakespeare continued to evolve in how it created and recreated Shakespeare's works both in and for lockdown. CtrlAltRepeat returned to Shakespeare in May for their third Zoom-to-YouTube production, *As You Like It* (see Chapter 9). Director Rachel Waring's adaptation took place in lockdown and transformed Arden from forest to online gaming environment. Waring's world-building marked an important step in CtrlAltRepeat's wider development of lockdown performance as they moved away from live-streamed performance and towards Virtual Theatre in the months that followed. New Lockdown Shakespeare projects also emerged. In Australia, Melbourne-based Circle in the Sand and the Alex Theatre teamed up with the International Actors Ensemble to perform full text staged readings of both history cycles, promoted as *Age of Crowns*, between May and September. In the UK, *A Midsummer Night's Dream* continued as a firm favourite. The Wet Mariners Theatre Company staged a Zoom-to-YouTube production of the play for the Willow Globe (*Y Glôb Byw*) in Powys, a theatre which hosted numerous Shakespeare-related events online throughout the pandemic. 60 Hour Shakespeare also performed a Zoom-to-YouTube production of *Dream* in place of their annual Spring Bank Holiday open air production on 25 May. Bristol and Bath-based Fresh Life Theatre Company's planned in-person adaptation of *Dream* also moved online as Charlie Day directed two pre-recorded films rethinking the play. *Helena: Ugly as a Bear* and *Hermia: Heaven unto Hell*, released on 22 May and 5 June respectively, were shot using smartphones by socially-distanced actors. Both offered a thirty-minute version of the play from the point of view of the female lovers, drawing attention to the play's inherent toxic masculinity. Those watching each film's YouTube premiere were rewarded with the one-off opportunity to interact with characters via Fresh Life's Twitter feed as the production developed. Live-tweeting acted as a paratextual device, informing and shaping readings of the production.

Where Fresh Life found the dark side of *Dream*, The Northern Comedy Theatre's *Doing Shakespeare* approached both Shakespeare's works and their performance during the pandemic more light-heartedly. Written in lockdown by David Spicer, *Doing Shakespeare* offered a metatheatrical commentary on the 'backstage' antics of Zoom rehearsal spaces (see Allred Chapter 3). Watching live via a Zoom Webinar, the audience dropped into the first rehearsal of the fictional Felching Players, where each actor had learnt a different Shakespeare play. Judith (Lauren Molyneux) revealed that, regardless of which Shakespeare play the company has staged, she had always performed *Pericles* – something which had gone unnoticed. Following Judith's lead, the company decided to do 'some Shakespeare', with each player performing the play they had prepared – testing, in rehearsal, the claim that 'you can get away with anything' when doing Shakespeare. This ultimately turned out to be true as *Shrew*'s 'Where did you study all this goodly speech?' (2.1.253) was answered by *Romeo and Juliet*'s 'In fair Verona where we lay our scene' (Prologue.2); and *Macbeth*'s 'Double, double, toil and trouble' (4.1.10) mashed up with *Lear*'s 'Blow winds, and crack your cheeks' (3.2.1). *Doing Shakespeare* launched Northern Comedy's *Doing...* series of online productions which parodied other elements of lockdown life, from Zoom quizzes to remote working.

Zoom performance and lockdown life were also parodied in Simon Evans's BBC sitcom *Staged*, starring David Tennant and Michael Sheen. The first two episodes aired on 10 June, with the entire series made available for UK viewers to 'binge' on iPlayer on the same date. *Staged* engaged with the rise of online performance through its narrative conceit of David and Michael (fictional versions of Tennant and Sheen) rehearsing a West End play over Zoom-style software. Although not filmed over Zoom, the series evoked the appearance and aesthetic of lockdown performance with characters primarily seen in separate windows on calls with each other. The play David and Michael were rehearsing was not Shakespearean, but Shakespeare was, nonetheless, a recurring theme within the series. Episode two, 'Who The F**k Is Michael Sheen?', centred around David and Michael delivering bad news to Samuel

L. Jackson (playing himself); at one point, the actors considered the merits of channelling Shakespeare's Henry V over Richard II – roles they themselves had played. As well as their identities as Shakespearean actors, both men were regularly characterized through their national identities. In the fifth episode, 'Ulysses', these identifiers merged in a call with fellow Shakespearean Adrian Lester (also playing himself), who encouraged David and Michael to '[lean] into their own true voice[s]' by performing Polonius's 'to thine own self be true' (1.3.78) in their respective Scottish and Welsh accents, gently poking fun at the idea of Shakespeare being a way to 'find yourself' during the pandemic. However, the pair's performances became increasingly caricatured and overlapped to the point of incoherence, suggesting not the finding but the losing of identity within lockdown – a topic explored throughout much of the sitcom's second series broadcast in January 2021.

Away from Zoom-based innovations, streamed content continued to appear from around the globe. In May, Shakespeare's Globe released, via YouTube, a recording of Cressida Brown's *Macbeth*, the most recent of its Playing Shakespeare with Deutsche Bank productions. Playing Shakespeare productions are aimed at UK schoolchildren and 'designed to break down walls to cultural access and empower teenagers to develop their creative curiosity' ('Family Shows' 2020). Not only was this the first time a Playing Shakespeare recording had been made available to the wider public, but *Macbeth* was also recorded in February 2020 shortly before Covid-19 cut its run short. In early June, *NT At Home* made Josie Rourke's Donmar Warehouse production of *Coriolanus*, starring Tom Hiddleston, available for a week, with a YouTube premiere on 4 June. Rourke was joined live by Hiddleston on her Instagram channel during the premiere, providing commentary on the streamed production. The result was cognitive overload – it was unclear whether the intended audience was meant to watch *Coriolanus* or focus on Hiddleston's paratextual commentary. In France, Thomas Jolly's thirteen-hour production of *Henry VI* was streamed in its entirety on Le Quai Angers's digital platform, during May; and La Comédie Française made the 2017/18 Production *La Tempête* available on 20 June.

Alongside ongoing projects such as *TSMGO* and Shakespeare Happy Hours, one-off live-streamed productions from theatre companies around the world continued throughout the summer. Philadelphia-based Arden Theatre Company performed their

FIGURE 11 *Katherine (Robyn McHarry), The Princess of France (Alix Dunmore), Rosaline (Marianne Oldham) and Maria (Lanna Joffrey) hold ladle parasols and eat bananas in The Factory Theatre Company's Love's Labour's Lost. Screenshot reproduced courtesy of The Factory Theatre Company.*

Zoom-to-YouTube production of *A Midsummer Night's Dream* twice on 5 June (see Broadribb Chapter 2). London's Factory Theatre Company adapted their anarchic prop-based style to a Zoom-to-YouTube production of *Love's Labour's Lost* for The Willow Globe. The company asked the audience to suggest, via YouTube's Live Chat, props to be incorporated into the performance. The suggestion of a banana proved particularly influential: being small, versatile and commonly found at home, bananas cropped up again and again throughout the production as makeshift props, costume adornments or mid-scene snacks. The result was gloriously nonsensical, as well as creating a sense of liveness by allowing the audience to influence the production whilst it was being performed.

At the end of June, the Old Vic became the first major London theatre to stream live performances from its stage through its *In Camera* season, beginning with a socially-distanced production of Duncan Macmillan's *Lungs* starring Claire Foy and Matt Smith. Audience members logged into a Zoom Webinar to view the performance, with director Matthew Warchus utilizing the software's familiar split-screen aesthetic to broadcast the production through two camera feeds simultaneously, creating the illusion of physical proximity between Foy and Smith. Warchus returned in September with *Three Kings*, written in lockdown by Stephen Beresford and performed by Andrew Scott; and Brian Friel's *Faith Healer* with Michael Sheen, Indira Varma and David Threlfall (see Wyver Chapter 1).

As the summer months brought the easing of lockdown measures in many parts of the Northern Hemisphere, digital performance had to compete with opportunities to venture further afield and enjoy being outdoors. The San Francisco Shakespeare Festival's annual outdoor performance was replaced with a technically ambitious production of *King Lear*, performed live from July to September by isolated actors in their own homes against green screens. The company's technical director, Neal Ormond, then edited their feeds together to create a sense of the cast sharing the same outdoor space. The Shakespeare Ensemble's *What You Will* sought to move the immersive promenade theatre experience online, transforming *Twelfth Night* into nine different simultaneous performance streams for viewers to switch between on the Ensemble's website (see Brown and Crystal Chapter 6). Tender Claws' 'The Under Presents: *Tempest*' utilized the Oculus VR headset to allow audience members to immerse themselves in an interactive adaptation of Shakespeare's play (see Sullivan Chapter 5).

In Brazil, Armazém Companhia de Teatro staged *Parece Loucura, mas há Método* (a loose translation of Polonius's 'Though this be madness, yet there is method in't' (2.2.202-203)) in mid-July. The Portuguese-language production, directed by Paulo Moraes, deconstructed Shakespeare's plays and emphasized audience control. In a parallel to Northern Comedy's *Doing Shakespeare*, the audience joined ten actors on Zoom, nine of whom performed characters from across Shakespeare, with the tenth acting as 'Master of Ceremonies'. In an interactive Shakespearean battle royale, the actors 'duelled' with translated monologues. Characters were voted out of the play by the audience, who chose whose stories they wanted to continue, making for a unique combination in each performance (Rosolen 2020). In Mexico, Teatro del Mundo staged *Variaciones de una Habitación (Shakespeare en Marzo)* ('*Variations of a Room (Shakespeare in March)*'), directed by Renata Wimer and performed live via Zoom. First performed in early July, the project was revived in August and again from February-May 2021. Promoted as '7

Women. 7 Rooms. 6 Cities. 9 Characters', Wimer's production took inspiration from Virginia Woolf's *A Room of One's Own* to explore the roles and identities of women today through intimate portraits of Shakespeare's women in isolation. *Variations of a Room* was truly international: actors based in Brazil, Italy, Mexico and the United States performed Shakespearean monologues in Italian, Portuguese, Spanish and English ('*Variaciones de una Habitación*').

Away from Shakespeare, Creation and Big Telly collaborated again throughout August to perform *Alice: A Virtual Theme Park* (dir. Seaton) via Zoom. The production was honoured as the Best Platform-based Production at The Off West End Theatre Awards in February 2021, as part of the ceremony's newly-created Online Commendations (OnComm). The Virtual Theatre adaptation of Lewis Carroll's *Alice* novels focused on an immersive and interactive experience rather than a narrative-driven show. Supported by Oxford-based AI developers Charisma, the production boasted multi-platform elements, including smartphone games in which audience members designed and raced hedgehogs against each other.

Also an OnComm winner was Tim Crouch's Virtual Theatre adaptation of his one-man show *I, Cinna (The Poet)*, performed for free and live via Zoom in July 2020. Crouch had concluded a run of the play at London's Unicorn Theatre in February 2020, just weeks before the first UK lockdown was announced; he expressed a desire to revive *I, Cinna* in 2020 because it felt more relevant than it had in 2012, the year he wrote it:

> In 2012, the original production of the play was interspliced with film footage of the UK riots of the previous year. In 2020, we widened our video palette to accommodate the widening global crisis – violent protest in Ukraine, Hong Kong, Palestine, Syria, Charlottesville, Catalonia, Lebanon and Chile.
> (Crouch 2021: 11)

The production was a digital transfer of the Unicorn show, with Naomi Wirthner directing Crouch both on the physical and virtual stages. *I, Cinna* fitted eerily perfectly into both the Virtual Theatre model and the current socio-political circumstances of the Western world. In the opening moments, Cinna spoke about 'standing in a queue for bread. Feeling not all there. Watching it all go on, but feeling not quite part of it'; virtually everyone who watched the performance would have experienced something similar whilst standing two metres apart from their fellow shoppers, waiting in line to enter their local supermarket. Caesar's assassination on the Ides of March was another coincidental detail which lent Crouch's play a chilling resonance. When Cinna told his audience to remember the date and that they were living through history, it was hard not to reflect on the lockdown that was either imminent or already in place across much of the globe around the Ides in mid-March 2020. Video clips usually projected behind Cinna on the physical stage were transmitted directly onto the screens of the audience's devices through Zoom. Some footage used was recognizably that of recent Black Lives Matter (BLM) protests, furthering the uncanny quality that Cinna's unstable Rome was in fact a place within our world right now.

On June 19, New York's The Public Theater released a short film on their YouTube channel entitled *#ToBeBlack*, in which thirty actors of colour collectively recited Hamlet's Act 3 Scene 1 soliloquy. Directed by Kimber Elayne Sprawl and self-recorded by the cast in lockdown, the film both commemorated Juneteenth in the United States and powerfully reclaimed Hamlet's words to speak to the social and political moment in the weeks following the murder of George Floyd on 25 May. Sprawl asked viewers to '[l]isten as Black actors across the nation explore the truth in the painful reality of being Black in America with Shakespearean text … to listen with empathy and to act in alliance with Black Lives Matter' (Gans 2020).

The BLM protests also formed the socio-political backdrop to Saheem Ali's adaptation of *Richard II*. Originally planned as The Public's annual *Shakespeare in the Park* production, *Richard II* was transformed by Ali and the company into a four-part radio play, performed by a predominantly BIPOC cast and broadcast from 13-16 July on New York radio station WNYC. The episodes were also made available internationally on The Public's website and as a podcast. As part of the paratexts which framed each instalment, presenter Vinson Cunningham announced *Richard II* as being dedicated by The Public and the cast to the BLM movement. The first episode opened with the sound of the protests which had taken place in New York on 3 June, the same day the home recording sessions by the isolated cast began. The play's resonance with the socio-political moment, and specifically the murder of George Floyd, was repeatedly emphasized, with James Shapiro describing it as 'a play about a murder which nobody wants to take responsibility for, that nobody really wants to speak about'. Whilst the finished performances offered a polished radio adaptation of *Richard II*, the paratextual elements of the episodes explicitly referenced the Zoom rehearsal process, making Ali's audio production a cousin of the digital theatre happening online (see also Andrew J. Hartley's student-led audio play in Chapter 12). The final fifteen minutes of the first episode in particular offered details of making the production during the pandemic, and the way in which this wove the BLM movement even more deeply into the fabric of *Richard II*. The protests were a constant presence in many of the actors' New York apartments in a manner that they would not be in sound-proofed recording studios. This not only contributed to the tension and raw emotion present within Ali's production, but even caused some cast members to question how relevant and justifiable it was to be taking part in such a production at that time – as Ali himself said, 'Should we be engaging in something that some dead old white guy wrote 400 years ago?'

Zoom continued to offer opportunities as a democratizing performance space for groups often marginalized in mainstream theatre. As part of Arizona-based Southwest Shakespeare Company's series of online Shakespeare play-readings, Oneida and Ojibwe theatre practitioner Ty Defoe was invited to direct a one-off production of *A Midsummer Night's Dream* on 11 July, with audience members both present on the Zoom call and watching via live-stream to the company's Facebook page. Performed by a predominantly BIPOC cast to raise funds for Covid relief in Native Nations, Defoe's production 'focused on activating the deeper "indigeneity" of the stories appropriated by Shakespeare in his play ... and using the play's performance for an audience as a form of "medicine" to bring healing to Native and viewers' communities' (Yim 2021). The deconstruction of traditional barriers through the digital performance space was prioritized through Defoe's 'IndigiQueer+' *Dream*'s fluidity of both gender and culture: '[Madeline] Sayet's Puck remade magic-making as Mohegan' by interspersing Mohegan words and phrases amongst Shakespeare's English, 'building out another layer of Shakespeare's character to now include an eastern American Indian woodland entity' (ibid.).

Serialized Lockdown Shakespeare productions also emerged on social media over the summer months. US-based Socially Distant Shakespeare began its YouTube web-series *Cymbeline in Quarantine* in mid-July, offering the play in bite-sized episodes filmed on Zoom and initially released weekly. The series embraced all aspects of Zoom as a platform, including the low-res and at times unsteady nature of its camera feeds. Manufactured glitch effects added in post-production amplified this sense of instability – perhaps mirroring *Cymbeline*'s somewhat erratic narrative and generic qualities. Sally McLean's multi-award-winning series *Shakespeare Republic: #AllTheWebsAStage (The Lockdown Chronicles)* released the first of its twenty-four short films in August through the *Shakespeare Republic* Facebook page. Actors from across Australia, the United States and the UK performed speeches from Shakespeare in contemporary settings. Tim Constantine's UK NHS key worker Hamlet lamented his existence as a 'rogue and peasant slave' (2.2.546); imprisoned in his dingy bedroom, Dominic Brewer's Richard II watched the pandemic and political unrest through rolling news footage; feeling the stresses of working from home, Jodi Haigh's Duke Senior stepped away from her laptop to find Arden in her garden (see Broadribb Chapter 2).

Having established themselves as leaders of the digital theatre industry, Creation moved away from the expansive, immersive worlds of their Big Telly collaborations to support external creatives in performing more intimate Shakespearean two-handers in September. *The Merry Wives of WhatsApp* (dir. Rickman) played out through a series of video calls between two middle-class suburbanites, Alice Page (Olivia Mace) and Meg Ford (Lizzie Hopley). Rickman's *WhatsApp* felt firmly rooted in 2020 not just through its lockdown setting, but also in its engagement with the play's potentially problematic elements. Falstaff became an unwanted deviant refusing to enter (or oblivious to) the post-#MeToo era. Like all characters other than Page and Ford, Falstaff was mentioned but never seen – a choice which lent his actions an additional seediness, aligning him with the all-too-familiar 'internet man' sliding into a woman's DMs with unwanted sexual advances. This reframing ultimately placed the power further into the hands of Page and Ford, who, with help from their cohort of 'Merry Wives' – the audience members themselves – put a misogynistic dinosaur firmly, and deservedly, in his place.

Creation's second September production was Nicholas Osmond's *Horatio! and Hamlet, or Zoom Delights Not Me*. Set within lockdown and structured as a Zoom call between the two characters, Hamlet (Ryan Duncan) spoke almost entirely using lines and speeches from *Hamlet*, whilst Horatio (Osmond) used mostly modern English, becoming both a contemporary version of Shakespeare's character and a fourth-wall-breaking commentator on Hamlet's angsty verbosity. As with Falstaff's sidelining in *WhatsApp*, Osmond regularly pushed Hamlet into the background to offer a postmodern critique of a character who has seemingly fallen out of favour with audiences and scholars alike in recent years. The result was a timely snapshot of how Hamlet might be viewed in 2020 – an entitled, whiny adolescent, epitomized in the online meme 'emo Hamlet'. In terms of the evolution of Lockdown Shakespeare, together *WhatsApp* and *Horatio!* ably demonstrated just how effectively digital theatre could be created with two people on a Zoom call six months into the genesis of the medium. Both productions were also brought back for a second run of performances in October and November, showing how the appetite for digital theatre among Creation's audience persisted and perhaps even grew.

As the tidal wave of archive streams steadily ebbed over the summer, newly-created productions became ever more prominent as creatives explored, experimented and pushed the boundaries of the new digital performance spaces which had emerged. Shakespeare remained an undeniable presence, but was increasingly joined by the work of other literary figures and new voices. Creatives played with the possibilities of Lockdown Shakespeare as well as creating pandemic-native work which spoke to both the digital medium and cultural moment of 2020.

Autumn: 'But now I am cabin'd, cribb'd, confined' (*Macbeth*, 3.4.25)

As autumn approached, many in the Northern Hemisphere prepared for the relative freedoms of the summer months to revert to the restrictions of the start of the pandemic with Covid-19 cases (correctly) predicted to rise as winter approached. The amount of newly released streams had waned over summer; but in September Shakespeare's Globe made a recording of another Playing Shakespeare production available via YouTube – Michael Oakley's *Romeo and Juliet* (2019). As the UK entered its second full lockdown for four weeks from 5 November, free streamed content once again became more prominent. Having previously focused on streaming recordings of musicals, *The Shows Must Go On!* announced a Shakespeare season, streaming a filmed production a week for four weeks on YouTube, beginning on 2 November with a 2012 recording of Simon Callow's one-person show *Being Shakespeare*.

Forced Entertainment, an award-winning, experimental theatre company based in Sheffield, UK revived its *Complete Works: Table Top Shakespeare* series in September to offer viewers something more eclectic. First performed in 2015 for both in-person and online audiences, this project involved a single actor sitting at a table and narrating the story of one of Shakespeare's plays with the help of a collection of household objects. With a tin of Brasso as Henry V, a gravy bowl as Cleopatra and a small black flower pot as Richard III, *Table Top Shakespeare* fused puppet theatre, found object art and durational performance. While in 2015 the project live-streamed the performers from a black box theatre space using a single camera, the 2020 'At Home' version featured actors at kitchen tables and office desks in their own homes. Each hour-long performance was pre-recorded in a single take, then released on YouTube over the course of nine weeks. Each week featured four free streams, with a live Zoom Q&A on Sundays offering the opportunity for actors and audience members to meet and discuss the pre-recorded performances. *Table Top Shakespeare* also brought the domestic intimacy, so characteristic of lockdown theatre, into this experimental project. As actors performed plays in their kitchens, living rooms and studies, they offered audiences glimpses into their own pandemic-disrupted lives.

Autumn saw many of the relative 'big players' in live-streamed and virtual Lockdown Shakespeare offer some of their most notable work. *TSMGO* began the final season in the First Folio series with three memorable productions. *Timon of Athens* (30 September) starred Ben Crystal as Timon exploring Shakespeare in Original Pronunciation, working the performance choice into his characterization of the Athenian gentleman's narrative journey. *Timon* was followed by *Macbeth* (7 October), performed by an all women and non-binary cast. The production pushed against the clichéd evil woman trope of an oversexualized Lady Macbeth manipulating her misunderstood husband; avoiding testosterone-fuelled displays of masculinity refocused the play on emotion rather than violence. *TSMGO* continued its championing of diversity through its production of *Antony & Cleopatra* (14 October), performed by a Global Majority cast and starring Mark Holden and Debra Ann Byrd in the title roles. The First Folio series ended the following month, almost exactly eight months after *TSMGO*'s first production, with *The Tempest* (18 November) – a production which not only concluded the canon, but also bid farewell to the project through a sequence of fantastical intertextual Shakespearean cameos from past productions included as part of Prospero's (David Collins) masque in 4.1.

In September, London's Southwark Playhouse offered a lower-cost fringe alternative to the more mainstream *Old Vic: In Camera* season, extending the reach of new, small-scale works and countering the 'theatre for free' model pushed by Big Theatre's streamed recordings. Typically filmed with socially-distanced actors and a minimal camera set-up, Southwark Playhouse live-streamed a new production each week throughout November and into the new year. Its first studio performance was a rehearsed reading of *Before After*, a new musical by Stuart Matthew Price and Timothy Knapman. This was followed by the OnComm-award-winning *Poltergeist*, a one-man show written in lockdown by Philip Ridley; and a series of minimally-staged musicals including Luke Bateman and Michael Conley's *The Fabulist Fox Sister* and Alex James Ellison's *Fiver*. *Public Domain*, a verbatim musical written and performed by Francesca Forristal and Jordan Paul Clarke premiered in January 2021. For the book and lyrics, Forristal and Clarke repurposed content from blogs, vlogs, social media posts and interview footage from both before and during lockdown, holding up a mirror to both the positive connectivity of social media and the darker impact of fake news and data breaches. *Public Domain* became one of the first digital productions written and developed in lockdown to receive an in-person transfer, with a limited run at London's Vaudeville Theatre in May 2021.

If the Shakespeare play which characterized the early months of the pandemic was *Dream*, then *Macbeth* arguably emerged as the defining play of the end of 2020. Following *TSMGO*'s live-streamed production, Big Telly performed their Virtual Theatre production of *Macbeth* at the Belfast Festival from 14-17 October, followed by a ten-day run in collaboration with Creation which concluded on Hallowe'en night (see Allred Chapter 3; Chapter 11). Shakespeare's Globe also streamed *Macbeth: A Conjuring* from 5-11 November, directed by Robert Hastie and Michelle Terry. Reuniting the cast of Hastie's 2018 production, this pared-back, socially-distanced version was offered as a pre-recorded film to watch on demand. The actors were seated as auditors on stage when not *on stage* acting, with the simple staging – a trio of stools, two placed downstage, a third upstage centre as a position of power to be jostled for – offering a metaphor for the three witches. With the empty Sam Wanamaker Playhouse in view, the absence of an in-person audience was keenly felt. This was a production self-consciously founded in theatrical closure and plague, the marketing materials exclaiming:

> In 1605 there was a plague. Theatres were closed. In 1606 Shakespeare wrote *Macbeth*.
> In 2020 there was a plague. Theatres were closed. In 2020 we read *Macbeth*.
>
> ('*Macbeth: A Conjuring*' 2020).

Much as plague forms an unspoken backdrop to *Macbeth*, so too did Covid-19 to this production. Face masks worn when not performing afforded anonymity to the actors, rendering them ubiquitous, observing even the most intimate moments. The necessity of social distancing meant that violence was implied rather than shown. Space between the actors gained a sense of tangibility – that there was perhaps some unseen controlling element moving between cause and effect, offering a palpable sense of the supernatural. In stark contrast was the physical touch of the Macbeths, played by married couple Terry and Paul Ready. An opening caption informed the audience that the Macbeths were in a bubble together; they alone were afforded the privilege of contact and their intimacy became dramaturgically important. As Macbeth drew away from Lady Macbeth, this distance through choice, rather than requirement, gained significance. In placing the action clearly within a closed theatre space now under the control of the witches, there were parallels with Big Telly's *Macbeth*: Seaton's production framed the Macbeths as under the *Truman Show*-like control of the witches operating and manipulating the world from the closed Theatre Royal Brighton.

Autumn also saw creatives, particularly young talent, push the boundaries of what they could achieve. On 3 October, Rosedale Shakespeare based in Austin, Texas, live-streamed their Zoom production, *The Gaming of the Shrew*, via Twitch – usually a platform used for video gaming live-streams. A modern adaptation of Shakespeare's *Shrew* written by Amber Elby and directed by Lemons Clemons, *Gaming* retold the story through characters playing 'Prisons and Princes', a tabletop game reminiscent of *Dungeons and Dragons*, tackling the problematic gender politics of Shakespeare's play through a 2020 lens. The following month, Fresh Life Theatre returned to *Dream* for a third time with *Mortal Fools* (dir. Day), a pre-recorded interactive 'choose-your-own-adventure' journey through the woods which placed Puck (Aaron May) at the fore. While each of *Helena*, *Hermia* and *Mortal Fools*, on the surface, acted as a (re-)telling and reframing of *Dream* from a single character perspective, *Mortal Fools* acted to reframe this reframing again, forcing the viewer to re-assess their understanding of the earlier iterations. In none of the three instalments was the audience rewarded with the satisfaction of a neatly tied up Shakespearean comedy, but rather the uncomfortable incompleteness of Shakespeare's darker narratives was stressed, with Day's adaptations appropriating lines from, inter alia, Hamlet, Petruccio and Angelo – some of Shakespeare's most notorious misogynists (see Allred Chapter 3).

Where *Gaming* and *Mortal Fools* explored the problematic elements of Shakespeare's comedies, UK-based Cross-Stitch Theatre found humour in Shakespeare's histories. In a manner reminiscent of Northern Comedy's *Doing Shakespeare*, Beth Atkinson's *Henry V Take 2* was a lockdown Shakespeare production about staging Shakespeare in lockdown (see Allred Chapter 3). A company formed during the pandemic, Cross-Stitch's first production in early August had been a pre-recorded Zoom-to-YouTube performance of *Much Ado About Nothing*. For their sophomore show, Atkinson was more ambitious, not only putting on a live

Zoom-to-YouTube production but also writing a metatheatrical take on *Henry V* '[i]nspired by the work of Mischief Theatre [most famous for their West End show *The Play That Goes Wrong*] and our own experiences of what can go wrong on Zoom' (Atkinson 2020).

Whilst Shakespeare offered a route to experiment within online playing spaces, creatives were increasingly moving towards original work to push digital performance in lockdown in new and ambitious ways. In late October, CtrlAltRepeat opened their second pay-per-view Virtual Theatre production, the OnComm-award-winning *Viper Squad*, which invited audiences to play the stereotypical action hero in a 1980s blockbuster where they could influence the outcome. Offering two hours of escapist fun set outside of 2020, the production felt like an antidote to the ongoing pandemic and proved popular; it was revived with enhanced technical features as *Viper Squad: Remastered* from January to April 2021 (see Allred Chapter 3). In the United States, Jared Mezzocchi and Elizabeth Williamson co-directed *Russian Troll Farm: A Workplace Comedy*, a new play written by Sarah Gancher which satirized Russian social media interference in the US election through a script inspired by real transcripts of the Russian government-funded Internet Research Agency. *Russian Troll Farm* was performed live via Zoom for five nights in late October and early November. The production not only tapped directly into the election Zeitgeist, but was also described by Mezzocchi as 'a site-specific performance for the internet', demonstrating how theatre-makers around the globe were seeing digital spaces such as Zoom as exciting new outlets for creative practice rather than a substitute for the physical stages closed off to them (Fuchs 2021a).

This was certainly true for Fake Friends' *Circle Jerk*, written by Michael Breslin and Patrick Foley, who also co-directed with Rory Pelsue. Where *Viper Squad* was an '80s nostalgia trip and *Russian Troll Farm* a hyperreal version of today, *Circle Jerk* offered a dystopian past-present-future mashup: 'a queer comedy about white gay supremacy, a homopessimist hybrid of yesterday's live theater and today's livestream (set in tomorrow's news cycle)' (Breslin et al. 2020). Breslin, Foley and Catherine Rodríguez played several characters in the multi-camera, multi-set production performed live at Brooklyn New York's Theater Mitu. Inherently metatheatrical, *Circle Jerk* moved deftly between registers, blending American reality TV, meme culture and TikTok style with Brecht, Chekhov and Fritz Lang. Shakespeare was also channelled through the Troll (Foley), a Caliban-like original inhabitant of Gaymen Island where the story took place. Speaking solely in rhyming couplets, the Troll lurked in corridors and dressing rooms on the edges of the narrative in pre-recorded prologue-like scenes which acted to aid transitions between the scenes performed live. Wearing its politics in a stark and provocatively surreal fashion, *Circle Jerk* offered a touchstone for America in a heightened state of questioning its national identity and values. Followed by Fake Friends' second live online production, *This American Wife*, in May 2021, *Circle Jerk* became one of the most celebrated digital productions created in lockdown when it became a 2021 Pulitzer Prize Finalist in Drama in June 2021 (see Allred Chapter 3).

If *Macbeth* was the Shakespeare play which reflected the lockdown mood, then *Othello* emerged as the play through which US-based productions continued to strive to address the systemic racial inequality which events throughout 2020 had highlighted. *Moore – A Pacific Island Othello*, written by Stephen Richter and directed by Justina Taft Mattos, premiered online on 3 November, having been filmed on stage two days earlier in the empty University of Hawaii Performing Arts Center in Hilo, Hawaii. In accordance with state Covid-19 restrictions, cast and crew wore facemasks, maintained social distancing, and actors who needed to be in physical contact with one another were placed in 'Ohana bubbles'. The pandemic made its way into the production – many characters wore facemasks throughout – but was firmly in the background to *Moore*'s engagement with 2020's social and political themes. A multilingual adaptation of *Othello* performed in English, Japanese, Korean, 'Ōlelo Hawai'i and French, and set in North Carolina, Hawaii, Okinawa and Seoul, *Moore* explored *Othello* in the context of twenty-first-century America. Othello became Nathan Ohelo Moore, a gunnery sergeant in the US marines, played by Richter (himself a former US marine), and the play's conflict was updated to an act of aggression towards the United States by North Korea. A partially gender-flipped adaptation, Iago became Lieutenant Karen Johanson (Evangeline Lemieux). Named 'Janis' in the original script, the change was seemingly made to reflect 'Karen' becoming a pejorative for 'a specific type of middle-class white woman, who exhibits behaviours that stem from privilege' – a term which Richter himself used to frame his contemporary reading of *Othello* (Nagesh 2020; Richter 2020). *Moore* further subverted *Othello*, having Karen manipulate the eighteen-year-old Desdemona (Heather Sexton), rather than Ohelo, into thinking her husband was having an affair. Karen's overt previous sexual relationship with Ohelo drove her desire for revenge, fuelled by her underlying racism. *Moore* also offered a chilling reversal of *Othello*'s conclusion: instead of punishment, Karen was ultimately rewarded highly for her crimes, which she successfully pinned on Desdemona – a damning indictment by Richter of the military and political landscape of America in 2020.

More productions and adaptations of *Othello* appeared online around the same time. On 21 September, the National Arts Club and Harlem Shakespeare Festival restaged their 2019 all-female production of *Othello* over Zoom. As part of its 'Othello 2020' programme, the Red Bull Theater live-streamed an informal benefit reading of Keith Hamilton Cobb's *American Moor* on 12 October. The event reunited Cobb and Josh Tyson, who had performed the

FIGURE 12 *Captain Cassiopeia Martinez (Joanne Pocsidio), Sergeant Emiliano (Kekai Mattos), Lieutenant Karen Johanson (Evangeline Lemieux) and Gunnery Sergeant Nathan Ohelo Moore (Stephen Richter) in Justina Taft Mattos's production of* Moore – A Pacific Island Othello. *Image reproduced courtesy of Stephen Richter.*

play at New York's Cherry Lane Theatre in 2019, in a Zoom-to-YouTube reading from their homes, joined by Ayana Workman who read the stage directions (Meyer 2020). This was followed on 19 October by a reading of Anchuli Felicia King's *Keene*, which responded to *Othello* in a way that was 'color-conscious, as opposed to "post-racially" colorblind, especially with respect to whiteness' (Brown 2020) (see Brown and Crystal Chapter 6). *Sofa Shakespeare*'s *Othello*, the project's eleventh production, was released on 13 November and performed by an entirely BIPOC cast to offer 'a platform for BIPOC voices to be elevated beyond the opportunities traditionally allowed' and to combat the 'systemic issue in the performing arts' of '[t]reating whiteness as the "default" for casting purposes' (Giolzetti 2020a, 2020b). The play's reach expanded beyond the United States: in South Korea, The Flow Theatre's *Othello against the Storm*, directed by Hyeon-Ok Song, was broadcast from Sejong University Choongmoo Hall in early November (Lee 2020).

Examinations of race, politics and history extended beyond *Othello*. On 7 October, Dathan B. Williams directed a Zoom-to-Facebook reading for Harlem Shakespeare of Leah Maddrie's *Just About Love*, a new adaptation of *All's Well That Ends Well* set during the Freedom Summer voting drive of 1964. From September to November, Merced Shakespearefest released its YouTube series *Ricardo II*, a bilingual modern-day serialization of *Richard II* adapted from their planned in-person production. Set against the mid-nineteenth century wrangling for California between the United States and Mexico, *Ricardo II*'s historical setting reflected the cultural and political division of the United States in 2020 (see Chapter 8). In the UK, an archive recording of Morgan Lloyd Malcolm's *Emilia*, filmed in 2019 at the Vaudeville Theatre in London, was made available to stream on demand in November and December on a pay-what-you-can basis. The stream allowed *Emilia* to reach a wider audience than it had done through its limited runs at both the Vaudeville and Shakespeare's Globe before; placed against the backdrop of the BLM protests, the play's strong intersectional feminist message resonated strongly in the closing months of 2020.

As the pandemic continued and digital theatre remained the dominant form of theatre, there was a sense of taking stock of the moment as 2020 ended. In December, the Old Vic launched

In Camera: Playback, offering audiences a second chance to stream recordings of *In Camera* productions. Over the final two weekends in November, Kolkata-based organization The Red Curtain International hosted the 2020 edition of its Good The@ter Festival online as a celebration of digital performance. Online shows were performed live for free from across the globe: Finland's Red Nose Company offered a physical comedy rendition of *The Emperor's New Clothes;* Singapore's How Drama performed its light-hearted observational comedy *Fat Kids Are Harder To Kidnap on Zoom*; and Big Telly revived its October production of *Macbeth*. Hijinx Theatre, a professional company of learning disabled and/or autistic actors based in Cardiff, UK, revived their interactive Zoom adaptation of *Metamorphosis*, first performed in August at Green Man Festival's online programme 'Field of Streams'. The adaptation of Franz Kafka's novella placed the narrative firmly within lockdown. Gareth (Gareth John), introduced as an audience member unable to work Zoom Webinar technology, offered a repeated refrain of 'I'm lost, I'm stuck on mute' – both literally and figuratively lost in the system. Whilst Zoom offered connection in a time of distance, Gareth represented those unable or uncomfortable with navigating digital platforms who had been left bewildered, alienated and disconnected. *Metamorphosis* ended with Gareth telling the abandoned, transformed Gregor (Morgan Thomas): 'I've found you. Everything's going to be okay' – poignantly reflecting the emotional toll of social distancing and isolation.

In December, UK theatre companies turned to festive fare, including numerous online versions of the traditional Christmas pantomime. Several theatrical adaptations of Dickens's *A Christmas Carol* appeared, including those of The Old Vic: *In Camera*, GSC and The Charles Dickens Museum. On 19 December, *TSMGO* performed a live adaptation of *A Christmas Carol* written by Ian Doescher, author of the *Shakespeare's Star Wars* books. The production told Dickens's story in iambic pentameter and cast Shakespeare's characters in Dickensian roles: Puck, Falstaff and Old Hamlet played the Ghosts of Christmas Past, Present and Yet To Come respectively. Shakespeare in Pieces continued to be a favourite format on social media. In the UK, Carlisle-based Shakespeare Switched Theatre Company launched its 'Twelve Days of Shakespeare', sharing gender-flipped Shakespeare monologues on their Twitter feed, starting on 7 December with Katie

McNulty performing as *Lear*'s Fool and Maryam Grace as *Shrew*'s Petruccio. The series featured many Lockdown Shakespeareans from around the globe, including *Sofa Shakespeare*'s Giolzetti and multiple *TSMGO* alumni.

Whilst Shakespearean performance was less prominent than earlier in the year, new productions continued to appear. On 14 December, Derby-based 1623 Theatre Company streamed *Queer Lady M*, directed by Ben Spiller and performed live by Shane Gabriel on Zoom earlier in 2020 after the production's tour had been cancelled due to the first UK lockdown. Beginning as a one-person cabaret drag act retelling the story of *Macbeth* from the point of view of Gabriel's 'Lady M', the show took a further metatheatrical turn midway through as Gabriel broke character and refused to let his Lady Macbeth die. The sense of stripping away the artifice of theatre was enhanced further over Zoom as Gabriel pulled down the black sheets which had formed his performance space to reveal racks of clothing – suddenly making the reality of the actor performing in isolation from a dressing room to a remote audience starkly clear. Gabriel's re-enactment of his childhood self rewinding and rewatching Nikolay Serebryakov's 1992 adaptation of *Macbeth*, part of *The Animated Tales* series, on a fuzzy VHS at his grandmother's house – specifically Lady Macbeth's invocation to 'unsex me here' (1.5.41) – was framed as profoundly influential on his adult identity and took on additional meaning and power. This scene and others gained an extra layer of nostalgia within lockdown, becoming visions of a seemingly simpler, pre-pandemic past.

The uplifting productions of Shakespeare's comedies during the spring and summer months had offered magical realms in which lovers united, offering an antidote to the enforced confinement and separation of lockdown. In contrast, the closing months of 2020 saw creatives increasingly turn to Shakespeare's tragedies to give voice to the emotional, cultural and political challenges of the pandemic and beyond. Lockdown performance still offered an escape for audiences, whilst giving creatives an outlet to contemplate, critique and – where necessary – condemn the events unfolding in the world around them. Digital spaces democratized this process, amplifying previously unheard voices in a way physical spaces had not in the pre-Covid world.

Winter/Spring: 'At the twelvemonth's end/ I'll change my black gown for a faithful friend.' (*Love's Labour's Lost*, 5.2.821–822)

Streamed on New Year's Day, *Ratatouille: The TikTok Musical* was the first lockdown theatre production of 2021 in the United States. The show was conceived and crowdsourced through a series of musical theatre TikToks, based on Pixar film *Ratatouille* (dir. Bird 2007), under the hashtag #ratatouillethemusical. The team behind *Circle Jerk* produced a filmed-on-Zoom charity production directed by Lucy Moss, featuring a star-studded cast including Tituss Burgess, Wayne Brady and Adam Lambert. The show was a symbol of hope for a closed Broadway and, through the musical's refrain 'Anyone can cook', a manifesto for a Broadway with fewer barriers to entry. Audience members chose what to pay for their ticket, with prices from $5 to $100 USD. The premiere stream on the website TodayTix sold 200,000 tickets; an encore stream received 150,000 views, allowing the show to raise a total of $2 million USD for the Actors' Fund (Odman 2021).

New Lockdown Shakespeare also emerged in the new year. In the UK, the RSC launched Michael Morpurgo's *Tales From Shakespeare* in January. Screened free to UK schools and at low cost to at home audiences, the series offered weekly recordings of five plays – *A Midsummer Night's Dream*, *The Tempest*, *Macbeth*, *Romeo and Juliet* and *The Winter's Tale* – aimed at six-to-sixteen-year-olds. For adult audiences, the company offered a first glimpse in lockdown of the Royal Shakespeare Theatre stage on 9 January in *Swingin' The Dream*, a collaboration with Theatre for a New Audience. A live-streamed staged reading and concert performance by socially-distanced actors in the empty auditorium, *Swingin' The Dream* offered a taster of a new work in progress based on the 1939 Broadway jazz musical adaptation of *A Midsummer Night's Dream*.

Romeo and Juliet became the Lockdown Shakespeare play of choice for the early months of 2021. The Public Theater teamed up with WNYC again for *Romeo y Julieta*, their second lockdown radio adaptation directed by Saheem Ali, which blended Shakespeare's English with a Spanish translation by Alfredo Michel Modenessi.

Where Ali's *Richard II* spoke to a divided America, *Romeo y Julieta* offered to unite the country through its inherent multicultural status. As Ayanna Thompson states: 'It's incredibly important in this moment … [to] acknowledg[e] that the United States is not all English speaking all the time … This is exactly the production we need right now, when our world is so angry and sick and fraught' ('Program Note/Nota De Programa' 2021).

Romeo and Juliet also resonated with theatre-makers in Tokyo. Ryunosuke Kimura, Artistic Director of Kakushinhan Theatre Company, cut the play down to just over an hour, set it in 'fair Tokyo' and explored how this fast-paced play about division and misunderstanding might function as 'a documentary of ourselves, living in the contemporary world during the times of the pandemic' ('In the Time' 2021). It was Covid-19 that stopped the Friar's (Daisuke Oyama) letter from getting to Romeo (Keiji Nemoto), and it was the miracle of unexpected, life-changing love that offered audiences 'a clue to surviving in this new era' marked by so 'many ruins and losses'. Performed in an empty theatre and live-streamed to YouTube in November 2020, then filmed and redistributed online from April-June 2021, and finally performed in a slightly modified version for one night only in front of in-person audiences, *Romeo and Juliet: In the Time of Corona* demonstrated the potential for a more flexible, hybrid form of theatre that might traverse digital and physical stages (Suematsu 2021).

Two lockdown versions of *Romeo and Juliet* appeared in the UK in February 2021. Available to stream from 13–27 February, Nick Evans's film was planned, shot and edited during lockdown and put technological innovation above everything else. Actors were filmed individually against green screens, then edited into a computer-generated theatre setting to create the appearance of sharing the same space (see Allred Chapter 3). In contrast, Douglas Rintoul's *Sharon 'n' Barry do Romeo & Juliet*, live-streamed via Zoom from Queen's Theatre Hornchurch in London, fully embraced the low-tech aesthetic of Lockdown Shakespeare. Joanne Seymour and David Nellist bubbled to perform the production together on stage as the titular married couple acting out *Romeo and Juliet* between them via Zoom from their living room. Sharon and Barry changed costumes on camera to perform multiple characters and narrated the action between scenes to 'cut all the boring bits'. A static camera captured the couple's suburban living room, viewed in Speaker View by the audience, giving the production the nostalgic aesthetic of a TV play. The balcony scene was *Sharon 'n' Barry*'s most memorable moment, highlighting Rintoul's invention and embrace of Zoom as a performance space just as much as the theatre's physical stage. The couple transformed their living room with strategically hung bedsheets and a Virtual Background of *Casa di Giulietta* in Verona, allowing Sharon's Juliet to 'stand' on the balcony with Barry's Romeo closer to the camera on the 'ground' below. After delivering a heartfelt rendition of the scene, the couple broke the illusion to embrace and congratulate each other on their performances – Romeo and Juliet's theatrical love immediately followed by Barry and Sharon's authentic marital affection.

January and February saw the live-streaming of Ivo van Hove's Dutch-language *Kings of War* (2016–) and *Roman Tragedies* (2007–). These epic productions, both of which had previously toured the world, were performed without audiences in Internationaal Theater Amsterdam's (ITA's) auditorium and live broadcast via Vimeo to remote audiences (see Wyver Chapter 1). Each production amalgamated three to four Shakespearean plays (from the Henriad and the Roman plays, respectively) and located the drama in a contemporary, media-drenched society. Before the pandemic, on-stage cameras had captured footage of the actors and relayed it to television monitors and large screens hanging in the playing space. For the live-streams, that footage also went out to viewers at home. ITA's social media accounts also invited viewers to watch behind-the-scenes interviews, vote on their favourite characters and interact with GIFs and memes during the performances. Productions already deeply immersed in the world of digital culture became even more globally networked through these streams, which formed part of ITA's monthly programme of live theatre broadcasts in lockdown. The process of filming in lockdown was also overtly on show: as the end credits rolled for *Kings of War*, a handheld tracking shot began on stage with the actors celebrating their performance, and then moved through the camera runs to the editing suite, looking down on the now-empty stage with monitors and mixing desks also in shot.

January into February also saw the first production by Creation Theatre's Digital Rep Company, newly-formed through funding from public body Innovate UK. Based on traditional fairy tales, *Grimm Tales for Fragile Times & Broken People*, directed by Gari

Jones, marked a change of approach for Creation. There was a sense of tangibility as actors performed at home within physical sets rather than against Virtual Backgrounds. While the audience attended via a Zoom call, the actors' feeds were manipulated through vMix OBS which afforded Creation greater scope to control the audience experience. The Digital Rep Company presented two early modern productions: *The Duchess of Malfi* in March, co-directed by Laura Wright and Natasha Rickman; and *Romeo and Juliet* in May, directed by Rickman. Both pushed the use of OBS further to allow isolated actors to appear together on screen – superimposed, multiplied, merging and overlapping. Colour filters created a heightened, surreal setting which took actors and audience out of the restrictions of Zoom frames. *Romeo and Juliet* also played with the hybridity of digital performance. The first half was performed live on Zoom, cutting to interval after the deaths of Mercutio (Dharmesh Patel) and Tybalt (Sebastián Capitán Viveros). The second half offered choose-your-own-adventure style gameplay via a website, with audience members taking control of their own experience. Taking a similar approach to Fresh Life Theatre's *Mortal Fools*, audience members chose between two tarot cards to decide which pre-recorded video to watch next. These decisions allowed a number of different versions of *Romeo and Juliet* to play out, including the chance to save the lovers. Live-action interactivity was built in through QR codes which gave access to live video and phone calls with actors who offered sonnets and speeches from other plays, as well as in-character improvised chat. The Digital Rep Company concluded their six-month tenure in June with *Keeping Up With Kassandra*, written by Funlola Olufunwa and directed by Anne Musisi, which mashed up Ancient Greek mythology with contemporary socio-political issues through the lens of reality TV, 1990s nostalgia and Nigerian culture.

A year after theatres closed across the globe, Big Theatre properly entered the made in and for Lockdown Shakespeare arena, with both the RSC and The National Theatre producing significant new work. From 12-20 March, the RSC offered *Dream*, an interactive adaptation of *A Midsummer Night's Dream* directed by Robin McNicholas and scripted by Pippa Hill. The production was a collaboration with London-based creative studio Marshmallow Laser Feast, and utilized motion capture suits and gameplay technology. Two tiers of tickets were available: £10 'Audience Plus' tickets allowed participants to interact with the live performance; and free tickets offered a viewing experience without interaction. Running at thirty minutes, the production offered a loose narrative: Puck (EM Williams) entered the forest to meet a series of sprites, before a violent storm destroyed their home – an eco-critical subtext which sought to address environmental issues. Interactive participants could help Puck by catapulting 'fireflies' (CGI balls of light) into the world to illuminate the forest at several points. Snippets of Shakespeare's play heard throughout the script became echoes of a *Dream* once seen rather than interpreted anew. The most successful element of the production was a sequence in which the audience saw both Williams the actor in the studio and, on the screen behind them, the rendered CGI Puck created through their motion capture suit. Puck had fallen and, much like *Peter Pan*'s Tinkerbell, the collective belief of the audience was needed to restore them to life. The interactive audience were asked to carefully choose where to plant a seed within the digital world; as the forest grew, Puck's strength returned and they were restored.

In the UK, BBC Four broadcast the RSC's *The Winter's Tale* on 25 April. Erica Whyman's production had been poised to open as theatres closed in March 2020. Filmed in the empty Royal Shakespeare Theatre in early 2021, the production sat between film adaptation and theatrical production. Actors projected into the empty auditorium as if addressing an imagined in-person audience, but elements and conventions of cinema and television crept in to undermine this theatricality. Leontes (Joseph Kloska) addressed asides not to the imagined in-person audience but rather down the camera lens to the audience at home.

Also originally intended as a 2020 stage production was Simon Godwin's *Romeo and Juliet*, produced by and set within the National Theatre. Broadcast on freeview channel Sky Arts in the UK on 4 April (and subsequently screened in the United States on 23 April on PBS), Godwin blurred the boundaries of theatre, film and real life – using the language of screen adaptation whilst also weaving the stage aesthetic into its fabric. Beginning with a distinctly neorealist aesthetic, the Prologue was delivered in a rehearsal room by Lucian Msamati – seemingly the production's director, later taking on the role of Friar Laurence – to the cast seated around him as if ready to begin work. The opening brawl started as stage fighting, then seemingly became a genuine scuffle between two of the actors, before segueing from realism to theatricality once again. The simplicity of the staging and filming made Romeo (Josh O'Connor) and Juliet's (Jessie Buckley) love feel honest and innocent, lifting the characters out of their pop culture memetic afterlives. Godwin also never felt the need to overtly explain or apologize for placing the National Theatre centre stage in his film. The location both stood in for Verona *and* played itself, the closed building causing key moments in the narrative. Friar Laurence was unable to warn Romeo of Juliet's faked death due to the heavy doors in the theatre's loading dock blocking his way, refusing to move having been inactive during the pandemic. Filmed over seventeen days by a bubbled cast, the tangibility of the performances was heightened; with no social distancing required, seeing actors able to physically perform in a way they hadn't been able to for more than a year resonated as a ray of hope for performance post-lockdown.

Where many of the Lockdown Shakespeare productions of 2020 had been developed rapidly either out of necessity or choice, the opening months of 2021 were characterized by productions that had benefited from time and certainty as it became clearer that in-person theatre would remain closed into the summer. The homespun aesthetic of early lockdown began to fade as bigger budget Big Theatre productions emerged – but the ethos of 'showing the working' continued through the presence on screen of rehearsal rooms and motion capture studios, camera runs and broadcast mixing desks. Blurring the boundaries between real and fictional, on stage and backstage, the components which, before the pandemic, would usually have been kept 'behind the scenes' were as visible and integral as the worlds created and the characters inhabiting each production. The mechanics of performance in lockdown, and the methods of bringing new productions into being, were just as important as the stories being told.

In the fourteen months from March 2020 to May 2021, performance during the pandemic has transformed from archive streams to filmed productions rehearsed, shot and edited under pandemic restrictions; from logging into Zoom for staged readings to transforming the software into a Virtual Theatre stage, interactive auditorium and television studio (sometimes all three at once); from a way to perform born out of necessity to a hybrid creative medium in its own right, characterized by both diversification and diversity. We introduced this Extended Year in Review as a snapshot of a moment in time, capturing the essence and evolution of digital performance in lockdown through examples which demonstrate the sheer variety, creativity and resilience of the companies, collectives and individuals which have emerged onto digital stages. Just as a snapshot offers the sense of a moment, it can only hint at what might follow. Where the digital performance spaces, mediums, practices and conventions which have developed might go next is hard to predict. The pandemic undoubtedly marks a time of significant professional and personal losses in the creative industries and, of course, the wider world. But, amongst the losses, gains have been made: performance spaces that are more diverse and democratic, atypical and accessible. We can only hope that, when Covid-19 finally relinquishes its grip on so many aspects of our lives, the positive steps forward it has instigated for the theatre industry will remain.

References

Atkinson, B. (2020), Twitter, 6 November. Available online: https://twitter.com/bethiatko/status/1324758331400114176 (accessed 28 November 2021).

Bell, H. (2021), 'Review of #lockdownshakespeare', *Shakespeare Bulletin*, 38 (3): 35–9.

Breslin, M., Foley, P., Rodríguez, C. M. and Sibert, A. (2020), 'About', *Circle Jerk*. Available online: https://circlejerk.live/about (accessed 28 November 2021).

Brown, D. S. (2020), 'About the play', Red Bull Theater. Available online: https://www.redbulltheater.com/keene (accessed 28 November 2021).

Cho, D. (2021), 'Digitally Mediated Shakespeare in South Korea', *Shakespeare*. Available online: https://www.tandfonline.com/doi/abs/10.1080/17450918.2021.1925333 (accessed 28 November 2021).

Crouch, T. (2021), 'A Poet Dreams', in C. Svich (ed.), *Toward a Future Theatre: Conversations during a Pandemic*, 9–13, London: Methuen.

'Family Shows' (2020), Shakespeare's Globe. Available online: https://www.shakespearesglobe.com/whats-on/macbeth-playing-shakespeare-with-deutsche-bank-2020-2/ (accessed 28 November 2021).

Fuchs, B. (2021a), 'Reverse-Engineering Zoom with Isadora', *HowlRound*, 4 January. Available online: https://howlround.com/reverse-engineering-zoom-isadora (accessed 28 November 2021).

Fuchs, B. (2021b), *Theater of Lockdown: Digital and Distanced Performance in a Time of Pandemic*, London: Methuen.

Gans, A. (2020), 'Over 30 Black Actors, Including Audra McDonald, André De Shields, and Renée Elise Goldsberry, Give Voice to Hamlet's "To Be or Not to Be" Monologue', *Playbill*, 19 June. Available online: https://www.playbill.com/article/over-30-black-actors-including-audra-mcdonald-andre-de-shields-and-renee-elise-goldsberry-give-voice-to-hamlets-to-be-or-not-to-be-monologue (accessed 28 November 2021).

Giolzetti, J. (2020a), Twitter, 17 September. Available online: https://twitter.com/sofashakes/status/1306667150115966977 (accessed 28 November 2021).

Giolzetti, J. (2020b), Twitter, 17 September. Available online: https://twitter.com/sofashakes/status/1306667150891859968 (accessed 28 November 2021).

'In the Time of Corona – by Ryunosuke Kimura' (2021), YouTube, 11 June. Available online: https://youtu.be/0cAf4WmjmYY (accessed 28 November 2021).

Koetsier, J. (2020), 'Massive TikTok Growth', *Forbes*, 14 September. Available online: https://www.forbes.com/sites/johnkoetsier/2020/09/14/massive-tiktok-growth-up-75-this-year-now-33x-more-users-than-nearest-competitor/?sh=67cefa994fe4 (accessed 28 November 2021).

Lee, H. (2020), personal email communication.

'*Macbeth: A Conjuring*' (2020), Shakespeare's Globe. Available online: https://www.shakespearesglobe.com/whats-on/macbeth-a-conjuring-2020/ (accessed 28 November 2021).

Makarov, V. (2020), 'Shakespearean Performances Online in 2020 Russia: A New Kind of Theatre, Delayed?', unpublished conference paper.

Meyer, D. (2020), 'Red Bull Theater Presents Virtual Reading of *American Moor*', *Playbill*, 12 October. Available online: https://www.playbill.com/article/red-bull-theater-presents-virtual-reading-of-american-moor-october-12 (accessed 28 November 2021).

Nagesh, A. (2020), 'What exactly is a "Karen" and where did the meme come from?', *BBC News*, 31 July. Available online: https://www.bbc.co.uk/news/world-53588201 (accessed 28 November 2021).

Odman, S. (2021), '*Ratatouille: The TikTok Musical* Raises Record $2 Million for Actors Fund', *The Hollywood Reporter*, 12 January. Available online: https://www.hollywoodreporter.com/lifestyle/lifestyle-news/ratatouille-the-tiktok-musical-raises-record-2-million-for-actors-fund-4115050/ (accessed 28 November 2021).

'Progam Note/Nota De Programa' (2021), The Public Theater. Available online: https://publictheater.org/media-center/series/romeo-y-julieta/castcreative--romeo-y-julieta-program-note-nota-de-programa2/ (accessed 28 November 2021).

'Report on "Zoom Kabuki "CHŪSHINGURA""(1) "The Great Prologue" to ACT III' (2020), *Kabuki Official Website*, 6 July. Available online: https://www.kabukiweb.net/news/2020/07/zoomkabuki_report1.html (accessed 28 November 2021).

Richter, S. (2020), '"Desi Don't Play That" – Female Iagos, Cassios, and the Emancipation of Desdemona'. Available online: https://mooreworldpremiere.sites.ucsc.edu/2020/06/10/desi-dont-play-that-female-iagos-cassios-and-the-emancipation-of-desdemona/ (accessed 28 November 2021).

Rosolen, D. (2020), 'Shakespeare chegou ao Zoom: como um grupo de teatro se adaptou à tecnologia para montar uma peça online em tempos de Covid-19', *Draft*, 7 October. Available online: https://www.projetodraft.com/como-um-grupo-de-teatro-montou-uma-peca-no-zoom-em-meio-a-covid-19/ (accessed 28 November 2021).

Smith, P. J., J. Valls-Russell and D. Yabut, eds (2020), 'Shakespeare under Global Lockdown', *Cahiers Élisabéthains*, 103 (1): 101–206.

Suematsu, M. (2021), personal email communication.

'*Variaciones de una Habitación*', Teatro del Mundo. Available online: https://www.teatrodelmundo.mx/variaciones-de-una-habitacion-extensa (accessed 28 November 2021).

'Visualised #3: National Theatre at Home' (2020), *One Further*. Available online: https://onefurther.com/blog/visualised-3-national-theatre-at-home (accessed 28 November 2021).

Yim, L. L. (2021) 'Review of Shakespeare's *A Midsummer Night's Dream* (Directed by Ty Defoe for the Southwest Shakespeare Company), Zoom, 11 July 2020', *Shakespeare*, 17 (1). Available online: https://www.tandfonline.com/doi/full/10.1080/17450918.2021.1892816 (accessed 28 November 2021).

Conclusion: Shakespeare after Lockdown

Erin Sullivan

In October 2020, the UK government embarked on a disastrous and short-lived media campaign. Aimed at getting more young people interested in careers in digital technology, it featured an advertisement with a photograph of a beautiful ballerina, carefully tying her pointe shoes. Next to the elegant image were the following lines:

> Fatima's next job could be in cyber.
> (she just doesn't know it yet)
> Rethink. Reskill. Reboot

Public backlash to the message was swift, particularly among those in the arts. 'This has to be a joke? Right?', tweeted the choreographer Matthew Bourne, while the writer Caitlin Moran commented that the government had apparently 'created a "Hopes & Dreams Crushing Department"' (Bourne 2020; Moran 2020). Even Oliver Dowden, the UK government's Culture Secretary, was quick to distance himself from the image. 'To those tweeting re #Fatima', he wrote, 'This is not something from @DCMS [The Department for Digital, Culture, Media and Sport] & I agree it was crass' (Dowden 2020). After nearly seven months of extreme hardship for those in the performing arts, the idea that their future might be in 'cyber' – itself a bizarre and vaguely dystopian term – did not fill creative practitioners with confidence. Though Dowden reiterated that he 'want[ed] to save jobs in the arts', and that his department was 'investing £1.57bn' in the sector, a sense remained that the government was uninterested in artists' contributions to society and that recovery from Covid-19 would be calculated in coldly financial terms.

Such a response would have been callous in any circumstances, but it was all the more egregious considering everything that artists had done to help people cope during such a difficult year. As this collection illustrates, creative practitioners around the world showed extraordinary generosity and ingenuity in the face of global lockdowns. This was particularly true in the case of smaller companies and freelancers, who continued to create despite their own financial precarity. To be told, then, that 'reskilling' was their best option was a profoundly dispiriting experience, made all the worse by the fact that the advertisement presented 'Fatima' as a woman of colour. 'Disabled people, people of colour, those from socially deprived backgrounds — it is these people who are stepping away from the precarious business of working in culture', Suba Das, the Artistic Director of HighTide Theatre, would comment the following spring (Higgins 2021). To a sector already struggling with a lack of diversity, especially in leadership roles, the government seemed to be saying that the arts were a luxury that only certain people could afford.

In other countries, the impact of the pandemic on the performing arts was sometimes similar and sometimes very different to what happened in the UK. While theatre-makers in the United States might have wished for the UK's comparatively generous furlough scheme, which paid a significant percentage of the wages of some (though by no means all) arts practitioners and staff, those in countries with more extensive welfare systems were supported more robustly. In Russian theatres, for instance, 'salaries were guaranteed by the state and no redundancies happen[ed]', though casts and crews suffered from the loss of nightly 'performance bonuses' (Makarov 2020: 2). Even in parts of the world where the impact of the pandemic was not so devastating, theatres still faced major challenges. In South Korea, for example, effective virus control measures meant that full lockdowns never took place, but performing arts venues struggled when audiences voluntarily stayed home (Cho 2021: 5). In New Zealand, where the government's elimination strategy virtually extinguished Covid-19, companies reliant on international touring, such as the Pop-Up Globe, went into liquidation (August 2021). No country's arts sector went untouched, though the extent of the harm varied greatly according to the severity of the virus within its borders and the financial support available from its government.

If one generalization across countries can be made, however, it is that freelancers and small organizations evolved faster and more inventively than their larger counterparts — both out of desire and need. In the UK, it was companies like Creation Theatre, Big Telly, *The Show Must Go Online* and the Shakespeare Ensemble that first started exploring the possibilities of digital performance platforms, while in the United States and Australia it was collectives like *Sofa Shakespeare*, *Shakespeare Republic* and Tender Claws that most energetically tested what togetherness might look like on them. 'Practically speaking, smaller and more nimble companies ... moved more quickly to producing online', Barbara Fuchs has written of both the Anglosphere and beyond, while Dukhee Cho has emphasized that it was 'The brave actions of "small theatres"' in South Korea that 'created a forum' for experimentation and evolution (Fuchs 2021: 11; Cho 2021: 4). Vladimir Makarov, in turn, has attributed the relative lack of made-for-lockdown productions in Russia to the comparatively small number of 'amateur and semi-professional collectives' in the country (2020: 6). Worldwide, pandemic theatre-making has been an unusually small-scale and grassroots phenomenon: digital technology has in many ways proved a leveller, allowing lesser-known practitioners to find new prominence on a global stage.

And yet, to suggest that going online democratized Shakespearean performance in a straightforward manner would be to gloss over how the internet reiterates and even magnifies existing inequalities. As Sonia Massai has argued, the digitization of theatre does not necessarily result in a more equitable and representative Shakespeare, particularly when it comes to the relations between big and little theatres, as well as Anglophone and non-Anglophone ones. Digital networks may make Shakespearean performance 'more expansive and less hierarchical', but they still privilege certain institutions, languages and countries (Massai

2021: 120). '[L]ocalities traditionally regarded as central and peripheral' are now 'intricately and inevitably interconnected', she writes, but we should not take this to mean that 'all localities, because networked, are automatically or necessarily endowed with the same access to resources, mobility or visibility within the network' (ibid.). Search engine algorithms, social media connections, myriad language and time zone differences, and engrained patterns of thinking continue to influence which digitally accessible productions of Shakespeare get noticed on a wider scale and which, in turn, do not.

This collection has showcased the diversity and inventiveness of Lockdown Shakespeare, not just from traditional centres of power but also from many different margins. The work of smaller companies and freelancers has been a particular focus, in the Anglophone world and beyond. And yet, the majority of the productions considered in its chapters are English-language and hail from either the UK or the United States: traditional centres of power if there ever were ones. It does seem, on the one hand, that made-for-lockdown, digital productions of Shakespeare's plays were especially abundant within these countries, due to a combination of the severity of Covid-19 mortality and lockdown restrictions there, the high number of freelancers and semi-professional collectives, the fragility of governmental support for them (both financial and ideological), and the far-reaching influence of Shakespeare in their educational and cultural systems.

On the other hand, it is clear that lockdown experimentation with Shakespeare was not an exclusively transatlantic or Anglophone activity. Projects like Merced Shakespearefest's *Ricardo II*, Armazém Companhia de Teatro's *Parece Loucura, Mas Há Método*, Shakespeare ZA's #lockdownshakespeare, and Sarah Hatchuel and Yu Umemiya's educational work in Montpellier and Tokyo powerfully demonstrate how creative practitioners around the world drew on Shakespeare as they tested the boundaries of digital performance — and vice versa. In this collection we have striven to illustrate the richness and breadth of made-for-lockdown Shakespearean performance, but we are keenly aware of our linguistic, cultural and personal limitations. There are undoubtedly more projects deserving of recognition, and we are excited by the ways in which other explorations of Lockdown Shakespeare, such as those that focus on archive recordings, are showing how existing patterns of theatrical transmission reassemble within a globalized and digitized landscape.

Pascale Aebischer, for instance, has demonstrated how the abundance of German-language Shakespeare recordings made available in spring 2020 by Thalia Theater, the Schaubühne, Deutsches Theater and Schauspielhaus Bochum, among others, resulted in a complex 'meshwork' of theatre-viewing in which 'productions from different cultures and time periods [were] unexpectedly brought into dialogue' (2021: 25). Old productions signified in new ways, especially as they interacted with one another in the minds of audience members such as Aebischer, who found herself dreaming again in German for the first time in decades. Special issues of reviews in *Cahiers Élisabéthains* and *Shakespeare Bulletin* have further illuminated the diversity of Shakespearean performance materials that have found new audiences during this pandemic, as well as the important and often very personal ways they have created meaning for scholars, teachers and theatre-makers around the world (Smith, Valls-Russell and Yabut 2020; Kirwan and Sullivan 2021). Such work shows how the adaptation and evolution of performance – during lockdown and beyond – is as much about reception as production. As investigation into this extraordinary time continues, we look forward to hearing more people discuss what Lockdown Shakespeare looked, felt and sounded like in their languages, cultures, personal lives and political contexts. We present our collection as a contribution to this evolving conversation — part of its beginnings rather than its end.

Because, as we all know, this pandemic is not finished with us. As I write this conclusion in June 2021, Chile, Hungary, Israel, the UK, the United States and a handful of other nations have passed 50 per cent population immunity through their vaccination programmes; at the same time, many countries are facing devastating further waves and uncertainty about vaccine supply. Even once – or if – global herd immunity is achieved, we will have to reckon with the economic, psychological and indirect health impacts of this pandemic. Somewhere amongst all this will be the state of theatre-making, at both the global and national level. This is not the first time, of course, that the world has faced a pandemic and found a way through it. The so-called Spanish flu of 1918–19 killed at least 50 million people worldwide, or more than ten times those lost in the Great War, while the Black Death of 1347–51 killed 40–70 million people in Europe, or roughly 30–60 per cent of the population (Honigsbaum 2009: xiii; Honigsbaum 2018).

Still, it may very well be the first time that large swathes of the globe are looking to restart after prolonged, and in some cases almost total, government-imposed shutdowns due to illness. In 1918–19 in the UK, for instance, there was no nationwide lockdown. Mark Honigsbaum has shown that while some schools closed for short periods of time, and some public venues had to ventilate their premises between gatherings, the official response was on the whole 'phlegmatic' (2009: 77–9, 104–5). In an interview about his career, the actor Arnold Ridley recalled falling ill with the virus while onstage in Birmingham, and how the director asked him to return to the show while he was still convalescing. 'Things in the theatre were desperate', he commented; his landlady, the stage manager and another cast member had died, and he was needed to help 'keep the curtain up' ('Spanish Influenza' 2016). Shockingly for listeners today, at no point does Ridley reflect on whether the venue should have closed. In the wake of a costly war, and in an era that predated most of the country's welfare services, there was little appetite and few resources for a full-scale shutdown.

The issue of what comes next, then, is almost wholly uncharted. Caridad Svich has emphasized how the pandemic, and all the global unrest surrounding it, has 'laid bare the fault lines of racial and class hierarchies that exist inside the precariat class' (2021: 1). Such a group encompasses the vast majority of practitioners celebrated in this collection, who have given so much while receiving so little. While none of them has done it solely for the money, neither should they be expected to do it irrespective of financial support. Svich suggests that rebuilding theatre after the pandemic might in fact be about 'debuild[ing]' it, and one of the first steps in such a process would be to make sure that the Fatimas of the future feel like there is a place for them there, culturally as well as economically (ibid.: 6–7). This would mean creating and supporting theatre-making that is less bounded, less hierarchical, less rule-governed — that celebrates excellence in all its forms and finds ways to share it widely and equitably around the world.

References

Aebischer, P. (2021), *Viral Shakespeare: Performance in the Time of Pandemic*, Cambridge: Cambridge University Press.

August, H. (2021), personal email communication.

Bourne, M. (2021), Twitter, 12 October. Available online: https://twitter.com/SirMattBourne/status/1315597677355204608 (accessed 28 November 2021).

Cho, D. (2021), 'Digitally Mediated Shakespeare in South Korea', *Shakespeare*. Available online: https://doi.org/10.1080/17450918.2021.1925333 (accessed 28 November 2021).

Dowden, O. (2020), Twitter, 12 October. Available online: https://twitter.com/OliverDowden/status/1315586209415073793 (accessed 28 November 2021).

Fuchs, B. (2021), *Theater of Lockdown: Digital and Distanced Performance in a Time of Pandemic*, London: Methuen.

Higgins, C. (2021), '"We Won't Be Bouncing Back"', *The Guardian*, 12 May. Available online: https://www.theguardian.com/culture/2021/may/12/bouncing-back-unsettling-truth-big-reopening (accessed 28 November 2021).

Honigsbaum, M. (2009), *Living with Enza: The Forgotten Story of Britain and the Great Flu Pandemic of 1918*, Basingstoke: Palgrave.

Honigsbaum, M. (2018), 'Why the Spanish Flu Defied Both Memory and Imagination', *Wellcome Collection*, 25 October. Available online: https://wellcomecollection.org/articles/W7TfGRAAAP5F0eKS (accessed 28 November 2021).

Kirwan, P. and E. Sullivan, eds (2021), 'Shakespeare in Lockdown', *Shakespeare Bulletin* 38 (3): 1–59.

Makarov, V. (2020), 'Shakespearean Performances Online in 2020 Russia: A New Kind of Theatre, Delayed?', unpublished conference paper.

Massai, S. (2021), 'Networks: Researching Global Shakespeare', in P. Kirwan and K. Prince (eds), *The Arden Research Handbook of Shakespeare and Contemporary Performance*, 114–31, London: Bloomsbury.

Moran, C. (2020), Twitter, 12 October. Available online: https://twitter.com/caitlinmoran/status/1315583381560852480 (accessed 28 November 2021).

Smith, P. J., J. Valls-Russell and D. Yabut, eds (2020), 'Shakespeare under Global Lockdown', *Cahiers Élisabéthains* 103 (1): 101–206.

'The Spanish Influenza Pandemic' (2016), *BBC Sounds*, 11 October. Available online: https://www.bbc.co.uk/sounds/play/p049wkyk (accessed 28 November 2021).

Svich, C. (2021) *Toward a Future Theatre: Conversations during a Pandemic*, London: Methuen.

INDEX

Abbott, Courtney 223
access 6, 9, 109–10, 128, 130, 131, 132, 138, 140, 144–5, 159, 168–9, 181–2, 188, 193, 203–4, 205, 213–15, 221, 227
Aebischer, Pascale 13, 61, 263
Ajala, Jamal 144
Alberti, Leon Battista 26
Aldridge, Sydney 154
Alfreds, Mike 66–7, 77, 84
Ali, Saheem 8, 169, 236–7, 250
Allred, Gemma Kate 37
Alwyn, David 71, 171, 173, 176, 179, 181
American Shakespeare Center (USA) 221
Anderson, Wes 55
Andrew, Geoff 56
Archer, Scarlett 73
Arden Theatre Company (USA) 8, 52–5, 58, 60, 232–3
Arledge, Roone 31
Armazém Companhia de Teatro (Brazil)
Parece Loucura 234, 262
Artaud, Antonin 113, 122
Askew, Hazel 131
Atkin, Leo 55–6, 57–8, 59
Atkinson, Beth 80, 243–4
Atkinson, Sarah 34
attention 107–11, 119–20, 121, 122
  attention economy 108
  controlled inattention 74

fascination (hard and soft) 111, 114, 116, 119–20, 122
audience behaviour 74, 199
audience agency 128, 129, 131, 133, 135–7, 145, 191, 234
audience participation 67–70, 89, 91, 92–4, 97–105, 116, 118–19, 121, 178, 180–2, 230–1, 233, 234, 238, 254
audience surveys 87–8, 98–105, 110
audio description 145, 222
audio drama 208, 209–20, 211, 213, 214, 236–7
Auslander, Philip 65

The Back Room Shakespeare Project (BRSP) (USA) 11, 38, 223
Ballet de l'Opéra national de Paris (France) 24, 36
Barclay, Al 68, 89, 94
Bard College (USA)
  Mad Forest 38, 229
Barker, Martin 75
Barnes-Worrell, Elliot
  'Thinking Out Loud: Quarantine Shakespeare' 227
Barton, Luke 73
Bateman, Luke 241
Bauer, Katrin 189
Beaulieu, Dan 134, 136, 139, 140
Belfast Theatre Festival 195

INDEX

Beresford, Stephen 39
Berliner Ensemble (Germany) 221, 261
Biden, Joe
    inauguration of 50
Big Telly Theatre Company (Northern Ireland) 6, 10–12, 14, 15, 69–70, 80, 87–105, 225, 235
    Macbeth 15, 60, 69–70, 71, 80, 83, 195–205, 242, 248
    The Tempest (see under Creation Theatre Company)
Big Theatre 1, 2, 9–10, 12, 205, 219, 241, 253, 255
Bizzocchi, Jim 27
Black, Tom 78, 173, 175, 179
Blake, Adam 173
Boehm, Claudia 168–9
'Bohemian Rhapsody' (song) 75–6, 153
Bonner, Frances 36
Brady, Wayne 250
Breslin, Michael 80, 81, 244
Brewer, Dominic 73, 75, 149, 151, 152, 154, 157, 158, 238
Bristol Old Vic (England) 66
British Broadcasting Corporation (BBC) (UK) 12, 221, 254
    Staged 24, 231–2
Broadway 132
Brook, Peter 47
Brooker, Charlie
    Black Mirror 175
Brown, Cressida 232
Brown, David Sterling 8, 127, 155
Brown, Joanna 175
Brucoli, Jenna 49
Buchanan, Judith 31, 32, 94–5
Buckley, Jessie 255
Bucknall, Joanna 66
Burgess, Tituss 250
Bushnell, Rebecca 120

Butusov, Yury 222
Byrd, Debra Ann 241

Cahiers Élisabéthains 13, 263
Caley, Olivia 175
Callow, Simon 240
Capaldi, Robbie 156
Carlson, Marvin 93
Cartwright, Edward 80
Cartwright, Kent 58
Castano, Juan 169
Caughie, John 30
Cena IV Shakespeare Sia (Brazil)
    Projeto A Web é um Palco 226
Chapman, John 12
Charles, Justin 51
Cheek by Jowl (England) 221
Cherry Lane Theatre (USA) 247
Cho, Dukhee 261
Churchill, Caryl 38, 229
Cimolino, Antoni 221
Circle in the Sand (Australia) 230
Clarke, Jordan Paul 2, 241
Clemons, Lemons 243
Cobb, Keith Hamilton
    American Moor 133–4, 246–7
Cochrane, Bernadette 36
Cohen, Maya 58–9
Coleman, Grantham 144
Collins, David 241
Collins-Hughes, Laura 67, 84
La Comédie Française (France) 232
commercial viability 88, 178–180, 260–1
community 89, 94–7, 101–4, 110, 111, 116, 118–19, 130, 139–40, 152–4, 158, 168–9, 182–3, 186, 188–94, 196, 203, 211, 222, 237
community and grassroots theatre 161–70, 261
Conley, Michael 241

INDEX

Constantine, Tim 238
Cook, Amy 93
Covid-19 pandemic 3–4, 45, 61,
    107, 109, 122–3, 127, 128,
    138, 151, 152, 162–3,
    176–7, 181–2, 196, 203, 236,
    239–40, 242, 255–6, 259–63
  'Bubbled' performers 24, 242,
    245, 251, 255
  mental and emotional toll 16,
    57–9, 104, 107, 109, 172,
    248
  as narrative device 69, 197,
    210, 212, 238–9, 248, 251,
    255
  pre-pandemic nostalgia 57,
    212, 249
  social distancing in performance
    66, 79, 83, 230, 233, 241,
    242, 245, 250
  socioeconomic inequity 7, 204,
    264
  theatre as antidote to 180–2,
    197, 244, 249
  Zeitgeist 79, 197, 244
Craiova Shakespeare Festival
    (Romania) 222
Creation Theatre Company
    (England) 37, 87–105, 133,
    225, 235, 238–9, 252–3, 261
  The Duchess of Malfi 38, 253
  The Tempest (with Big Telly
    Theatre Company) 10–11,
    12, 14, 24, 67–9, 71,
    87–105, 195–6
Cross-Stitch Theatre (England) 11,
    79–80, 243–4
Crouch, Tim
  I, Cinna (The Poet) 235–6
Crystal, Ben 6, 8–9, 76, 127, 149,
    152, 158, 240
CtrlAltRepeat (England) 6, 11, 15,
    52, 53, 79, 171–83

As You Like It 175–7, 230
Midsummer Night Stream 37,
    38, 78–9, 80, 171, 172,
    173–5, 223
Viper Squad 70–1, 72, 180–2,
    244
cultural capital (Shakespearean)
    97, 104, 133, 146, 155, 232,
    237, 262
Cunningham, Vinson 236

Dae-hak-ro Arts Theatre (South
    Korea) 222
Dailey, Dan 27
Danae, Xdzunúm 134, 136
Darley, Acndrew 33
Das, Suba 260
Day, Charlie 71, 230, 243
Day, Doris 27
Deafinitely Theatre (England)
    221
Defoe, Ty 237
Dehenny, Elizabeth 75–6
digital divide (*see also*
    Globalization [and digital
    culture]) 7, 130, 144–5
Digital Theatre Transformation
    (AHRC/UKRI-funded
    project) 14, 87–8
Dillon, James 6, 171, 172, 174,
    178–82
Dinnen, Zara 120
disability 6, 138, 144–5, 204, 222,
    248, 260
distraction 108–11, 120, 122
diversity and inclusion 9, 133–4,
    138, 140–5, 150, 153–5,
    168–9, 190–1, 214–5, 222,
    227, 228, 241, 256, 260–2,
    264
Doescher, Ian 248
domesticity 48–51, 53, 66, 69,
    79–80, 102, 114, 120, 156,

157, 158, 173, 188, 191,
  201–2, 212, 226, 227, 228,
  237, 240
Doran, Gregory 1, 2
Dowden, Oliver 259–60
Duncan, Ryan 89, 95, 239

Earl, William 46
Ehren, Ashleigh 50–1
Eisenstein, Sergei 26
Elby, Amber 243
Ellison, Alex James 241
embodiment 93–5, 97, 116, 120,
  121–2, 164
emotion 14, 15, 103–4, 118, 119,
  138–9, 140, 165, 186, 191,
  194
  emotional bandwidth 109–10
empty auditoria (productions
  performed within) 11, 39,
  66, 242, 245, 250–2, 254
Engleman, Ashley 49
entrainment 94, 102
ephemerality 78–82, 91, 96, 169
environmental issues 128, 254
escape rooms 229
Evans, Nick 82, 251
Evans, Simon 231
event-connectedness 65–6, 68
Exit Productions (England)
  Jury Duty 179, 229–30

FaceTime 38, 224
The Factory Theatre Company
  (England) 233
Faiers, Meryl 192
Fake Friends (USA)
  Circle Jerk 81, 244, 250
  This American Wife 80–2, 245
Fandom 74
Fantova, Marketa 224
Fernhout, Roeland 35
Figgis, Mike 28, 29, 34, 36, 37, 38

film and cinema 1, 14, 25–32, 47,
  56–9, 82–3, 103, 115–16,
  129, 131–3, 165, 208,
  211–12, 214, 223–4, 236,
  250–1, 254–5
  black and white 51, 56–9, 212,
    224
  close-ups 212
  filming process (for theatre) 35,
    81, 164, 167, 210, 212
  montage 26, 103
  post-production 167–8, 238
  pre-recorded material 48–51,
    78, 94–6, 176, 200–2, 229,
    242, 245, 251
Finch, Rebekah 171, 177, 181–2
Fischer-Lichte, Erika 65
The Flow Theatre (South Korea)
  247
Floyd, George 7, 77–8, 236–7
Foan, Helen 134
Foley, Patrick 80, 81, 244
Folger Theatre (USA) 3, 221
Forced Entertainment (England)
  *Complete Works: Table Top
    Shakespeare* 240
Ford, John
  'Tis Pity She's A Whore 223
Forristal, Francesca 2, 241
Foy, Claire 39–40, 233–4
flexibility 127–46
Flores, Cathryn 165–7, 169
Floyd, George 7, 8, 77–8, 236,
  237
Frankenheimer, John 27
Freedman, Bryan 53
freelance creatives 88, 260–2,
  264
Fresh Life Theatre Company
  (England) 8, 11, 230
  Mortal Fools 71–2, 243, 253
Friedberg, Anne 25, 30
Fry, Stephen 226

INDEX

Fuchs, Barbara 13, 261
funding and pay (in the arts) 88, 128, 131, 143, 145, 156, 159, 221, 260–2, 264

Gabriel, Shane 249
Gajic, Thea 227
Gance, Abel 26
Gancher, Sarah 244
Garfield, Paula 221
gender and sexuality 135, 136, 141, 153–5, 204, 237, 240, 243
    casting 8, 155, 237, 241, 245–6, 248
    #MeToo 238
    misogyny 155, 243
    toxic masculinity 230, 241
Gendron, Vanessa 224
Gibson, Adam 149, 157, 158
Gilpin, Debbie 12
Giolzetti, Julia 48–51, 226, 249
Globe on Screen 66
globalization (and digital culture) 8, 150, 151, 158, 182–3, 203–4, 261–4
Glover, Donald 47
Gobran, Sarah 225
Godard, Jean-Luc 47
Godwin, Simon 254
Gordon, Michael 27
Gordon, Simon 82
Gorman, Samantha 112, 116, 117, 121
Goslinga, Janni 35
Grace, Maryam 248
Green, Jesse 39
Green Man Festival (Wales) 248
Greenaway, Peter 28, 38
Gross, Paul 144
Guest, Janet 6
Guildford Shakespeare Company (GSC) 225–6, 248
Gutiérrez, Alejandro 163, 166

Hagener, Malte 30
Haigh, Jodi 238
Hale, Harker 166
Hambley, Heike 162–4, 167–9
Harlem Shakespeare Festival (USA) 246, 247
Harley, Nicky 195, 199–203, 205
Harris, Jeremy O. 228
Hastie, Robert 242
Hatchuel, Sarah 34, 35
Hawkes, Terence 60
Herdman, Dennis 70, 195, 200–1, 204, 205
HEWILLNOTDIVIDE.US 45–6
Hiddleston, Tom 232
Higgins, Annabelle 73
Hijinx Theatre (Wales) 248
Hill, Pippa 253
Hill-Corley, Lisa 8, 149, 151, 153, 158
Hitchcock, Alfred 34
Hodgson, Sarah 187
Holden, Mark 241
Holehouse, Lucy 192
Holger-Madsen 26
Holmes, Sean 2
HOMEShakes (Italy) 226
Honigsbaum, Mark 264
Hopley, Lizzie 238
How Drama (Singapore) 248
Huck, Amy 224
Hudson, Rock 27
Hunter, Alasdair 135
Hunter, Jay 56
Hurley, Colin 136
hybridity 34–5, 167–8, 174, 196, 202, 256

immersive theatre 67–72, 89–91, 105, 115, 122, 130, 178–82, 225, 234–5
inclusion *see under* diversity and inclusion
Ingram, Emily 52, 149, 156

Internationaal Theater Amsterdam
  (ITA) (Netherlands)
  Kings of War 34–5, 251
  Roman Tragedies 34–5, 251
International Actors Ensemble 230
internet connection (and failure)
  80, 94, 131, 140, 187, 200,
  209, 211
improvisation 94, 99, 117
isolation 6, 11, 17, 56, 59, 66,
  104, 111, 116, 127, 128,
  129, 130, 138, 142, 145,
  163, 186–7, 189–90, 197,
  211, 221, 226–7, 236,
  248–9
Ivan Franko National Academic
  Drama Theatre (Ukraine)
  222

Jameson, Fredric 46, 49
Jermyn, Deborah 36
Jhala, Amba Suhasini Katoch 136,
  137
John, Gareth 248
Johnson, Boris 1
Jolly, Thomas 222, 232
Jones, Gari 252–3
Jones, Kalina 48
Jonze, Spike 47
July, Miranda 47
Jumbo, Cush 41
Juneteenth 236
Jury Games *see under* Exit
  Productions

Kabuki 229
Kageyama, Takashi 222
Kahn, Joseph 33
Kakushinhan Theatre Company
  (Japan) 251
Karim-Cooper, Farah 142
Karp, Arian 134
Kelly, Gene 27
Kidd, Michael 27

Kimura, Ryunosuke 251
King, Anchuli Felicia
  Keene 144, 247
Kirwan, Peter 12, 82
Klapisch, Cédric 24
Kloska, Joseph 254
Knapman, Timothy 241
Knight, Suzanne 78, 171, 172, 180
Koh, Sun-Woong 222
Koolschijn, Hugo 35
Korsunovas, Oskaras 222
Kōshirō, Matsumoto 229
Kurata, Hiroaki 136, 137
Kwei-Armah, Kwame 40–1

LaBeouf, Shia 45–6
Laight, Ryan Dawson 92
Lambert, Adam 250
Lanier, Douglas 48
Lanier, Jaron 120
Lawrence, Francis 33
Lee, Ang 30
Lemieux, Evangeline 245
Lenson, Adam 12
Lewis, Rhodri 92
Lieberman, Anna Faye 52–6
Liedke, Heidi 95–6, 98, 102
Liu, Dana 53
Liveness 14, 31, 65–84, 89, 94–6,
  102–4, 121, 131–2, 196,
  200–2, 204, 233
Lloyd Malcolm, Morgan
  Emilia 247
Lloyd Webber, Andrew 2, 220
Lowman, Diane 191
Lucas, George 27
Lucrezio, Nathan 27
Lyly, John
  Gallathea 6

McAnally, Aonghus Óg 195, 198,
  202, 204
McAnespie, Lucia 69, 195,
  199–201

MacDowell, James 47, 54–5
Mace, Olivia 238
McGuire, Patrick 51
McIntyre, Paula 197
McLean, Sally 11, 55–6, 57, 238
MacMahon, Madeleine 68, 89, 92–3
Macmillan, Duncan 39, 233
McNicholas, Robin 253
McNulty, Katie 248
McMinn, Mark 73
Maddrie, Leah
  Just About Love 247
Madianou, Mirca 7
Makarov, Vladimir 261
Maleedy, Kieran 79
Manovic, Lev 26, 35
Marlowe, Christopher
  Dr Faustus 209, 214
Marshmallow Laser Feast (England) 253
Martin, Trayvon 141
Masloboishchikov, Serhii 222
Massai, Sonia 261–2
Mattos, Justina Taft 8, 245
May, Aaron 243
memory 93, 96–7
mental health 138, 139, 187, 190, 212
Merced Shakespearefest (USA)
  Ricardo II 16, 161–70, 247, 262
Mercury, Freddie 75–6
Met Opera Live in HD 25, 33
metamodernism 14, 45–61
metatheatricality 37, 79, 196–7, 231, 243–5, 249
Metcalfe, Ryan 82
Mezzocchi, Jared 12, 17, 244
Michlin, Monica 35
Middleton, Thomas
  The Witch 223
migration and displacement 165
Miller, Frank 30

mirror neurons 93, 96
Mischief Theatre (England) 244
Mitchell, Justin 53
Mitchell, Katie 34
Modenessi, Alfredo Michel 250
Molyneux, Lauren 231
Monáe, Janelle 47
Moor, Patrice 130
Moraes, Paulo 234
Moreno, Itxaso 68, 88, 90–1, 96–8, 104–5, 225
Morrison, Benedict 28
Moss, Lucy 250
Msamati, Lucian 254
multilingual theatre 161–70, 245–6, 247, 250–1
music 23–4, 53–4, 90, 131, 137, 157, 165–7
music video 33
Musisi, Anne 253
Myles, Robert (Rob) 6, 8–9, 10, 11, 52, 72, 73, 77, 149–59

Nair, Anirudh 128, 136, 138
National Arts Club (USA) 246
National Health Service (NHS) (UK) 77, 238
The National Theatre (England) 3, 220–1, 232, 253, 254–5
  NTLive 25, 36, 66
Nellist, David 251
Nemoto, Keiji 251
Neuls, Kelly 51
neurodiversity 6, 182, 204
Nguyen-Cruz, Maria 165
Nichele, Haylee 119, 120, 121
1918–19 influenza pandemic ('Spanish flu') 263–4
non-linear storytelling 132–3
The Northern Comedy Theatre (England)
  Doing Shakespeare 79, 231, 234, 243
Novelty 120

Nri, Cyril 227
Nuñez, Ángel 162–5, 167, 169
Nyong'o, Lupita 169

Oakley, Michael 240
object theatre 156, 240
O'Brien, Richard 187
O'Connor, Josh 255
O'Donovan, Crissy 69, 84, 195–6, 199, 203–4
Old Vic (London, England) 11
  In Camera season 39–40, 66, 233, 241, 248
  Lungs 39–40, 233
  Three Kings 39, 234
Olufunwa, Funlola 253
Open Broadcast Software (OBS) 69–70, 229, 253
Original Pronunciation 240
Ormond, Neal 234
Osmond, Nicholas 239
Ostermeier, Thomas 222
Overton, Shawn 167
Owens, Sinéad 94
Oyama, Daisuke 251

Paddenburg, Ilke 35
Parillon, Amelia 8, 78
Pastor, Krzysztof 222
Patel, Dharmesh 6, 69, 195, 198, 200–1, 204–5, 253
Pawarroo, Andrew 8, 75, 149, 151, 157, 158
Payne, Alexander 56
Peachey, Sarah 9, 72, 149, 151, 155, 159
Pelsue, Rory 244
Penny, Katheryne 27
Pérez González, Ricardo 169
Pfeiffer, Matt 52, 54
Phelan, Peggy 65, 67, 91
Phoenix, Sid 37, 52, 78, 79, 171–4, 176–83, 223
Plague and Black Death 187–8, 264

playfulness 53–5, 58, 60, 96–7, 117–18, 119, 233
play-readings 11–12, 150–1, 172, 185–94
political unrest and protests 162, 163, 165, 167, 212, 213, 235–6, 237, 264
  2011 UK riots 235
  2020 Black Lives Matter protests (*see* race)
  2020 US Presidential election 213
  Yellow Vests demonstrations (France) 212
popular culture 48, 50–1, 228, 248, 255
Pop-Up Globe (New Zealand) 261
Poreia Theatre (Greece) 222
Porter, Darcy 48
Posner, Aaron 221
postmodernism 14, 46–7, 49, 50, 51, 52, 56, 239
Powell, Jakeem Dante 80
Prague Shakespeare Company (Czech Republic) 224
Presence 65–7, 108, 119–23
Price, Matthew 241
props 48, 52, 156–7, 188, 200, 228, 233, 240
Prokofiev, Sergei 24
Public Domain (2021 musical) 2, 241
The Public Theater (USA)
  Richard II 8, 236–7
  Romeo y Julieta 169, 250
  #ToBeBlack 236
Punchdrunk (London, England) 122, 130
Purcarete, Silviu 222
Pye, Valerie Clayman 74, 78

Queen's Theatre Hornchurch (London, England) 251
quirky sensibility 54–5

race 7–9, 15, 127–8, 134–5, 140–4, 153, 155, 161, 163, 165, 168–9, 204, 236–7, 245–7, 260, 264
  antiracism 134, 155
  Black Lives Matter (BLM) 7–9, 51, 134, 140–2, 236–7, 247
  global majority 9, 135, 141–2, 241
  racism 78, 138, 140, 144, 155, 246
  unconscious bias 141–3
Reading Early Plays (REP) 193–4
Ready, Paul 242
realism 121, 229
Reaney, Mark 113
Red Bull Theater (USA) 12, 223, 246–7
The Red Curtain International (India)
  The Good The@ter Festival 202–3, 248
Red Nose Company (Finland) 248
Redpath, Emily 82
resistance 127–46
Rheingold, Howard 113
Rhodes, Matthew 76, 149, 153, 158
Rice, Emma 66
Richter, Stephen 245
Rickman, Natasha 225, 238
Ridley, Arnold 264
Ridley, Philip 241
Rintoul, Douglas 251–2
Roberts, Guy 224
Robinson, Chris 89, 92–3
Rodríguez, Catherine 81, 244
Rodriguez, Robert 30
Rönkkö, Nastja Säde 45–6
Roodt, Lee 227
Rose, Renee 134, 137, 140
Rosedale Shakespeare (USA)
  The Gaming of the Shrew 243

Rotterdams Philharmonisch Orkest (Netherlands) 23–4, 36
Rourke, Josie 232
Royal Shakespeare Company (RSC) (England) 1, 66, 79, 215, 221, 250, 253–4
Ruelas, Greg 166
Ryan, Larissa 49

Salt, Barry 26
San Francisco Shakespeare Festival (USA) 234
Sambrooks, Anna 173
Sanders, Bernie
  mittens meme 50
Saraf, Shubham 226
saucy priests 73
Sayet, Madeline 237
Schaubühne Berlin (Germany) 3, 222, 263
Schneider, Rebecca 93, 97
Scott, Andrew 39
Scuola Teatrale d'Eccellenza (Italy) 227
Seaton, Zoë 10, 60, 68, 69, 81, 82, 83, 87, 92, 95–7, 195–200, 202–4, 225, 235
Secret Cinema (England) 172
Sedgman, Kirsty 66, 77, 83
Sénéchal, Héloïse 192
Seome, Amanda 227
Serebryakov, Nikolay 249
Serratore, Nicole 81
Sexton, Heather 246
Seymour, Joanne 251
Shakespeare, William
  All's Well That Ends Well 247
  Antony and Cleopatra 151, 154–5, 240, 241
  As You Like It 175–7, 227, 230, 238
  The Comedy of Errors 58–9, 156
  Coriolanus 232

INDEX

Cymbeline 238
Hamlet 41, 50–1, 76, 139, 145, 209, 221, 222, 227, 229, 232, 234, 236, 238, 239
Henry IV, Part 2 227
Henry V 79–80, 232, 240, 243–4
Henry VI plays 73, 232
History cycles 230
Julius Caesar 35, 207, 227, 235–6
King John 31, 74
King Lear 47, 156, 188, 221, 222, 227, 231, 234, 249
Love's Labour's Lost 80, 221, 233
Macbeth 15, 60, 69–70, 71, 79, 80, 83, 157, 195–205, 209, 210, 211–12, 221, 227, 231, 232, 241, 242–3, 248, 249, 250
as material for digital theatre 47, 91–2, 104–5, 172, 173, 187
Measure for Measure 153, 222
The Merry Wives of Windsor 238
A Midsummer Night's Dream 2, 8, 52–8, 71–2, 73, 76, 78–9, 80, 171, 172, 173–5, 222, 223–4, 226, 230–1, 233, 237, 242, 243, 250, 253–4
Much Ado About Nothing 56
Othello 8–9, 134, 144, 155, 188, 222, 227, 245–7
Pericles 6, 231
Richard II 16, 161–70, 226, 232, 236–7, 238, 247, 251
Richard III 222, 240
Romeo and Juliet 24, 48–9, 82–3, 169, 187, 226, 227, 231, 240, 250–2, 253, 254–5

The Sonnets 11, 226, 227
The Taming of the Shrew 77, 231, 243, 249
The Tempest 10, 14, 24, 32, 67–9, 71, 87–105, 108–23, 153, 222, 223, 225, 232, 234, 241, 250
Timon of Athens 240
Titus Andronicus 153, 226, 227
Twelfth Night 15, 127–46, 209, 210–11, 214, 226, 234
The Two Gentlemen of Verona 72–3, 151, 222–3
The Two Noble Kinsmen 187
The Winter's Tale 75, 79, 153, 250
Shakespeare Bulletin 13, 263
Shakespeare Ensemble (international)
What You Will 8, 15, 127–46, 234
Shakespeare Happy Hours (USA) 223
Shakespeare's Globe Theatre (England) 2, 3, 11, 73, 79, 94, 132, 135, 221, 226, 232, 240, 242, 247
Sam Wanamaker Playhouse 11, 242
The Shakespeare Institute (England) 12, 16, 185–94
Shakespeare in Pieces 11, 226–8, 248–9
Shakespeare Republic: #AllTheWebsAStage (The Lockdown Chronicles) 11, 55–9, 60, 238, 261
Shakespeare Switched Theatre Company (England) 248
Shakespeare ZA (South Africa) #lockdownshakespeare 226–7, 262
Shake-scene Shakespeare Theatre Company (England) 223

Shapiro, James 237
Shaughnessy, Robert 94
Sheen, Michael 24, 231–2
Shin, Jae-Hoon 222
Shochiku Company (Japan) 229
The Show Must Go Online
  (*TSMGO*) 6, 8–9, 10, 11,
  12, 15, 52, 53, 72–8, 80,
  133, 138, 149–59, 173, 188,
  222–3, 240–2, 249, 261
The Shows Must Go On! (YouTube
  channel) 220–1, 240
sign language interpreting 6, 145
Simon, Herbert A. 108
Singleton, Keith 90, 92
site-specific theatre 89–91, 167
1623 Theatre Company
  (England) *Queer Lady M*
  249
60 Hour Shakespeare (England)
  230
Smalley, Phillips 26
Smith, Jodie 192
Smith, Matt 39–40, 233–4
Smith, Zadie 47
Socially Distant Shakespeare
  (USA) 238
social media 87, 110, 121, 123,
  226–7, 241, 252, 262
  Facebook 27, 90, 113, 168,
    222, 226, 237–8, 247
  Instagram 227, 232
  TikTok 11, 28, 107, 122, 123,
    228, 245, 250
  Twitter 11, 12, 71, 110, 193,
    227, 230–1, 248, 259
  WhatsApp 192, 238
Soderbergh, Steven 30
Sofa Shakespeare 48–51, 60, 226,
  247, 261
Song, Hyeon-Ok 247
sound design 157
Southwark Playhouse (London,
  England) 2, 11, 241

Southwest Shakespeare Company
  (USA) 237
Spence-Hyde, Simon 68, 89, 90
Spicer, David 231
Spiller, Ben 249
split screen 13, 14, 23–41, 233–4
Sprawl, Kimber Elayne 236
Stewart, Patrick 11, 227
Stoakley, Giles 89, 91, 92–3
Stratford Festival (Canada) 3,
  221
subtitles 165, 208, 222
Sullivan, Erin 65, 68, 71, 72–3,
  74, 77
Svich, Caridad 12, 13, 17, 264
Sweete, Barbara Willis 33
Sylvester, Katie 166
Syme, Holger 35

Tanenbaum, Isaiah 49
Tangibility 52, 53, 68, 80–1, 82,
  156–7, 174
Tata, Ashley 38, 229
Taylor, PK 90, 92
Taylor, Samuel 223
teaching 6, 16, 186, 190–1,
  207–15, 220, 232, 262
Teatro del Mundo (Mexico)
  Variaciones de una Habitación
  234–5
Teatr Praktika (Russia) 229
technophobia 96–7, 104
television 11, 14, 23–4, 26–8,
  30–3, 56, 111, 129, 133,
  165–6, 200, 227, 254
  streaming platforms 137,
    221–2, 231
Teller 221
Tender Claws
  'The Under Presents: *Tempest*'
  15, 108, 112–23, 234, 261
Tennant, David 24, 231–2
Terry, Annabelle 90, 95
Terry, Michelle 2, 221, 242

Thalia Theater (Germany) 3, 221, 263
Thane, Em 136
Theatre broadcasts and recordings 33–6, 39–41, 65–6, 74, 77–8, 82, 109, 110, 111, 132, 220–2, 232–3, 262–3
Theatre for a New Audience (USA) 250
  Mad Forest 38, 229
theatre history (early modern) 192–3
Theatre Royal Brighton (England) 70, 196, 243
Théâtre Royal de la Monnaie/De Munt (Belgium) 222
theatricality 96–7, 104
Thomas, Morgan 248
Thompson, Ayanna 142, 251
ticket prices 88, 221–2
time zones 116, 187, 191, 211, 262
Toneelgroep Amsterdam *see under* Internationaal Theater Amsterdam (ITA) (Netherlands)
Torres, Kathia 51
translation 59, 165, 167, 208–10, 237, 263
Tree, Herbert Beerbohm 31
Trump, Donald 45–6
Turner, Luke 45–6, 47
Tutty, Sam 82
24 (television series) 34, 35, 36
Twigg, Kathryn 190
Twitch (live-streaming website) 243
Tyson, Josh 246

University of Hawaii at Hilo's Performing Arts Center (USA)
  Moore – A Pacific Island Othello 8, 245–6

University of North Carolina at Charlotte (USA) 207–8
University of Paul Valéry Montpellier 3 (France) 208

van den Akker, Robin 46, 60
van Hove, Ivo 34, 35, 252
Varjack, Paula 12
Vaudeville Theatre (London, England) 241, 247
Vermeulen, Timotheus 46, 60
videogames 108, 175, 230, 235
  Animal Crossing: New Horizons 175
  and coordination 114
  multiplayer 119
  'The Under Presents' 15, 112, 114–15, 116, 118
virtual reality (VR) 15, 108, 112–23, 234
  market penetration 113
  Oculus 112–13, 234
  theatre as 113
Virtual Theatre 10, 15, 67, 69, 79, 178–9, 196, 225, 235, 242, 244, 255
Viveros, Sebastián Capitán 253
vMix 37, 69–70, 253

Waghorn, Jennifer Moss 192
Wallace, David Foster 47
Warchus, Matthew 39, 41, 233–4
Waring, Rachel 171, 172, 175–7, 182, 230
Waseda University (Japan) 208–9
  Waseda Institute Players 209, 210–11, 213
watch parties 74, 110, 221
web series 161–70
Weber, Lois 26
Webster, John
  The Duchess of Malfi 29, 38, 253
Welton, Martin 104

The Wet Mariners Theatre
Company (England) 230
Wheatley, Ben 56
Whedon, Joss 56
Whishaw, Ben 227
White, Gareth 99–101
Whyman, Erica 254
Wiggins, Martin 185–6, 192–3
Wilde, Oscar 172
Williams, Dathan B. 51, 247
Williams, EM 254
Williams, Raymond 46
Williamson, Elizabeth 244
The Willow Globe (Wales) 230, 233
Wimer, Renata 234
Wirthner, Naomi 235
Wolfgang, William 162–5, 167–9
The Wooster Group (USA) 29, 221
World Health Organisation (WHO) 3
working from home 7, 107, 109–11, 129, 231, 238
Workman, Ayana 247
Wright, Edgar 30

Young, Sandra 142
Young Vic (London, England) 40–1
YouTube 10, 16, 24, 49, 71, 77, 131, 137, 145, 168, 213, 214, 220–2, 247
  Live Chat 72–8, 83, 150, 153

Zoom (video conferencing software) 10, 16, 51–2, 78, 112, 129, 131, 140, 144, 162, 188, 224, 255
  audience (un)familiarity with 181–2, 205, 248
  Breakout Rooms 71, 178, 225
  Chat 6, 76, 99, 182, 186, 189–94
  Gallery View 6, 52–3, 68, 80, 37–8, 52, 53, 94, 103, 205, 224, 225, 199
  as narrative setting 37, 52, 70, 79–80, 173–4, 223
  as performance space 12, 24, 31, 37–8, 51–4, 60, 68–9, 79–80, 87–8, 91–105, 135–7, 151, 158, 171–4, 176–9, 181, 188, 196–201, 204, 209, 211, 223–5, 229, 231–2, 234–9, 244, 249, 252–3
  pets on camera 68, 73
  Poll (feature) 225
  recorded performances 78, 99, 102–3, 243
  rehearsal process 198, 237
  screen names 73, 174
  as social and connective space 139–40, 164, 167, 192, 203, 231, 240
  as teaching space 190–1, 207–8
  Speaker View 37–8, 80, 133, 205, 225, 251
  Spotlight (feature) 67, 69–70, 94, 97, 99, 101, 182, 199
  Virtual Backgrounds 53, 67, 70, 92, 94, 96, 129, 157, 173, 188, 196, 199, 224, 229, 252, 253
  webinar 231, 233, 248
Zoom-to-YouTube 10, 11, 15, 72–8, 52, 67, 76, 150, 171, 172, 173, 178, 221–4, 230, 233, 243–4, 247

www.ingramcontent.com/pod-product-compliance
Lightning Source LLC
Chambersburg PA
CBHW052214300426
44115CB00011B/1675